₁ BILL OF RIGHTS

of Human Rights and Fundamental Freedoms.
, Chapter 44, assented to 10ᵗʰ August 1960.

prived thereof except by due—

ndividual to equality before the
tection of the law;
ion;
h;
nbly and association; and
ress.

nada shall, unless it is expressly
the Parliament of Canada that it
standing the *Canadian Bill of Rights*,
plied as not to abrogate, abridge or
ze the abrogation, abridgment or
of the rights or freedoms herein rec-
G-in particular, no law of Canada
applied so as to
the arbitrary detention, imprison-
ny person;
ze the imposition of cruel and
nt or punishment;
ho has been arrested or detained
e informed promptly of the reason
detention,
tain and instruct counsel with-

by way of *habeas corpus* for the
of the validity of his detention
se if the detention is not lawful;
ibunal, commission, board or other
el a person to give evidence if he is
otection against self crimination or
nal safeguards;

e) deprive a person of the right to a fair hearing in
accordance with the principles of fundamental justice
for the determination of his rights and obligations;

f) deprive a person charged with a criminal offence
of the right to be presumed innocent until proved
guilty according to law in a fair & public hearing
by an independent and impartial tribunal, or of
the right to reasonable bail without just cause; or

g) deprive a person of the right to the assistance of an
interpreter in any proceedings in which he is involved
or in which he is a party or a witness before a court,
commission, board or other tribunal, if he does not
understand or speak the language in which such
proceedings are conducted.

3. The Minister of Justice shall, in accordance with such
regulations as may be prescribed by the Governor in Council,
examine every proposed regulation submitted in draft form
to the Clerk of the Privy Council pursuant to the *Regulations
Act* and every Bill introduced in or presented to the House
of Commons, in order to ascertain whether any of the
provisions thereof are inconsistent with the purposes and
provisions of this Part and he shall report any such in-
consistency to the House of Commons at the first convenient opportunity.

4. The provisions of this Part shall be known as the
Canadian Bill of Rights.

*" I am a Canadian, a free Canadian, free to speak without fear, free to
worship God in my own way, free to stand for what I think right, free to
oppose what I believe wrong, free to choose those who shall govern my
country. This heritage of freedom I pledge to uphold for myself and
all mankind."*

The Right Honourable John G. Diefenbaker, Prime Minister of Canada,
House of Commons Debates, July 1, 1960.

ONE CANADA

MEMOIRS OF THE RIGHT HONOURABLE

JOHN G. DIEFENBAKER

ONE CANADA

MEMOIRS OF THE RIGHT HONOURABLE

JOHN G. DIEFENBAKER

✳

THE YEARS OF ACHIEVEMENT
1957 - 1962

MACMILLAN OF CANADA

TORONTO

Canadian Cataloguing in Publication data

Diefenbaker, John G., 1895-
One Canada

Includes indexes.
Contents: [1] The crusading years 1895-1956. —
[2] The years of achievement 1956-1962.

ISBN 0-7705-1331-X (v.1).   ISBN 0-7705-1443-X (v. 2).

1. Diefenbaker, John G., 1895-   2. Canada -
Politics and government—1935 -   * I. Title.

FC616.D53A36   971.06′42′0924   C75-10480-5
F1034.3.D5A36

Printed and bound in Canada by Hunter Rose
for The Macmillan Company of Canada Limited
70 Bond Street, Toronto M5B 1X3

TO ALL OF THOSE GOOD FRIENDS
AND SUPPORTERS
WHO SHARED WITH ME
A VISION OF ONE CANADA,
UNITED, PROSPEROUS,
AND FREE

LIST OF ILLUSTRATIONS

✳

*Photographs not otherwise credited are from
Mr. Diefenbaker's personal collection.*

(A number of photographs in Mr. Diefenbaker's personal
collection bear no source identification. The publishers
would be pleased to correct any omissions from this list
in future printings.)

PREFACE

In this, the second volume of my memoirs, again I have
been fortunate to have at my disposal the historical and
research assistance that a project of this magnitude requires. I wish to pay special tribute to John A. Munro for
his sterling contribution to the preparation of this work.
To Dr. John H. Archer of Regina, and to those of my
long-time friends and associates who gave of their val-
ued advice and counsel, I also give my warmest thanks.
I acknowledge with gratitude the continued support of
the Canada Council.

FOREWORD

In this second volume of *One Canada* the reader will encounter both the vision and the substance of the Right
Honourable John G. Diefenbaker's national stewardship. Here we have an authoritative account of Mr.
Diefenbaker's years as Prime Minister of Canada. No
tender cloak of forgetfulness obscures either the issues or
the personalities of these years. His judgments are sharp
and to the point; his arguments lucid and full of arresting
detail; his overview of the nation of which he was first
minister profound in the simplicity of its presentation.
Mr. Diefenbaker's love of Parliament emerged with force
in the first of these volumes; his reputation as a House of
Commons man will stand the test of time.

From the excitement of the 1957 campaign, through the
forming of his first government and the legislation
brought before a Parliament for the first time graced at its
Opening by the presence of Her Majesty the Queen, to
the calling of the 1958 election and the campaign that followed, the reader is gripped by the accounting of the
master raconteur. There follows in four chapters the most
revealing and important account of Canadian foreign policy by any former Prime Minister in our history. With a
candour that is as refreshing as it is rare in this sort of exposition, Mr. Diefenbaker documents Canada's relations

with Britain and the Commonwealth, the United States, France, Germany, the Soviet Union, China, the United Nations, and the world at large. In consequence, Canada's foreign policy considerations emerge as never before. These chapters should serve to confound those who contend that there is but one effective approach to the advancement of Canadian interests abroad. Hereafter, the initiates of the cult of quiet diplomacy will have to do more than indulge in liturgical cant to convert students of Canadian external policy to their point of view.

For the rest, it will take more than the purple prose and acid pen of some journalist to counter the record and the reason set forth between these covers. The Atlantic Provinces, Quebec, Ontario, the Prairie Provinces and British Columbia, the Yukon and Northwest Territories: each found a place, both individually and collectively, in his One Canada concept. Northern and national development, agriculture, aid to small business, technical and higher education, job creation, and export sales promotion involved policies to unite the nation as a whole. Native rights, women's rights, the rights of those less privileged—the aged, the disabled, the veterans—the welfare of the unemployed and the average Canadian were part of a social justice program wide in its compass. French language rights were made effective as never before. With sound philosophy, the institutions that make this nation strong were buoyed and given new life. And most important, Canadians were for the first time given a Bill of Rights to ensure their fundamental freedoms. Not only did Mr. Diefenbaker honour most of his specific promises made to the nation on the hustings, he and his government eased the Canadian economy to full recovery from an inherited recession and kept inflation to the lowest level in the Western world. The record is opened to examination and independent assessment. Here then is the significance of this volume and of the one to follow, which will complete Mr. Diefenbaker's prime-ministerial period.

Fortunately, most historians are reluctant to pass judgment on a period or a person until passions are cool and the necessary facts are at hand. Before any verdict is possible, particular realities must be reordered, reworked, and made to show their significant side. All contemporary documentation is but grist for the historians' mill. Yet some contemporary works may be as siren songs in diverting the historian from his independent path.

Historiographically, the period of the Diefenbaker government was in danger of suffering a fate even worse than that accorded the period of the R. B. Bennett government. To all intents and purposes the Conservative régime that governed Canada from 1930 to 1935 has been treated by Canadian historians as an aberration in the great Liberal scheme of things Canadian. A major work on R. B. Bennett has yet to be written. Had Mr. Diefenbaker failed to provide us his account of his national stewardship, we might have had worse than nothing in its stead.

John A. Munro
John H. Archer

ONE CANADA

MEMOIRS OF THE RIGHT HONOURABLE

JOHN G. DIEFENBAKER

CHAPTER ONE

※

As the polls closed in Prince Albert constituency on the evening of 10 June 1957, the unofficial reports on the results in the Atlantic provinces, Quebec, and Ontario were confirmed. It was apparent that for the first time in many elections, the results in the West would be decisive in determining the outcome of a general election. The Conservative Party had come out of the Atlantic provinces with 21 of a possible 33 seats. While Liberal strength had held in the Province of Quebec, I was pleased, none the less, that we had more than doubled the party's 1953 representation, from 4 to 9. (In 1940, under Manion, we elected 1; in 1945, under Bracken, we elected 1; in 1949, under Drew, 2.) Indeed, without those nine seats in 1957, this volume, if written at all, would be concerned with other matters. In Ontario we had made large gains, increasing our strength from 33 to 61. The result was that at the Manitoba border the Conservatives and the Liberals stood virtually neck and neck, with 91 and 97 seats respectively. Even with four provinces and two territories still to be heard from, the Conservative Party was assured of its finest electoral hour since the Right Honourable R. B. Bennett won the election of 1930. Although we did not make a sweep of the three Prairie Provinces, we broke the back of the infamous Gardiner machine as the Liberal victories fell from a 1953 total of 17 to 6. When the vote was counted in British Columbia, the Progressive Conservative Party had a total of 112 seats in the new House of Commons as compared to 105 for the Liberals, 25 for the CCF, and 19 for Social Credit. The people of Canada had spoken. The next move was up to Prime Minister St. Laurent. Would he heed the message and resign, or would he choose to meet the House and seek the support of the smaller parties?

It was in these uncertain circumstances that I flew from Prince Albert to Regina that election evening to speak to the people of Canada over the national networks of CBC television and radio. I remember my emotions as I spoke. It was for me a moment of deep dedication rather than of elation, and my first words were ones of gratitude and appreciation for the wonderful support that thousands of people, without regard to party consideration, had given me. I said in part:

My fellow Canadians . . . If we are called on to form a government, I give you this pledge: in everything we do, we will try to achieve those things which represent the hopes and yearnings of all Canadians, however humble. I say to you . . . I shall keep the faith. When I accepted the leadership of this party I said to the party and to the people I would be guided by those words from the scriptures: "He who would be chiefest among you shall be the servant of all." That is my dedication. If I may say a personal word, I would ask for your prayers so that everything I may do will be those things which are inherent in everyone who believes in divine guidance.

The Conservative Party in Canada was on the verge of emerging from twenty-two years in the political wilderness. I was one of the few knowledgeable not surprised at the election result. Indeed, some of the more prestigious of the Parliamentary Press Gallery pundits had proclaimed that my election as party leader marked the final step on the road to national oblivion for the Conservative Party. I have been told that following the convention vote, members of the *Winnipeg Free Press* offered to bet that we wouldn't have sixteen seats after the next election. I might comment that had I followed the advice of these experts we would have arrived at oblivion soon enough.

I had spent most of a lifetime contending against those less enlightened forces in the Conservative Party who in their blindness actually seemed to find some comfort in defeat at the polls, election after election. My ambition was to open the Conservative Party to the average Canadian. This issue was joined almost immediately at a press conference following my election as leader on 8 December 1956. I was asked what I planned to do about Social Credit. I replied that if the Socreds wanted to join us that would be fine; that I could not see any reason for their existence as a separate federal party; that while some might have certain peculiar monetary ideas, they nevertheless believed in free enterprise; that their general philosophy was a small-"c" conservative one; and that since we had a common purpose, there was no reason why we should continue to oppose each other to the benefit of the Liberal Party.

Well, those who thought like the *Winnipeg Free Press*'s Bruce Hutchison and Max Freedman considered this the last straw. Their estimates of my chances of success were now even further reduced. The verdict seemed unanimous. Leading Social Crediters, such as British Columbia's Premier W. A. C. Bennett, rejected my position out of hand. What he thought in 1958 when the nineteen Social Crediters elected in 1957 turned to zero, I do not know.

In 1956, however, Bennett was in good company. Establishment Tories were scandalized by the thought that we might welcome the Socreds into our ranks. Jim Macdonnell, Conservative M.P. for Greenwood and Opposition financial critic for many years, was horrified. When I saw him in Toronto a few days after the convention, he gave me a lecture on what the financial establishment would and would not accept. I listened patiently. He concluded by pointing out that his father had been close to Sir John Macdonald. Macdonald, he said, would now turn over in his grave! I suggested that since he belonged to the financial circles to which he referred, he might go to work on winning their support. He thought that this was a waste of time, that we didn't have a chance. Actually, I found this reassuring: Macdonnell had been wrong in his prognostications concerning every past leader and election. I told him, "Your attitude gives me new hope." The Canadian Broadcasting Corporation's television cameras recorded for time immemorial the facial reactions of J. M. Macdonnell, Richard Bell, the Honourable Earl Rowe, George Nowlan, and Léon Balcer as they stood in collective lament when the results of the first ballot were announced at the leadership convention. Apparently they could not understand how anyone not sanctioned by their group could possibly be chosen. There was no doubt that they regarded my being chosen leader an unmitigated disaster, a catastrophe, a judgment that they now considered proven beyond doubt.

Nevertheless, my first task, so far as possible, was to heal the wounds and to unite the party. I knew we would face an election within the year. I invited George Drew to remain in Parliament as my desk mate in the House of Commons. His health did not permit it. Although our personal relations were not close, I was never aware, nor am I now, of any animosity between us. Indeed, when his health subsequently did improve, I appointed him our High Commissioner to Britain.

It was equally important to party unity that my two opponents in the contest for leadership not be left to brood

upon their defeats. Davie Fulton, the Member for Kamloops, British Columbia, had come into the House in the
general election of 1945. He had promised me his support
for the 1948 leadership convention but decided, in the
event, that his position as National President of the
Young Progressive Conservatives precluded his openly
supporting anyone. His subsequent decision to contest
the leadership in 1956 was, at best, a notice served upon
the future, although it is more than possible that he was
disappointed with his 117-vote total. He seemed surprised
when I called him following the convention, but pleased
at my request that he help. He agreed at once.

I visited Donald Fleming in Toronto in the convention
afterweek. He had contested the leadership in 1948 and
1956, running third in 1948 and second in 1956. I found
him still surprised and somewhat angry at his relatively
poor showing. But Fleming was a good, tough, able, and
dependable party man. He willingly assumed the responsibilities that I asked of him and did his best to secure the
active co-operation of his fellow Toronto members. I
never had reason to question his loyalty from that meeting to his retirement from politics because of a family
difficulty in early 1963.

At the national organization level, I was able to convince Brigadier Beverley Matthews, distinguished Toronto lawyer and corporate director, to continue to perform those very necessary financial functions for the
party that he had begun under George Drew. This was
extremely important. A leader must have someone he can
trust implicitly in this most sensitive area. He must build
a wall to preserve the anonymity of those who donate
funds to the support of his party and thus preserve his
own independence of action.

National Headquarters presented my most difficult
early problem. The National Director of the party at the
time of the convention was Bill Rowe (son of the Hon.

Earl Rowe). I was advised that there might be a mass exodus of the Headquarters staff following my election. I did not regard this as a misfortune, given the apparent hostility of some of them to the prospect of my leadership in both 1948 and 1956. Their depression at my success and fear lest I bear a grudge against them (although this was far from my intention) would hardly guarantee their effectiveness. However, with an election looming on the horizon, continuity at the senior level was important; otherwise there might be no organization at all when the election was called. I approached Bill Rowe and asked him to stay on. I pointed out to him that I was not concerned over the fact that he had worked against me during the convention. He assured me that this was now in the past and that he would be only too happy to remain in his position at National Headquarters. Within a week there were rumours in the press of his resignation, although he denied responsibility for leaking these stories. Within two weeks of my election, and before I received it, I read his letter of resignation in the *Ottawa Journal*.

I find it difficult to describe the troubles I passed through between my election as leader and the opening of the House of Commons a month later. The whole of the party apparatus had to be geared to an election footing. The campaign committee had to be set up, itineraries for national and regional tours detailed, publicity arranged, an election manifesto readied, and strategy at the upcoming session of Parliament considered and determined. These were matters requiring time and attention. What I did not need was a National Headquarters full of people whose chief desire was to torpedo me so as to bring about a new leadership convention as quickly as possible.

Fortunately I was not alone. As I mentioned earlier, Donald Fleming and Davie Fulton started immediately to work, as did many of my long-time friends: W. R. (Bill)

Brunt and Dave Walker, who had supported me through three leadership conventions and elections; Gordon Churchill, M.P. from Winnipeg; Ted Rogers, Toronto; Lyle Jestley and M. J. O'Brien, Vancouver; George Cloakey, Calgary; Fred Hadley and Ed. Topping, Prince Albert; Tupper McConnell, Moose Jaw; Arthur Pearson, Lumsden; H. E. Keown, Melfort; Paul Lafontaine and Gérald Morin, Montreal; Bob Coates and Bob Muir, M.P.s, and Don Haggart from Nova Scotia; William Browne from St. John's, Newfoundland; Daniel Johnson, future Premier of Quebec. These men became the organizational group at the centre of the 1957 campaign. In addition, Premier Leslie Frost put his own tremendous energy and ability and the considerable talents of his Ontario organization at my disposal. But most important was the decision of Allister Grosart to accept the position of National Director of the party, first on a three-day-a-week basis, and later full time. It was he who turned Rowe's resignation from a disaster to a blessing. As I have written in Volume I, Allister Grosart had brought great skill and ability to the management of my 1956 campaign for the leadership, as he had to the campaign of George Drew in 1948. I must note before leaving the topic of organizational problems that when I moved into the office of the Leader of the Opposition, it was staffed entirely by Drew appointees, among them Derek Bedson, now Clerk of Manitoba's Legislative Council. Bedson and the others who agreed to continue on an *ad hoc* basis until after the election served me well and ably.

When Parliament opened on 8 January, we in the Conservative Opposition faced a supremely arrogant Liberal government. They seemed to be of a mind with the newly retired palace guard of the Conservative Party, except that they could not have been happier with the election of anyone as Conservative Leader than they were with mine. Indeed, they were in ecstasy. They boasted that my election had rendered the Liberal government impregnable! This, they said, was simply a case of an election taking place at an early date, when Mr. St. Laurent would be returned. They had no more idea that defeat was coming than the man in the moon. I recall travelling to Montreal in early January. I was by myself and carrying my own bags as I checked into the Windsor Hotel. At the desk I met one of St. Laurent's Cabinet Ministers, who looked at me and said, not unkindly, "Well, I see you're getting in practice for what you'll be doing in the future."

It was on the afternoon of 8 January 1957 that I took my place in the House of Commons as Leader of Her Majesty's Loyal Opposition. In responding to the kind words and official welcomes from the Prime Minister and the leaders of the two other parties, I said in part:

I love this chamber, for however much we may disagree—and when strong men have strong opinions on occasion they use strong language to express them—we retain that conformity with the tradition of respect for one another. It is in that spirit that I thank the Prime Minister and the other honourable members for what they have said.

... The essence of our system of government, the basic foundation, is the right of each of us to disagree. The Prime Minister paraphrased, I think, the words of Tierney, who over one hundred and forty years ago said . . . "The function of an opposition is to propose nothing, to oppose everything and to turn out the government." With the first two obligations, I am in disagreement, but I say, sir, that in this year of grace the third would seem to be one worthy of adoption.

The Speech from the Throne reflected the overweening confidence of the Liberals, as did the budget that followed. Scant attention was paid to the economic difficulties looming on the horizon (and these only the government then understood). If the Speech from the Throne and the budget were to be taken as the Liberal

Party election manifesto, their message was that house-keeping was enough, and that the Canadian public was fortunate to be so blessed in its rulers. In fact, the government was open to legitimate criticism on many fronts. It devoted the largest part of the Throne Speech to questions of external policy, and to the creation of the United Nations Emergency Force in the Middle East and Canada's role therein. But it left unanswered the question of giving Egypt's Nasser effective control of that force, and of what would happen if and when he ordered the force from Egyptian territory.

On the budget, we scored the government for over-taxing and thus creating inflation and hurting investment, for giving advantage to big business over small business, for not helping the poorer provinces, and, most of all, for the parsimony of the six-dollar increase in the Old Age Pension. The Minister of Finance, Walter Harris, and his Cabinet colleagues had established a situation in which they earned the description of the "six-buck boys".

On the subject of agriculture, we struck hard against government inaction on unfair and illegal United States dumping practices; against refusing cash advances to farmers on unsold crops; for not recovering the British agricultural market; and for not investigating the agricultural price spread. Generally, we made the case made many times before by the Conservative Party for establishing the equality of farmers in the Canadian economy. I made yet one more plea for the building of the South Saskatchewan Dam. I was able to take a clear stand in opposition to economic continentalism and against some of the more baneful effects of foreign ownership, such as the lack of industrial research or of processing in Canada.

The recently completed preliminary report of the Gordon Royal Commission on Canada's Economic Prospects, tabled in the House in January, had turned out to be of considerable embarrassment to the St. Laurent government. As I remarked in the House on 11 February, I thought it strange that this Commission, which was to be the chart, the compass, of Canada's future for the next twenty-five years, had become something in which the government showed little interest. I wanted to know what portions of the report would receive the government's imprimatur. We knew that there were certain portions of the Gordon Report, dealing with the threat posed to Canadian economic independence by United States ownership, that had already received the utmost condemnation from powerful ministers in the Liberal government. I was, I explained, concerned not with American investment in Canada *per se*, but with the degree to which the investment in Canada by foreign corporations was uncontrolled. The necessary criterion was whether such investment operated for the benefit of Canada. What was needed was a *national policy* to provide a dynamic influence on the economy, and a sense of *national* purpose and *national* destiny.

Thus, the question of northern development became the issue that clearly separated the Conservative Party, under my leadership, from the Liberals. I had this to say on 11 February 1957:

... In so far as northern Canada is concerned, there can be no question whatever that in the territories there has not been a policy of vision in keeping with the tremendous potentialities of that area. There is no question of constitutional division of responsibility between the dominion and the provinces in the Northwest Territories. In that area there are vast resources that should be developed, with the state making possible that development by providing the means and the climate for private industry to develop and expand. I can see this northland of ours with developments envisaged by D'Arcy McGee in his magnificent speech at the time of Confederation as he saw that great Canada. I can see cities in northern Canada north of the Arctic Circle. There are vast power potentialities in that area. I can see cities developing there as they are developing today in Norway, if only the government would catch the vision of the possibilities.

In emphasizing the question of northern development and northern vision, I advocated a twentieth-century equivalent to Sir John Macdonald's national policy, a uniquely Canadian economic dream. The Liberals were coming to believe that what was good for General Motors was not only good for the United States but good for Canada. My advocacy of a northern development policy was not suddenly produced. Indeed, in July of 1956, I spoke in the House of the need for a national vision to equalize economic opportunities everywhere in Canada. The emphasis in that debate was on the federal government's responsibility to ensure an equality of development throughout the Dominion, with emphasis on processing, scientific education, and research in Canada, stimulated if necessary by tax concessions. The party convention's Resolutions on Policy in December 1956 added weight to these positions.

Any difference in emphasis between my earlier pronouncements and those in 1957, however, may be attributed to the influence on my thinking of Dr. Merrill Menzies, who in early 1957 had just completed his postgraduate work in economics in the United Kingdom. Interested in northern development, he wrote a thirty-page brief on the subject which he sent to his brother-in-law, Dr. Glen Green, a close friend of mine in Prince Albert, who brought it to my attention. Although Menzies' concept was no less than spectacular, initially I was not deeply impressed with it; I did not think that it could be implemented as practicable policy. I put it aside. Shortly thereafter, I reread it while travelling by train to Ottawa. My interest was caught, and I decided to seek more detailed data on Menzies' proposals.

Certainly, if any political leader in our history was ever

amenable to a coherent and comprehensive proposal for northern development, it was I. I had had an infatuation with the north throughout my life. As a boy of ten or eleven I often imagined that I was a participant in the expeditions of Sir John Franklin, Captain Robert Falcon Scott, or Sir Ernest Shackleton. I remember well the newspaper reports of Robert E. Peary's expeditions, and my dreams would have been fulfilled had I been with him on his journeys. I read all that I could find about the north and northern exploration. I remember being privileged to introduce Roald Amundsen to an Eclectic Club meeting in the Third Avenue Methodist Church in Saskatoon in 1926, the year he flew over the North Pole. He was on a lecture tour to raise funds for his next expedition. The Eclectic Club was a young men's club in five Saskatchewan cities and towns: Regina, Saskatoon, Prince Albert, North Battleford, and Lloydminster. In 1926, I was chosen as chairman. Vilhjalmur Stefansson, too, was one of my heroes. In September of 1957, when Dartmouth College gave me an honorary degree, Stefansson came to see me and, busy as I was with my new duties as Prime Minister, I felt honoured to spend two or three hours talking with him on northern questions.

Throughout my life, I have had the ambition to travel to the North Pole. It is an ambition not realized. Indeed, it was not until 1941 that I finally had the opportunity to travel to the Yukon. I remember spending two very early morning hours wandering about Dawson City. Everything was in a state of shocking disrepair and decay. When I returned to Ottawa I urged the government to make some effort to restore this historic town. Not until my government was in office was this done.

As I reread Menzies' proposals, they inspired in me the dream of opening Canada to its polar reaches. I could see a Canada that answered not only the description on the main doorway of the House of Commons, "Canada from

Sea to Sea", but "Canada from Sea to Seas". Today, these ideas are regarded as the fundamental policy for the development of the north. The name I ascribed to them at the time of the 1957 election was "the New Frontier Policy". John F. Kennedy borrowed it in 1960 (without attribution) and used it to great advantage. Of course, because our northern development policy turned out well, many today claim credit for it but, other than Menzies, had nothing to do with it. As things turned out, although I advanced the idea of the New Frontier in my speech opening the 1957 election campaign in Toronto's Massey Hall on 25 April 1957, it did not really kindle the public imagination until the opening of the next campaign in Winnipeg in February 1958.

The 1957 election took place on 10 June. And, although the House of Commons was dissolved on the evening of 12 April 1957, Mr. St. Laurent had taken the unusual course of giving me advance notice in February. The Gallup Polls at the time all seemed to confirm that St. Laurent's "Uncle Louis" image was good for one more victory. On the eve of the election, they assigned the Liberals a startling 48 per cent of the popular vote. I am fond of dogs and I have often observed that dogs have their own appropriate treatment for poles. As I travelled back and forth across the country, I had not the slightest doubt on what the outcome would be. Mr. St. Laurent, on the other hand, told me after the election: "I never dreamed that our defeat was possible."

A typical day on the 1957 campaign trail would begin at about seven a.m. with a meeting between me and Gordon Churchill, who was my chief political adviser on the campaign. We would review my itinerary for that day and look over what had been said the day before by the leading political figures of all parties, including our own. As for the latter, there is nothing more frustrating than to discover that one of your lieutenants has made a speech somewhere that not only has failed to gain support where he was speaking but has lost the party support in some other constituency. We would then decide on the particular matters that should be stressed in the day ahead. Perhaps twice a week I would make a series of phone calls to various people across the country on whom I had learned to depend on policy matters.

The people who accompanied me in addition to Gordon Churchill were Derek Bedson, my Private Secretary, George Hogan, who was in charge of train and itinerary arrangements, Dr. Merrill Menzies, as Research Assistant, Fred Davis, as press liaison and public relations man, and my personal secretaries. In addition, Mr. Harry Willis, Q.C., of the Ontario Conservative organization acted as an advance man, travelling to each of the places on my itinerary two or three days before my arrival to make certain that all the appropriate arrangements had been made.

Normally, there would be one major speech per day complemented by two or three short and specific public announcements. Into each I endeavoured to work some new aspect of our platform. Saturday, 25 May, to take a day at random, I was en route from Kamloops Junction to Edmonton on the Canadian National Railways Supercontinental. My itinerary read as follows:

8.35 a.m.	Platform appearance, Jasper
11.00 a.m.	Platform appearance, Edson
1.55 p.m.	Arrive Edmonton
2.15 p.m.	Press conference, Macdonald Hotel
2.45 p.m.	Television interview, Macdonald Hotel
3.15 p.m.	Leave hotel for airport
3.30 p.m.	Depart for Peace River by plane
5.00 p.m.	Arrive Peace River
5.30 p.m.	Public meeting
8.00 p.m.	Leave for Grande Prairie
8.30 p.m.	Arrive Grande Prairie

10.30 p.m.   Leave for Edmonton
12.00 midnight   Arrive Edmonton

I do not know how many miles I travelled during the 1957 campaign, nor in how many different planes, trains, and cars. Every day, excepting Sunday, was a full day. In large auditoriums and small meeting halls, on railway platforms, and on main streets, I met the people of Canada. The Conservative Party had a message to deliver and an alternative government to offer. The Liberals stood on their record of economic stability, blind to the problems of structural maladjustment in the agricultural sector, blind to the problems of regional under-development, and blind to the problems of penetrating and developing our northern frontiers. They were further caught in a web of their own weaving in that the problem of our massive trade imbalance was the direct result of their policies of integrating the Canadian economy with that of the United States. C. D. Howe, the economic czar of the St. Laurent government, had pursued economic continentalism with unchecked vigour in the post-war decade.

In contrast, we offered a policy of positive government, although not unnecessary government—a distinction worth noting. We saw the historical origins of our policy in the first Conservative ministry in Confederation. Macdonald had known instinctively that the goals of an economically independent and viable Canada could not be realized except by positive, even heroic, government action to ensure the establishment and development of east–west lines of communication and trade. His railway, immigration, settlement, and tariff policies were all testimony to this. Macdonald's national policy had been fully enunciated in 1878. It was now 1957 and the Liberals continued to demonstrate that they had not learned the fundamental truths concerning Canada's very existence as a nation. We were offering a new national policy of regional and northern development. Our objective was to continue Macdonald's historic task of nation-building within the context of modern requirements and circumstances. We wanted to get government back to the people, to involve them more intimately in the shaping of their own destinies, to release their energies, their enthusiasms, and their imagination. We wanted to make ours an Elizabethan Age worthy of its predecessor, an age of adventure and high endeavour. Government, in our view, was as much a matter of inspiration as it was of administration.

We presented the Canadian people with a grand design for national development which ultimately required the co-operation of the federal and provincial governments. Perhaps the most succinct statement of our initial policy was contained in the Speech from the Throne read to the Canadian Parliament and people by Her Majesty Queen Elizabeth II on 14 October 1957. It said in part:

My ministers believe that a National Development Policy carried out in cooperation with the provinces, and in the territories, is needed to enable all regions of Canada to share in the benefits to be realized in developing the resources of this great nation. It is their intention to propose to you from time to time programmes and projects to implement this policy. As an immediate start upon a programme of more extensive development in the Atlantic Provinces, you will be asked to authorize, in joint action with the provincial governments, the creation of facilities for the production and transmission of cheaper electric power in those provinces. You will also be asked to provide assistance in financing the Beechwood Project which has been under construction in New Brunswick. My ministers will advance this National Development Policy further by initiating new discussions with the Government of Saskatchewan in order to make possible the early commencement of construction of the dam on the South Saskatchewan River. My ministers are pressing for a favourable settlement of international problems in connection with the Columbia River to clear the way for a joint programme with the Province of British Columbia to develop the immense power in the waters of this river.

And this was only a beginning. We would soon move forward with policies designed to provide access to the resources of our northern frontier. As I told the people assembled in Massey Hall in Toronto 25 April 1957: "The North, with all its vast resources of hidden wealth—the wonder and the challenge of the North must become our national consciousness."

The Massey Hall meeting was the first in our 1957 campaign. It was a magnificent meeting. My friend Joel Aldred flew in from Hollywood just for that evening to act as chairman. Premier Leslie Frost of Ontario was in fine form and gave me a more than generous introduction. I might note that Mr. Frost had had some doubts about the wisdom of launching the national campaign in Toronto. He felt that Ontario's capital was the one city in Canada that inspired resentment in almost every other part of the country. I was insistent, however. When I considered my family origins, both paternal and maternal, I was attracted by the personal symbolism of starting this first great national campaign in Toronto. Premier Frost, once the decision had been taken, was not one of those Conservatives who argued that Massey Hall was too large. My response to those people was: "If we can't fill it, we might as well forget the whole campaign." We filled it.

I have never had a ghost writer to draft my speeches for me. My course was to ask friends and colleagues for opinions on various matters; to check the editorials of the major newspapers, some of which would be critical; and to instruct my staff as to the data I required by way of fill-in. Political intelligence and public opinion demand that a leader not only have the fullest information at his finger-tips, but have a refined sense of its historical context. During the elections of 1957 and 1958, Allister Grosart was generally the one who acted as conduit in collecting my speech materials. As an adviser, I found him possessed of sound common sense and wise counsel.

It has been said of me that when I speak I always have three speeches: the one I intend to make, the one I give to the press that I don't use, and the one I finally deliver to the audience. It is amazing what audiences can do for a speaker. To me an audience for or against has a profound effect, and each new audience has its unique effect. They can move one in a way far beyond anything that any speech writer can imagine. To read a prepared text to an audience is to miss it all. When I stand before my audience, I know the message I want to put over. I begin in a rather uncertain manner. If something has arisen that permits a jocular reference, I make it. I try to get the sense of the audience and to gain their attention. To understand in my own mind what particular matters are of interest to them, I immediately launch into a series of topics that could be discussed. When I find a positive general reaction to one particular subject, this is where I begin in detail. People would not attend meetings if they did not want to hear; there is in each one present, except for the rock-ribbed party supporter, an open mind even though it may not be admitted. Of course, I welcome audience participation. Anyone who wants to interrupt is free to do so. If it is a question seeking information, it is answered; if it is one designed to be destructive, the answer is not always what the questioner expected. It is a study to watch people in an audience; to see a husband and wife during a speech, sitting side by side. She decides to applaud a little; he gives her a poke as if to say: "You stop now. You're going too far." Then, after a while, to her surprise, he begins to applaud.

Some say that the day of public meetings is over. This

new generation of political leaders apparently cannot deliver a speech without reading it; consequently they cannot hold their audiences. Nor have they found an effective replacement for public meetings. Ninety-nine per cent of those whom I have observed on radio or on TV are not able to convey any sense of their individual personalities. A teleprompter turns speakers into amateur announcers.

An old-time politician indulged in baby-kissing; some of the more modern have carried the kissing proposition to others older in years. Neither technique was ever attractive to me. It is true, however, that one has to adopt those things which, if they are in keeping with one's feelings rather than one's aspirations, bring about political results. I found that there were many people who were attracted to meeting a candidate or the leader of a party on the street. I experimented with this method and it worked. It was described as Main-Streeting. Going down the street, meeting with individual electors, has found its way, not only into the language, but also into the activities of all Canadian parties.

There have been variations where the candidate makes a speech, using various means to attract attention from the back of a truck, car, or train. I think of the United States governor in one of the Southern states who ran on the platform "Pass the biscuits, pappy." That was it. He handed out biscuits. (Until recently, one could not have done that in Canada; handing out biscuits would have contravened the Elections Act.)

Other campaigners followed the course of having shows with them. I never did. I relied on meeting the people. This has a double advantage. They meet you and they pass on a word of encouragement to others. People feel when you meet them in this way, either Main-Streeting or by railway, that they are part and parcel of your thinking, and that they have been personally recognized, as they have been, by the fact that you have chosen to visit with them. Their problems are your problems; their heartbreaks, your heartbreaks.

Now and then you run into someone who is offensive—not critical, just offensive. I think of one person in my own constituency who, when I came along the street to shake his hand, said, "I wouldn't shake hands with you. Never shake hands with a Tory. Never. Never. Never." "Well," I said, "I admire you for your clarity of expression and your loyalty to your party." You would be surprised to know that two elections later he was among my best supporters. That shows the influence of personal contact.

I began this kind of campaigning in 1953. I would go by car, actually a cavalcade of ten or fifteen cars. I remember the first time. In one town after another I would meet people and get to chatting with them. By six o'clock in the afternoon, when we should have completed the entire journey, we would have gone only half-way. One of my very good supporters, who at all times had an innate desire to use words of size and prestige, regardless of whether they applied or not, said, "Now let's get down to brass tacks. The next time we go on one of these 'calvacades', the artillery has to be lived up to in every particular. When we say we're going to be at a certain town, we're going to be there." By "artillery", he, of course, meant the itinerary, but he made a good point. To be too late is to lose goodwill and votes.

From time to time, I have adopted new systems. To get around as fast as possible I decided three elections ago to use the helicopter. To assure a good turnout in every village and town visited, attention must be paid to the necessary advance work: advertising the time of each visit on radio and TV, and on the morning of the tour getting a group of young people out to the small towns en route to put up posters and remind key supporters of the meeting.

The turnouts were amazing. I also follow the course, when using a helicopter, of dropping down to meet farmers in their fields. In a single helicopter tour I can cover twelve or fifteen towns and villages and visit with hundreds and hundreds of people.

To return to the particulars of the 1957 campaign: on the Liberal side, Jimmy Gardiner was a great campaigner; C. D. Howe was not. Howe never dreamed that things were going as they were. Howe had prestige, properly earned, and I had a very great admiration for him. But the Right Honourable C. D. Howe had no more use for Parliament than Satan has for Heaven. Although these were not his words, his attitude was: "Who's going to stop us if we want to do anything?" His arrogance was well established—his "What's a million?" approach to the public's business. In my campaign speeches I would bring out one thing after another, and I would end every point with: "Where are we going—and Howe?" Everyone laughed. There were occasions when I came to the end of a sentence, and the crowd, anticipating my next word, started to say "and Howe".

Then, of course, there are the breaks that take place in a campaign. In the last few days of the campaign in Toronto, a youngster by the name of William Hatton, encouraged by others in the Youth for Diefenbaker movement (among them my present Executive Assistant, Keith Martin), made his way to the platform where Prime Minister St. Laurent was speaking. Carrying a Diefenbaker sign, he was shoved off the stage by a Liberal official. Down he went several feet to the concrete floor. He appeared to be seriously injured. The crowd was outraged. The next day I devoted part of my speech to new methods for quieting perverse people who did not agree with government policy: "Shove them off the platform. If they break their necks, that's just too bad."

The turning point in the campaign, though, was a meeting that I will always remember, in Vancouver on 23 May. Olive and I rode in an open car from the Hotel Vancouver to the Georgia Auditorium. There were thousands on the streets. On the way to the meeting, a great tall chap, rugged in appearance, came up to the car. "Hello, John. I bet you don't remember me." I did, and said so. He went on. "I bet you can't tell these people the last time you saw me." I said, "Do you want to know? You were in the dock charged with murder." He turned around to his companions. "I told you so-and-sos he wouldn't forget me."

The auditorium was crammed: close to ten thousand people. My speech rolled along until I committed an unpardonable sin. I asked a question. Never ask questions on the platform, unless of someone who isn't there. After pointing out how the Liberal Party hadn't acted, I asked, "What would the Conservative Party do?" And away out there in the balcony was a Cockney chap with a loudspeaker who roared, "Nothing." The audience laughed. (The best hecklers are old-country Englishmen. In the old country they call them "trined 'ecklers", and they are good.) I was concerned; you can have an audience laughing with you, but not at you. I ploughed along rather insecurely for about three or four minutes, trying to work out in my own mind something that would offset that interruption. Finally, in relation to another aspect of policy, I asked, "And what did the Liberal Party do?" Apparently my friend up there was receiving the adulation of those surrounding him for his magnificent effort in interruption. From that same location, from that same horn, there was another loud "Nothing". I thanked him very much, and said I appreciated the reformation that had taken place within the last few minutes. That turned the situation around. When the meeting was over there were hundreds to shake hands. I saw a fellow trying to work his way through, and I said, "You come here. They're holding you back." He said, "I'm your 'eckler and I'm going to vote for you too."

Actually, there were no major problems during the campaign, although there were some minor ones. I wanted to get Charlotte Whitton to run in the constituency of Renfrew South. She could have won very easily; she was raised in that area. Typical of Charlotte, she wouldn't say yes and she wouldn't say no. I spent an hour with her in my office one morning discussing the question. That finished me; Gordon Churchill had to take over. When I went into the House at eleven o'clock, he was with her; when I came back at one, she was still saying the same thing over and over again. She phoned me next day and said, "I think I'll go to the convention." I thought it a fine idea. She said, "I want to come with you." I told her that I couldn't do that; if I brought her out, the other candidates could complain that the nomination had been rigged in her favour. "Well," she replied, "I haven't said whether I'm going to be a candidate or not." We left it at that. She arrived on her own. My speech was to be broadcast locally at five p.m. The convention began in the early afternoon. No candidate was to speak for more than five or ten minutes. I don't know how long Charlotte spoke, but it was over an hour. And she ended up by saying, "I will not run!" The result was that instead of having forty-five minutes on the radio, I had five minutes.

No matter where I spoke, I felt that I was speaking to all Canadians. I gave them a picture of the kind of Canada I wanted to achieve, from the north to the south, from the east to the west. When I went to the Province of Quebec, I did not go there to make all kinds of promises, as so many Conservatives had done over the years. I told my Quebec audiences: "I'm not going to promise you anything except that your rights shall be maintained. In many cases, in too many, you've been denied equality. That will end as far as I'm concerned." I did not go into Quebec to tell the people, "You're wonderful." I brought no such message. If I were to say to the people of Vancouver or Calgary or Winnipeg or Toronto or Halifax, "You're the most wonderful people in the world," I know what my audience would do. Everyone who had a wallet would reach to see whether it was still there.

I have a great admiration for the people of Quebec, although I have found it difficult sometimes to understand their attitude in relation to France. France forsook her Canadian colonists forever in 1763. I said so. Further, never at any time did I run away from the fact that so many French Canadians had concluded (there being no effective argument offered to the contrary) that the monarchy ought to be removed. I simply pointed out that French Canadians from their earliest days have always had a monarch; that in 1774 had it not been for the British monarchy they would not have achieved freedom of religion, for it was Westminster that provided this fifty years before the same rights were attained in Great Britain. I said, "You want a republic. Let me go back to the period of the American Revolution. Had it not been for French Canada, the Americans would have won in 1775 and '76 when they attacked Canada. French Canada stood firm. One has only to ask the question: 'What language rights would French Canada have as part of the United States?' "

My reading of the discussions prior to Confederation revealed convincing evidence that the Fathers of Confederation intended to build "One Canada", while at the same time assuring the French minority of its rights of language, education, and religion. I have always contended that these rights must remain inviolate and that they cannot be changed without the agreement of the federal Parliament and of all the provinces. I believed that Quebec at heart was conservative-minded, but that propaganda, poured out endless times by unnumbered political agitators, had sold the idea that as a party we were against the rights and aspirations of the people of the Province of Quebec. Even in 1957 the Liberal Party was still fighting with the slogan that Louis Riel should not have been executed in 1885.

In an address in Montreal on 12 March 1957, I clearly stated what the Conservative Party would do:

1) It will bring about a united Canada. Our first aim is "ONE CANADA" in which there will be equalization of opportunity for all parts of Canada.
2) We will maintain the Constitution and Provincial rights thereunder which we consider as a sacred trust which shall be maintained in fact as in law.
3) We will halt the ever-increasing trend to centralization of power in Ottawa whether directly taken or indirectly through taxation measures which deny to the Provinces and in consequence to the Municipalities their fair share of the taxation dollar. Is evidence necessary to establish this trend?

The concentration of taxation in the Federal Government since the war is shown by the fact that in 1939, of the Net General Revenue—44% of the total taxation levied was taken by the Federal Government, 32% by the Provincial, and 24% by the Municipal governments.

On the basis of the latest taxation statistics available 71.2% went to the Federal coffers, 15.8% to the Provincial, and 13% to the Municipal governments.

The concentration of taxation in the central Government will, if unchecked, dilute Provincial rights as effectively, if more slowly, than would actual amendment of the Constitution. This trend must be stopped.

The views of the Government were revealed in the speech given by Prime Minister St. Laurent to the Canadian Bar

Association two years ago when he spoke of the increasing demands of the people on the Central Government, and used these words:

"If those demands are to be met it naturally follows that the Government has to be endowed with the necessary powers and financial means to make that possible. . . . Only in that way can a democratic government remain democratic."

That theory enunciated by the Prime Minister would set at naught the Constitution.

4) *We will restore Parliamentary Government.*

Parliament has been treated as an unmitigated nuisance and the people's elected representatives dominated by the Cabinet. Father may know best but that is not Democracy.

5) We will put a stop to the Federal Government going into business which, in recent years, has developed into an insidious form of creeping socialism.

6) We will provide needed help to the agricultural industry by providing for expanding markets and to alleviate the detrimental effects of the squeeze in which farmers are now and have been irreparably caught between rising costs of production and falling farm prices.

7) We will respect the right of Labour.

8) We will maintain the Social Security Measures.

There is every indication that the Liberal Party will endeavour to lead people to believe that Social Security Measures will be diminished or abolished by our Party. Let that question be answered once and for all by this declaration.

We have fought the battles of Parliament to maintain the Constitutional rights of the minorities and of the Provinces. It was the Conservative Party under Macdonald and Cartier that created these Constitutional rights. It is this Party that will maintain them.

The Party that gave Canada Confederation and the Federal System of Government believes that that Constitution must be preserved and maintained and that the Agreement of

Confederation must not be subject to the whims of majorities in Parliament.

In recent years we have fought these battles although the support given the Conservative Party in point of numbers elected in the Province of Quebec has been small. Having taken this stand have we not the right to ask for active and effective support with members from this Province to join with members from all parts of Canada in maintaining the vital and abiding principles of Confederation.

At the beginning of the campaign in 1957, it was said that I was anti-French Canadian. And this despite the fact that I had always been the friend of French Canadians in my province who had not forgotten that I had acted successfully on the appeal of Ethier and Boutin, two French-Canadian school trustees who had been convicted of permitting too much French-language instruction in their local school. It was claimed in 1957 that so far as I was concerned all I intended to do was secure the support of English Canada and forget about Quebec. They knew this was not true; not one syllable, not one word, not one line in any speech I ever delivered conveyed any other idea than that I was for "one Canada, one nation". I have never uttered a disparaging word about French Canada either indirectly or at all.

But the Liberals thought they had something and, with the active support of the Balcers and that ilk, contended that Gordon Churchill, a dominant figure in my campaign, had originated a plan, which they said was Conservative Party policy, that we would work to secure support in English-speaking Canada and would forget about Quebec. That was false propaganda and they knew it. What Gordon Churchill had said in effect was this: "Quebec has not voted Conservative in election after election in this century, but it's of singular interest that whenever the Conservative Party has taken office, French

Canada has given the party considerable support. That was so in 1911 when Robert Borden formed a government; that was so in 1930 when R. B. Bennett did the same." In other words, his advice was: "Have a national policy and whatever the Liberal false propaganda may be, when the people of Quebec realize that a Conservative Party can win, they'll do what they did in those past two elections."

Quebec thus received the same assistance for its candidates as every other province in the campaign. I went in there and spoke to no greater or lesser an extent than in any other province, excepting Ontario. A French Canadian is no different from anyone else, but he knows one thing. He knows sincerity and he knows political camouflage. I decided on the course to be followed; the words of Sir George-Etienne Cartier sum it up: "First of all let us be Canadians." I used those words and added to them: "Canada has need of French Canada and French Canada has need of Canada: without subservience, with equality." There were to be no false promises, no hypocrisy for the sake of votes. I simply appealed to them on the ground that Liberal propaganda sought to make dupes of them. "You ask why you're disregarded? Well, the Liberal Party has you in the palm of its hands. You are just puppets. They count you that way." It is of interest that the lowest number of seats won in Quebec under my leadership was greater than the sum of the seats won by Bennett in 1935, Manion in 1940, Bracken in 1945, and Drew in 1949.

Quebec's Premier, Maurice Duplessis, did not actively support me. I never chatted with him for more than fifteen minutes in all the years excepting at conferences of premiers, and then only briefly. The only time he ever telephoned me was from the airport in Quebec in September of 1959 when he was en route to the northern part of his province, where he passed away. It is a strange thing. He said that when he returned to Quebec, he was going to be in touch with me; he had a number of matters that he wanted to discuss. But he did not return. He was followed in office then by Colonel Paul Sauvé, a close friend of mine. Daniel Johnson was the most important Union Nationale personage to support publicly the Conservative Party in 1957.

In Ontario, it was Premier Frost. No man in public life did more than he for the Conservative Party in that election. In Nova Scotia, the Honourable Robert Stanfield, Premier since 20 November 1956, worked very hard for our candidates, as he did in subsequent elections, particularly in 1965. The Honourable Hugh John Flemming worked tirelessly in New Brunswick. But in 1957, from the very beginning of the campaign, it was Frost who said, "We're going to win." I have read that Dalton Camp played a major role in the 1957 victory. At the time, I knew nothing of him whatever; and he did not operate under an assumed name at that time. At the convention in 1967 he was never referred to by name: he was "Mother". After his conduct at the 1966 Annual Meeting, it was understandable that he would operate under a name other than his own. In 1957, however, he was nothing.

Very important to our 1957 success was the agricultural policy we presented at Brantford on 7 May. We pledged, when returned to power, to take action at the federal level to improve the condition of agriculture so that our farm people might successfully re-establish their rightful position in our economy, so basic to our national welfare.

To this end, we committed ourselves to:

1. Maintain a flexible price support program to ensure an adequate parity for agricultural producers, based on a fair price-cost relationship.
2. Include a definite formula in the Agricultural Prices Support Act for arriving at support prices, such for-

mula to allow for variation in production and demand
for individual products.

3. Establish the formula and support prices in consultation with representative farm organizations, which
would be announced each year well in advance of the
production period, as required.

We favoured producer marketing boards as a method
of marketing agricultural products, and promised every
possible encouragement and support for their establishment, when desired by producers, in co-operation with
the provinces. The principle of cash advances on farm-
stored Western wheat had been advocated time and time
again by the Conservative Party in Opposition. We were
pledged to a policy of extending and easing the farm
credit problem. We promised to co-operate with the Prairie Provinces in developing a more realistic crop insurance plan, and to work with all the provinces in establishing a proper program of soil and water conservation
on a national basis. We took firm positions on freight
rates, agricultural dumping, and expanded foreign markets. Mountains of wheat were piling up in the West as
high as Everest. Markets were lost, right and left. Those
in Trade and Commerce simply accepted this situation as
inevitable. We did not, and the farmers knew we meant
business.

In discussing our 1957 election platform, I have left until the last our program of social justice. This was an essential part of my national vision. To me, government not
only had to be *of* and *by* the people, but most positively
for the people. Unless government concerned itself with
the problems of the individual working man and farmer,
unless government was cognizant of the problems of the
small businessman and not just of the corporate giants,
unless government acted in the interests of our senior citizens, our veterans, our blind and disabled, unless government sought a basic equality of citizenship, of oppor-

tunity, and of well-being for all our peoples, then government had lost sight of its true purpose. I argued that the Liberals had long since forgotten the fact that human betterment is the essence of government. Their six-dollar-a-month increase in the Old Age Pension amounted to a mere twenty cents a day. The result was that our pensioners were receiving less in purchasing power in 1957 than in 1951. The same position applied to the war pensioners and retired civil servants. The record is clear. Liberal policies were meagre and mean. I stated the position of the Conservative Party in our very first campaign meeting:

In connection with Social Security we propose to set a figure high enough to meet the needs of our older citizens, and to make necessary adjustments thereafter on a cost of living basis. My mind goes back to my early days. . . . I believe I know the needs of the average man and woman. My pledge to you is that you will receive adequate and fair treatment in keeping with the responsibilities of the state to assure a reasonable equality to all our citizens.

On the question of a Canadian Bill of Rights, I stood as firmly for it in 1957 as I had during the preceding years, despite some opposition. It has been critically remarked in relation to the first volume of these memoirs that there is nothing in Hansard to indicate my position on the question of the banishment of the Canadian Japanese from the west coast of British Columbia during the Second World War. Indeed, on 23 April 1947, on a question of privilege in response to a statement by Stanley Knowles, M.P. from Winnipeg North Centre, I said on this very subject:

I want to say that my attitude has never changed, and aspersions such as those [in reference to my alleged support of the Order-in-Council ordering the forced removal of the Japanese

Canadians from the Pacific Coast] do not detract from that fact. I am opposed to any discrimination against Canadians, regardless of their race or creed.

Stanley Knowles, to his credit, apologized for suggesting that I supported the Order-in-Council in question. Three weeks later, on 16 May 1947, I said this in the House:

What would a Bill of Rights do? . . . It would assert the right of the individual; it would assert the right of a minority to be protected in the exercise of its rights, against the majority. It would, above all, assure that each of us would have a legal right to be heard in the courts of this country.

Or as I said on 24 March 1952:

A Bill of Rights would do something more; it would make Parliament freedom-conscious. It would make Parliament realize that rights are to be preserved. It would make Parliament more cautious in passing laws that would have the effect of interfering with freedom. It would act as a landmark by means of which Canadians, through Parliament, would have redeclared those things which have made Canada great. It would preserve those spiritual wells in legislative form without which freedom cannot survive. It would give to Canadians the realization that wherever a Canadian may live, whatever his race, his religion or his colour, the Parliament of Canada would be jealous of his rights and would not infringe upon those rights which are dear to us all. . . .

I regarded a Canadian Bill of Rights as fundamental to my philosophy of social justice and national development. My focus was on the individual betterment of Canadians. If historic freedoms were not protected, then my programs to ensure a climate of expansion and development from Atlantic to Pacific, then my concern that all Canadians should enjoy a reasonable share of the good life, then my vision of the "New Frontier", would be for nought. "One Canada" stood for prejudice towards none and freedom for all. There were to be no second-class citizens, no discrimination based on race, creed, sex, or economic station in the Canada of my dreams. "Let us be Canadians first" was a message that only the most gross distortion could portray as anything other than a call to a realization of our full potential as a nation of free people. It was a clarion call that many Canadians heard for the first time in 1957 and 1958. Their response speaks for itself.

The 1957 campaign ended for me on the evening of Saturday, 8 June 1957. I held my last meeting, as I always do, in the town of Nipawin, in the eastern portion of Prince Albert constituency. I remember that it was a large meeting, ably presided over by Mrs. Wright. When I remarked to my audience in an almost casual way, "On Monday I'll be Prime Minister," it was obvious that many thought I had passed beyond the pale of responsibility.

Sunday we were at home in Prince Albert. On election Monday, Olive and I voted and waited for what fortune might bring. Allister Grosart was with us, as were those many friends who had made it possible for me to be elected in Prince Albert in 1953, when the returns from Eastern Canada began to come in. When the news came through that the Right Honourable C. D. Howe had been defeated in Port Arthur, I remarked that the list of defeated Liberal ministers reminded me of Scotland after Flodden. It was suggested that, whatever the outcome, I should be prepared to go on national television and radio, and that it would be wise to prepare a couple of speeches, one in the event that we won, and one in the event that we lost. I said, "One. We're not going to lose."

When I was defeated in election campaigns, and it was a frequent enough occurrence between 1925 and 1938, Mother always said that sooner or later things would turn out well. My abiding memory of my mother is on election

night in 1957. She was in hospital in Saskatoon. I went to
see her. By then, it was generally being said over the radio that I would be called upon to be Prime Minister. My
mother said to me, "You've been given the opportunity to
do something for your country. Do not forget the poor
and afflicted. Do the best you can as long as you can."
And that was the last time that she, with her Highland an-
cestry and their refusal to exult, ever said anything about
the fact that I had become Prime Minister of my country.
With regret that day, I thought how wonderful it would
have been if my father had lived to see his dreams come
true. It had been a long, long journey from our arrival at
Fort Carlton fifty-four years before.

There was a real celebration in Prince Albert on election night, 1957. Not only was I on the verge of forming a
government, I had more than doubled my 1953 margin of
personal victory. I stayed at the party long enough to
make a little speech of thanks to those who made the
election result possible. Then I went to bed. The next
morning, with Duff Roblin, M.L.A. and Leader of the Opposition in the Manitoba Legislature, my brother Elmer, and
my devoted friends Fred Hadley, Tommy Martin, and
Harry Houghton, I went fishing.

CHAPTER TWO

※

THE LIBERAL HIGH COMMAND may have been staggered, even stunned, by the election results, but I suspect that no one had cause to view them with greater dismay than Blair Fraser, Ottawa editor of *Maclean's* magazine, whose magazine had been put to press before the election results were in, assuming that the universe would unfold as it always had. He had written, with supreme Liberal confidence, on the return of the St. Laurent government to power: "For better or for worse, we Canadians have once more elected one of the most powerful governments ever created by the free will of a free electorate. We have given that government an almost unexampled vote of confidence, considering the length of its term in office."

I can only imagine how trying the world was for all these mainstays of the Liberal Party those first few days following the election. For me, there were no ringing telephones, no hurried consultations, no meetings with the press. I was fishing on Lac La Ronge. And, for a trout fisherman, the northern and eastern portions of the lake are in a class by themselves. Those too-few halcyon days were interrupted by a message from Mr. St. Laurent asking me to meet him in Ottawa as quickly as convenient, a reminder that the events of 10 June were indeed reality.

The limitations of this reality, however, were demonstrated one day as I was fishing out of sight of and some distance from my companions. One of the local game wardens approached me and demanded to see my fishing licence. His only concern was whether or not I had a valid fishing licence, and properly so. I might say that he looked at me with unveiled suspicion while I fumbled through my pockets in search of it. Finally I found it. He examined it. Satisfied, he left. Had I not had one, and I might easily have forgotten to get one the morning after the election, I am sure he would have proceeded to do his duty. It would have given my prime-ministership a rather unusual beginning.

Olive and I arrived at Uplands airport, Ottawa, at 7.35 a.m. on Friday, 14 June 1957, having paid our own way on a regular commercial flight. Later that morning, I saw Mr. St. Laurent in his East Block office on Parliament Hill. He told me that the Right Honourable James G. Gardiner and one or two others in the Cabinet considered that he should stay on until the House met, and that their ability to continue as the government should be determined on a confidence motion. Mr. St. Laurent, however, felt that the people had spoken. He said that unless the soldiers' vote brought about a substantial change in the election result, he would resign.

As I left our meeting, the press judged from the expression on my face that Mr. St. Laurent was going to continue in office. Blair Fraser joined me as I walked towards my office in the Centre Block. I referred to his editorial: "Blair, you must feel very much like a lawyer who, knowing he has a good case, argues it with enthusiasm. Concluding that his position is impregnable, he then to his amazement finds that the lawyer on the other side has produced an authority binding the reverse of his argument on the court." Although he laughed, I detected a certain lack of enthusiasm for my analogy. I might have reminded him of an earlier article in *Maclean's* on 1 December 1953, in which he suggested that I lacked the stamina ever to become a party leader.

The soldiers' vote changed only one seat, and Mr. St. Laurent announced his decision to resign on 17 June. I am unable to recall my reaction when I was sworn in as a member of the Privy Council of Canada and Secretary of State for External Affairs. (There is no oath of office for the Prime Minister.) Naturally, it meant for me the opportunity to achieve some of those things I had advocated over the years. From my earliest days I wanted to become one of the leaders of my country. I wanted to bring about the realization of an ideal that went back to my collegiate days: one Canada, one Nation. I wanted to end discrimination within this country. I wanted to do something for the poor and the afflicted. I saw the difficulties of the farmer. I knew what it was to be a common labourer. I knew what it was to have lived in a home in which every dollar had to be carefully spent. I had always believed that some day I would have the opportunity now presented. This was one of the reasons why, while often rejected, I was never dejected by defeat. June 21, 1957, was the culmination of a long, long trail to the mountain peaks. If I may adapt Lincoln's reply to the Congressional Committee on 9 February 1865 as a description of my feelings, it was with deep gratitude to my countrymen for this mark of their confidence; with a distrust of my own ability to perform the duty required; yet with a firm reliance on the strength of our free government, and the loyalty of the people to the just principles upon which it is founded; and above all with an unshaken faith in the Supreme Ruler of nations, that I began the tasks of government.

My first task had been to form a Cabinet. This is a difficult and trying responsibility. The considerations of region and religion that normally complicate decisions of Cabinet appointment were in my case made doubly difficult by the fact that only one of our members had had any previous Cabinet experience, an experience limited to a few weeks in 1935. A Prime Minister cannot pick all the best men and women to serve with him. Every province must be represented. There must be a Catholic from Ontario and a Protestant from Quebec, and so on. Thus A and B may be selected, whereas C and D, who are better qualified, may be left aside. Because Ontario and Quebec had between them 160 of the 265 members in the House of Commons, one was obliged to begin the process of Cabinet selection there. There had been 24 possible Cabinet portfolios under the previous administration. I settled on 23, although all were not filled by separate ministers on 21 June when we went to Government House to be sworn in. Ontario had given the Conservative Party 61 of a possible 85 seats in the House of Commons, or 72 per cent; those 61 seats represented 54 per cent of our total strength. Ontario, to begin with, had five ministers in my government, including one without portfolio. Quebec had given us 9 of her 75 seats in the Commons, or 12 per cent; those 9 seats represented 8 per cent of our strength. The three ministers appointed from Quebec amounted to 33 per cent of our members from that province; Ontario's five appointments represented only 8 per cent of her members. Nevertheless, when the Cabinet was sworn in, editorials appeared in the French-language press criticizing me for not appointing more French-speaking ministers from Quebec. Two of the three ministers in question were French Canadians. To this number I added the Deputy Speaker of the House of Commons, a Parliamentary Assistant, and our Deputy Whip.

I might note that when I first entered the House of Commons in 1940, there were only four French-Canadian ministers in the Cabinet: Messrs Lapointe, Cardin, Casgrain, and Dandurand, the latter being Minister without Portfolio and Government Leader in the Senate. When Mr. Lapointe died on 26 November 1941, Mr. St. Laurent was appointed to replace him. But Mr. Casgrain resigned on 15 December 1941 and Senator Dandurand died on 11 March 1942. When Mr. Cardin resigned on 11 May 1942, the only French-speaking Quebec member in the Cabinet was Mr. St. Laurent. This went on for a period of five months, despite the fact that the Liberal Party had a bloc of sixty Quebec members. Yet the press at the time was not critical of Prime Minister King.

The process of making my first Cabinet was not fully completed until 9 October, five days before the opening of Parliament, when Senator John Haig was made Government Leader in the Senate. The Canadian ministry as it then looked:

Prime Minister and President of the Queen's Privy Council for Canada
   The Rt. Hon. John G. Diefenbaker
Minister of Public Works and A/Minister of Defence Production
   The Hon. Howard C. Green
Minister of Finance and Receiver General
   The Hon. Donald M. Fleming
Minister of Veterans Affairs
   The Hon. Alfred J. Brooks
Minister of Transport
   The Hon. George Hees
Solicitor General
   The Hon. Léon Balcer
Minister of National Defence
   The Hon. George R. Pearkes
Minister of Trade and Commerce
   The Hon. Gordon M. Churchill
Minister of Justice and Attorney General and A/Minister of Citizenship and Immigration
   The Hon. E. Davie Fulton
Minister of National Revenue
   The Hon. George C. Nowlan
Minister of Agriculture
   The Hon. Douglas S. Harkness
Secretary of State
   The Hon. Ellen L. Fairclough

Minister of Fisheries
   The Hon. J. Angus MacLean
Minister of Labour
   The Hon. Michael Starr
Postmaster General
   The Hon. William M. Hamilton
Minister without Portfolio
   The Hon. James M. Macdonnell
Minister without Portfolio
   The Hon. William J. Browne
Minister of Mines and Technical Surveys
   The Hon. Paul Comtois
Minister of National Health and Welfare
   The Hon. J. Waldo Monteith
Minister of Northern Affairs and National Resources
   The Hon. F. Alvin Hamilton
Secretary of State for External Affairs
   The Hon. Sidney E. Smith
Leader of the Government in the Senate
   The Hon. John T. Haig

I might say that although the above listing is according to the formal order of precedence, I regarded all my ministers as equals. To let one minister know that he is in a department of a secondary nature is to bring about internal jealousies that can result in weakening a Cabinet. Naturally, there are some portfolios that have become senior in the public mind; but the suggestion that one is senior and another junior in the relations of a Prime Minister and the members of his Cabinet is the last thing I would want to develop. This is not to say that questions of precedence were not on occasion of considerable importance to some of my colleagues.

I think that one of the weaknesses of our system today is the increase in the number of Cabinet Ministers. Some contend that there should be a Cabinet within the Cabinet. Certainly the number of Cabinet Ministers in the present government, coupled with the number of Parliamentary Secretaries, is of such a size as to be ineffective.

In point of fact, I think that there should be a marked reduction; otherwise the Cabinet is simply a glorified extension of the House of Commons. Most important, a large Cabinet encourages a large bureaucracy, with the consequence that the bureaucracy takes control.

I will not discuss all my Cabinet appointments, but I feel that I should talk about some of them. To begin with, I asked Howard Green, Member of Parliament from Vancouver since 1935, to become my Minister of Public Works and Acting Minister of Defence Production. What I desired most was assurance that in the awarding of government contracts the integrity of the government would be unchallengeable. This was a matter of establishing clearly the moral tone of our government. The public deserved no less than full confidence that their business was being scrupulously attended to. I was not only certain of Howard Green in my own mind, I knew that no one would ever conclude that improper or under-the-table influences could determine the awarding of any major government contract while he was the minister responsible. (I say "major" because those are the only contracts subject to personal examination by the minister.) Personal integrity remained a principal consideration in my appointment of Green's successors as Minister of Public Works, the Honourable David Walker and the Honourable Davie Fulton.

As to Donald Fleming, there was never any doubt in my mind that he should be a member of the Cabinet. Initially, however, there was some question as to whether he should be Minister of Finance or Secretary of State for External Affairs. I discussed the question with him. He indicated that he would be happy with either portfolio. Finally, I decided that, given his study of finance and his capacity for detailed analysis, he would make an extraordinarily good Minister of Finance; and in my opinion he was just that. He was not only highly competent, but also more than careful with the people's money at every level of expenditure. He came to epitomize fiscal responsibility, even though the period of recession that the St. Laurent government had bequeathed us forced him into a program of deficit financing.

J. M. Macdonnell had been Opposition financial critic under Drew. However, Members generally regarded his speeches on financial questions as being less than admirable. When I told Olive the names of those I had chosen, she, without attempting to interfere in any way, said, "You haven't included Jim Macdonnell." I said that I could not. She suggested that it would break his heart. I reconsidered, and because of his war record and his many years of work for the party in the House and on the hustings, I decided to make him Minister without Portfolio. Following the swearing in at Rideau Hall, he told Olive that because I had forgiven him his subterranean plots against me over the years, he would never again be disloyal. It was not long, however, before he returned to his former ways. It was without regret that I accepted his resignation in August 1959.

I asked Davie Fulton to become Minister of Justice and Attorney General and Acting Minister of Citizenship and Immigration. While his experience as a lawyer was limited, he had a good knowledge of the law and an interest in penal reform and in the revision of the criminal code, which was filled with inacuities and anomalies that impaired its relevance to contemporary problems. What is more, he was a strong supporter of human liberties. Perhaps a little too abstract and detached to be effective on the stump, he was nevertheless a good parliamentarian, a close student of the rules, and an excellent debater. I had been much impressed by his performance during the 1956 Pipeline Debate; in my view, that was the high point of his parliamentary career. He was politically ambitious, and, as Prime Minister, I had always to consider this when reviewing his recommendations to Cabinet. Further, he was not politically wise: three of his great finds as officials and assistants in the Department of Justice were Guy Favreau, subsequently Minister of Justice under Pearson, Marc Lalonde, Minister of Health and Welfare under Trudeau, and Michael Pitfield, the present Clerk of the Privy Council. And this is to say nothing about his 1963 venture into British Columbia provincial politics against the Honourable W. A. C. Bennett. To help him, I made David Walker his Parliamentary Assistant. Mr. Walker not only had a considerable practical knowledge of the law but was a fine administrator.

In 1956 George Hees had initially considered himself a serious contender for the leadership of the party. A cross-country tour to line up support changed his mind. He then decided to support me. George's principal asset was his personality; everything he undertook he espoused with great enthusiasm. His initial portfolio was Transport, where he did his best. In 1960, I transferred him to Trade and Commerce, where he distinguished himself in the promotion of Canada's external trade. Frankness, however, demands recognition that a considerable portion of this success was due to the shrewdness of his Executive Assistant, Mel Jack. When I first spoke to Hees about Transport, he asked me whether I wanted Mel Jack in my office. I most certainly did, but I decided that it would not be fair to take him away from Hees. George needed the advice and counsel that Jack could provide.

Léon Balcer, Member for Trois Rivières, was first elected to the House of Commons in 1949. He was, perhaps, my most bitter opponent in 1956. When the convention decided that I should be Leader, he and his wife immediately rose and, with their group from Quebec, left the convention. His wife is reported to have said at the time that the blinds of Quebec would be forever drawn on my leadership. She would have made this so had she been able. Balcer was a past National President of the Conservative Party and an important member from Quebec. Although I found him honest, both as Solicitor General and subsequently as Minister of Transport, no uxorious control have I ever known to equal that in which he was enmeshed. I mention both Balcer and Macdonnell as examples of personages whom I included in the Cabinet who over the years had done everything they could to prevent my becoming Leader. I did not quarrel with their past activities. I believed—wrongly, however—that in the Cabinet their plotting would cease.

Gordon Churchill was a distinguished educator and a front-line soldier in both world wars. He was also a parliamentarian of unusual ability. He was a man of strong opinions, with 'a capacity to explain and clarify in the course of debate which was as effective as it was uncommon. As a parliamentary strategist, Churchill was recognized by members of all political parties. It was a great loss to Parliament when, in 1968, he could endure no longer what he considered vacillation instead of courage by the Conservative Party on the important issues facing us. You have but to read the debates to know his ability. He served in my government as Minister of Trade and Commerce, Minister of Veterans Affairs, and Minister of National Defence. He was one minister who never failed to tell me frankly his views. When Churchill disagreed, I reconsidered. In 1957, the Department of Trade and Commerce was a Grit hive. If there was any department of government permeated by the divine-right theory of the previous administration, this was it. I needed a strong minister to change all that, and Gordon Churchill was my choice.

For Minister of National Defence, I chose Canada's hero of heroes and soldier's soldier, Major-General George Pearkes, v.c. He supported me at both the 1948 and 1956 leadership conventions, and there are no words to express my regard for him. He was the personification of modesty, despite the fires of adulation that glow around those who win the Victoria Cross. Yet he could speak to the General Staff, to the senior officers, with an authority that they recognized. He brought about the signing of the NORAD Agreement shortly after we took office. In 1960, I had him appointed Lieutenant-Governor of British Columbia. He and Mrs. Pearkes will be remembered always for the outstanding manner in which they discharged their responsibilities in that office.

One of the portfolios that gave me concern was External Affairs. Having decided that it would take me some time to find the appropriate person to fill it, I took the portfolio myself as a temporary expedient. In September of 1957 I was at Dartmouth College speaking on the subject of Canadian–American relations. Among those present was Dr. Sidney Smith. Smith had a remarkable scholastic and educational record, and was a profound student of international affairs. He had been Dean of Dalhousie Law School, President of the University of Manitoba, and at the time in question was President of the University of Toronto. He had a political mind, and, as I have already written, in 1942 it had been all arranged by the Warwicks in the party from Toronto and Montreal that if Mr. Bracken would not stand for the leadership, Sidney Smith would. I asked him to give consideration to resigning the presidency of the University of Toronto in order to become Canada's Secretary of State for External Affairs. When he agreed to do so, I appointed George White, the Member for Hastings–Frontenac, to the Senate. Dr. Smith contested the nomination. He won it and was elected in the by-election that followed. Parliament proved a novelty to him, and it took him some time to get used to it. He told me on one occasion that he found it difficult. However, just before he died, he told me: "You know, I'm finally begining to understand this institution." There were some who told me that I should have realized that he was overdoing it, but I didn't. His very sudden death on 17 March 1959 was a tragedy for all of Canada.

Michael Starr was the obvious choice for Minister of Labour. He knew labour problems from experience, both as a labour man and as an employer. His constituency (Ontario) had a large union membership, and he had served as Mayor of the city of Oshawa before being elected Member of Parliament. I first met Michael Starr when I campaigned for him in the Ontario by-election of 1952, which he won. I have never lost my original regard and respect for him. He was one of the best Ministers of Labour in our history. Of Ukrainian parentage, to me his life epitomizes all those who have come to Canada from abroad to become Canadians. For I see Canada not as a mosaic but rather as a peopled garden in which the flowers of different lands lend richness and beauty and the strength of their diversity to our body politic.

Douglas Harkness was a good administrator, a hard worker. As Minister of Agriculture he was thorough, but he antagonized every group of farmers who came to Ottawa or made representations to the Department of Agriculture. There were complaints from farm organizations that they were being treated by him in a peremptory if not cavalier manner. I had to bring about a change; had I not, the farmers would have turned against the government simply because of the unalloyed truculence of the Minister. It was then I decided that Defence would be a natural for him. He had a very good record in the Second World War and I thought that he would adopt an attitude towards the senior Defence officers similar to the one he had towards farmers. I was mistaken.

I did not appoint Alvin Hamilton to the Cabinet until 22 August 1957. He had started his career as a farm labourer at Delisle, Saskatchewan, the area that produced the famous Bentleys of National Hockey League fame, and had gone on to university to become a teacher. During the war he had served as a flight lieutenant with the RCAF in Asia. He had more electoral defeats before his first victory in Qu'Appelle in 1957 than any other member of the Cabinet, but defeats never discouraged him. I had not intended to bring him into my first Cabinet. He accompanied me across the country in late July, 1957. As we discussed farm problems and the ideas of Dr. Menzies, which were as novel to him as they had been to me, I decided that he would make a good Minister of Northern Affairs and Natural Resources. Initially, I had given this portfolio to Douglas Harkness, along with the acting responsibility for Agriculture. Harkness now was given Agriculture on a permanent basis. In 1960 I moved Hamilton to Agriculture when I appointed Harkness to Defence. He deserves special mention for the notable initiative that resulted in ARDA (Agricultural Rehabilitation and Development Act). Although this is legislation that I will discuss in detail in Chapter Nine, let me note here that not even the most determined efforts of our Liberal successors could destroy this achievement.

Over the years, I had taken the position that the women of Canada deserved and had the right to expect representation in Cabinet. Mrs. Ellen Fairclough, a Certified Public Accountant, attractive and able, and by this time an experienced Member of the House of Commons (having been first elected in a by-election in 1950), was an obvious choice for a portfolio. She was the first woman to become a member of the Queen's Privy Council for Canada, and was an outstanding Minister of the Crown. This was long before the days of "women's lib", but it is significant that in every case involving the appointment of Royal Commissions and the like by my government, women had their representatives. Canada's first woman ambassador was also appointed under my government.

William J. Browne from Newfoundland was a Rhodes Scholar, a man of courage and loyalty. First elected to the House of Commons in 1949 (he was defeated in 1953, but re-elected in 1957), he regarded Smallwood as a charlatan. I regretted that I was not able to give Browne a departmental portfolio; although he never showed any resentment, he must have been disappointed. When I reorganized my Cabinet in October 1960, I appointed him Solicitor General.

J. Angus MacLean, D.F.C., from Prince Edward Island, was a natural choice for the Cabinet. The hair-raising story of his escape from being arrested by the Gestapo after his plane was shot down during the Second World War, and the months and months it took him to travel through France to Spain, is a saga. First elected to Parliament in 1951, he has never failed to have the respect of the House of Commons, something that cannot be purchased. He was reliable and sincere, and although he did not speak frequently, he showed his ability as an orator at the caucus following the defeat of my government in 1963. As Minister of Fisheries, he was a success.

Waldo Monteith, a chartered accountant, came from a Perth, Ontario, family which has made a worthy contribution for generations to the public life of this country. Before he became Minister of National Health and Welfare in August 1957, he was one of my best friends and very trusted colleagues, and so he has remained. He deserves much credit for Canada's national Hospital Insurance scheme.

William McLean Hamilton of Montreal impressed me because he had overcome a lifelong physical disability. I felt that he would be an inspiration to others who were similarly handicapped. As Postmaster General, he made important progress in eliminating patronage practices in his department.

Alfred Brooks, Member of the Legislature of New

Brunswick from 1925 to 1935 and Member of Parliament from 1935 until his appointment to the Senate in 1960, was ideal for the portfolio of Veterans Affairs. He had served in both world wars, rising from the rank of corporal to major in the First World War, and to the rank of colonel in the Second. As Minister of Veterans Affairs, he held the affection and respect of the veterans and brought about an important advancement of their rights.

Then there was George Nowlan from Digby–Annapolis–Kings in Nova Scotia, who had served ably in the Nova Scotia Legislature and in Parliament. He had strongly opposed my candidacy at the 1948 leadership convention. In 1956, he assumed an air of neutrality and prevented the Nova Scotia delegation from indicating how they might vote by a show of candidates' badges or banners, when all the while he worked assiduously to defeat me. Despite his long-established opposition to me, I made him Minister of National Revenue. When Cabinet changes were made in 1962, I made him Minister of Finance.

I have often been asked why I appointed those people to Cabinet who had so vigorously opposed my leadership. Abraham Lincoln, who had included several in his Cabinet who had been his strong and bitter antagonists, was asked why he had done so. He is reported to have replied to the effect that he liked to have them around so he could see what they were doing. Unfortunately, I trusted my colleagues; but, then, in the early period of my prime-ministership I had no reason not to. I was quite pleased with my first Cabinet; I thought my ministers as talented and competent as any; certainly they were higher in general quality than those in preceding Liberal governments. Their performance during our period of minority government in 1957-58 was without question a worthy one.

The special prerogatives of the Prime Minister were set

out by Prime Minister Mackenzie King in an Order-in-Council (P.C. 3374) on 25 October 1935. It was provided that only the Prime Minister could recommend:

Dissolution and Convocation of Parliament

Appointment of

    Her Majesty's Privy Councillors for Canada

    Cabinet Ministers

    Lieutenant-Governors

       (including leave of absence to same)

    Provincial Administrators

    Speaker of the Senate

    Chief Justices of all courts

    Senators

    Sub-Committees of Council

    Treasury Board

    Committee of Internal Economy, House of Commons

    Deputy Heads of Departments

    Librarians of Parliament

    Crown appointments in both Houses of Parliament

    Governor General's Secretary's Staff

Recommendations in any Department

More important in many ways was the convention that gave the Prime Minister total control of Cabinet discussion. Each minister had the right to place any matter on the agenda for Cabinet consideration. The Prime Minister alone has the right to decide which matters shall actually be discussed in Cabinet. When a particular item is passed over, it automatically goes to the bottom of the next Cabinet agenda. If passed over again, it is not included in the next agenda. Prior to the First World War, the Prime Minister had been *primus inter pares*, first among equals, in his Cabinet. Over the years, and primarily because of his ability to control Cabinet decisions, he became *primus sine paribus*, first without equal.

The above Order-in-Council is lacking in another important particular: diplomatic appointments at the head-of-post level. I had many times expressed my view that Canada was ill served by the practice of virtually limiting External Affairs appointments abroad to departmental professionals. In consequence, the Department had built up an inbred élite of "personalities" which had been allowed to establish its own rules, a kingdom within a kingdom where diplomatic initiatives and negotiations were too often governed by democratically irresponsible perceptions of Canada's needs. I wanted to change this. I thought that something midway between the Canadian practice and that followed in the United States, where almost every head of post was a political appointee, would serve Canada well. If individuals, not necessarily learned in foreign affairs, but successful in their own fields of endeavour, were from time to time encouraged to focus their intelligence and ability on Canadian external relations through appointment to our missions abroad, the foreign-service establishment might recover from its atrophy. I also believed that a Canadian Ambassador or High Commissioner, if he so desired, ought to be free to make his representations and views known to the Prime Minister.

I have mentioned that I appointed the Honourable George Drew as High Commissioner to Britain. There was a feeling in External Affairs that this appointment should have gone to one of their establishment. Yet Drew proved to be an outstanding representative in London. He and his wife performed their duties in such a way that Canada had representation in London that was not just quiescent and bending. He understood the British people and tried to do everything he could during his term of office to bring about the closest of close relationships between the United Kingdom and Canada, and between Canada and the Commonwealth. He had strong opinions on Britain's entry into the European Common Market, which I shared. Drew's appointment was based on those principles that bring about the best of relations within families: recognition of differences, but the recognition also that the unity of a family is not destroyed by differences.

M. J. (Mickey) O'Brien of Vancouver was another. He would have brought new life, new verve, new views, and new vitality to the Department of External Affairs had he been appointed an ambassador. He was a stellar example of what an Irish immigrant can do with ability and determination in a new land. Everything was arranged for his appointment. Authoritative sources in the press predicted it. But at the last moment, Mickey decided his business demanded that he stay in Vancouver. I feel certain, however, that having made that decision, he later deeply regretted it. The indomitable and brilliant Charlotte Whitton had already been confirmed in her appointment as Ambassador to Eire when she lost her temper in Ottawa City Council and applied physical force to the person of a member of the city's Board of Control. Of necessity, her appointment was terminated before it had begun: another "first" for Charlotte.

Appointments at the deputy-minister level also received my fullest consideration, after consultation with the appropriate minister. When a government had been in power as long as the Liberals, it was natural that many public officials absorbed the political faith of the government, which in their opinion seemed destined to endure forever. Following the election in 1957 one or two high-ranking public servants suggested that my government would be at best short-lived. Another gave up his position because of an indiscretion in April 1958. The suggestion had been made by the British government that if we wanted to bring about a change in the balance of our foreign trade, this might be achieved by establishing free trade between Britain and Canada. It was not a formal offer but a suggestion, advanced, I think, with some degree of authority. Only four or five Canadians knew about this proposal. One morning I received a report that on a flight to Toronto the Deputy Minister of Trade and Commerce, Mitchell Sharp, had been discussing the British proposal with his seat-mate, who was not a member of the Civil Service. When this came to my attention, I called in the Clerk of the Privy Council and told him to get in touch with Mr. Sharp. He called Sharp, who immediately resigned; thus, he was never faced formally with the question.

There were a number of other occasions when leaks took place which, to say the least, were not helpful to my government. Pearson and Pickersgill, having been civil servants themselves, knew all the higher-echelon public servants. Perhaps there were a number of high-ranking public servants who should have been dismissed without delay when we took office, but I was one who was extremely reluctant to remove civil servants on the sole ground that they had served another administration. I thought that course most unjust, a view that I came by naturally. My father had joined the federal Civil Service under the Laurier administration. When the Conservatives came into office in 1911, there was strong pressure to remove all those who had been appointed under the previous administration. This, fortunately, was not done. Had my father been dismissed, it would have changed my entire life, and for the worse.

The most important consideration is to have ministers who do not allow themselves to be led around by their deputies, and who are not cowed by their deputies' superior command of relevant data. The Civil Service is there to advise on, but not to determine, policy. A minister is there to see that government policy is carried out within his department, or to know the reason why. That said, had I been returned to office in 1965, there would have been some major changes made. It became obvious as soon as we were out of office in 1963 that there were quite a number of senior people in the public service, about whom I had not known, who had simply been underground, quietly working against my government and waiting for the Liberals to return to power.

Below the deputy-minister level, the Civil Service Act had set up a commission to supervise appointments to the Civil Service, to ensure that all selections be based on competition, and to eliminate patronage appointments. The Act provides that there shall not be more than three Commissioners, appointed by the Governor-in-Council; each Commissioner to hold office for a period of ten years during good behaviour, and to be eligible for reappointment for not more than a further ten years. It is revealing that immediately before the 1957 general election, the recently appointed Chairman of the Civil Service Commission, Stanley Nelson, who was well below the compulsory retirement age of sixty-five and had served less than two years of his second ten-year term, was retired, very much against his wishes. Another Commissioner, A. J. Boudreau, who had served only eight of his ten years, was moved to the post of Canadian Consul General in Boston. The third seat on the Commission had been vacant since the retirement of Charles Bland the previous year. Arnold Heeney, Paul Pelletier, and Miss Ruth Addison, three career civil servants, all having been associated with leading Liberal ministers, were appointed to fill the vacancies. These appointments were open to a serious implication. If the Liberal cabal had wished to ensure their own stranglehold on the machinery of government, even in the event of their party's electoral defeat, their most certain way of doing so would have been to entrench Liberal Party sympathizers in the Civil Service Commission for the next ten years. The Civil Service Act stipulates that, except as otherwise provided in the Act, neither the Governor-in-Council nor any minister, officer of the Crown, or board of commission shall have any power to appoint or promote any employee to a position in the Civil Service. All appointments shall be made by the Commission, and only upon competitive examination. The federal Civil Service, exclusive of the employees of Crown corporations, had grown, in round figures, from 46,000 immediately prior to the outbreak of the Second World War to 115,000 by the war's end and to some 185,000 when we came into office. Given the fact that both Heeney and Pelletier had for many years been employed on the Prime Minister's and the Privy Council's staffs and that Miss Addison had been promoted quickly in the "Howe kindergarten", we were right to be suspicious. A situation existed in which there was some possibility that the Liberal Party in Opposition could vitiate the endeavours of the Conservative Party in power. Fortunately, Canadian civil servants were generally of a high professional quality. Indeed, on acquaintance, I was impressed with the qualities of Arnold Heeney. So much so, in fact, that I appointed him as our Ambassador to Washington.

It is the Prime Minister who appoints not only the Chief Justice of the Supreme Court of Canada, but all the provincial Chief Justices. This was a right with which I took great care lest someone become Chief Justice who might not discharge fully the responsibilities of that position. Of all the appointments I was called upon to make, I regarded those to the judiciary of critical importance to the well-being of society. While political considerations have their place in the appointment of judges under our system, they should apply only when the person under consideration is an outstanding lawyer and has the additional merit of personal courtesy. I endeavoured at all times to impress on my colleagues the necessity of established professional and personal merit in these appointments, and not just the fact that the party had benefited from the contribution of the individual concerned. As an example, when a vacancy for the position of Chief Justice of Saskatchewan arose, I chose the Honourable Justice E. M. Culliton, who had been appointed as a Puisne Judge of the Court of Appeal by the St. Laurent government. Earlier, he had been a minister in the Liberal government of the Honourable W. H. Patterson. I think it is only fair to add that under the Trudeau administration several judges have been appointed who were never members of the Liberal Party.

Some appointments were, of course, relatively easy to decide upon. Louis Rasminsky was the natural choice for Governor of the Bank of Canada. He should have been appointed governor in 1955, but the St. Laurent government decided that under no circumstances could they consider appointing a Jew to head the Bank. Theirs was a viewpoint that did not appeal to me.

Other appointments were somewhat more difficult: for example, the office of lieutenant-governor. There is often popular confusion about this position. A lieutenant-governor is not *per se* a representative of the Queen. He is simply an appointee of the Government of Canada to carry out the duties of the Crown at the provincial level of constitutional responsibility. Originally he was the principal federal check on provincial government, but this is no longer so. During our term of office there was only one occasion when a lieutenant-governor exceeded his authority. The Lieutenant-Governor of Saskatchewan, the Honourable Frank L. Bastedo, was an able, strong-minded, free-enterprise Conservative. When the Mineral Contracts Alteration Act was passed in 1961 by the Saskatchewan Legislature, he reserved it for the signification of the Government of Canada. Bastedo considered this legislation (1) *ultra vires* of the provincial legislature and (2) contrary to the national interest. No Provincial act should ever be reserved except on the request of the federal Cabinet. When I brought his reservation before Cabinet, royal assent was immediately advised. In announcing our decision in the Commons on 5 May 1961, I drew the attention of the House to the fact that in 1882 the Governor-General-in-Council, in a Minute-of-Council transmitted to the Lieutenant-Governors of each province, noted:

The Lieutenant Governor is not warranted in reserving any measure for the assent of the Governor General on the advice of his Ministers. He should do so in his capacity of a Dominion Officer only, and on instructions from the Governor General. It is only in a case of extreme necessity that a Lieutenant Governor should without such instructions exercise his discretion as a Dominion Officer in reserving a bill. In fact, with facility of communication between the Dominion and provincial governments such a necessity can seldom if ever arise.

I added: "That was in 1882. In view of the development of communications since, it is evident that nowadays there should be ample opportunity for Lieutenant-Governors to confer with the federal government before reserving a bill."

On 1 August 1958, we had considered in Cabinet the question of the federal power to disallow provincial legislation. We had then before us a petition for the disallowance of the British Columbia Mineral Property Taxation Act. My view was that we should not exercise this power. The Minister of Justice in 1927 had held the view that the federal government should not exercise disallowance on grounds of constitutional validity. I agreed; this was a matter for the courts. Disallowance on grounds that legislation might be objectionable in that it was contrary to the national interest and the national policy had not been exercised since 1936. In both the British Columbia and the Saskatchewan cases, "national interest" could not be properly defined in terms of political principle or point of view but had to include, as Justice Minister Fulton noted, "matters of practical or physical effect".

The position of lieutenant-governor is one that requires a broad knowledge of public affairs; and I have concluded that this office should be filled only by former parliamentarians, whether provincial or federal. The Honourable Paul Comtois, an agronomist in private life, had a sound grasp of constitutional traditions. I made him Lieutenant-Governor of Quebec in October 1961. He was an experienced politician who had served in the Cabinet as Minister of Mines and Technical Surveys since 21 June 1957. A man of sound judgment, he steered his office away from political trouble. There is, however, another side to this. The Honourable Earl Rowe, P.C., whom I appointed Lieutenant-Governor of Ontario in 1963, had over thirty years' experience in the House of Commons. It is not for me to judge how he discharged his responsibilities, but when he opened the Legislature of Ontario on 23 October 1963, he allowed the text of his Throne Speech to be broadcast publicly before he delivered it in the Legislature.

Some have contended that the office of lieutenant-governor is a constitutional anachronism. Nothing necessary to the carrying out of the parliamentary system is an anachronism. To dispense with royal assent in a constitutional monarchy is unthinkable.

The Governor General who invited me to form a government upon Mr. St. Laurent's resignation was His Excellency the Right Honourable Vincent Massey. Mr. Massey, the first Canadian Governor General, had assumed office 28 February 1952. He was a remarkably sound, learned, wise, and thoughtful man. He understood the monarchy and appreciated its contributions to good government. He fully understood that historically allegiance to the Crown had provided Canada a *raison d'être*, and that but for it Canada might have ceased to be an independent nation and become part of the United States. Although he had occupied various positions in the Liberal Party, including the presidency of the National Liberal Federation, at no time, when I asked his views, did I ever have reason to believe that he in any way permitted his party background to divert him from giving me the best advice possible. I do not believe that past political activity necessarily denies appointment as Governor General. Mr. Massey's term of office was due to expire when we assumed office. I was pleased to recommend that he continue in office, and he did so until 1959.

He might have been annoyed towards the end of his tenure, however, had he known that I was obliged to advise the Queen that during my period as Prime Minister there would be no titles for Canadian citizens. Her Majesty had desired to reward Mr. Massey as a personal expression of her gratitude for his fine service as Governor General of Canada. I personally was in the position where I might have received high and prestigious honours, but I made it clear I could not accept them. For example, in 1958 when I was in Malaya, Prime Minister Tunku Abdul Rahman offered me his country's highest decoration. I automatically turned it down. Another example was that of John T. Williamson, the famed Canadian diamond king, whom the British government was prepared to recommend for a knighthood. As Williamson was still a Canadian citizen, my government was asked what our attitude would be. We discussed this at length in Cabinet, and while his was a meritorious case, and particularly so because he was critically ill, we decided we could make no alteration in our stand.

It was my responsibility to recommend to Her Majesty a successor to Mr. Massey. I did not consider myself as bound to select a Canadian for this purpose. As a matter of fact, I was attracted by the idea that former Prime Ministers from various parts of the Commonwealth might from time to time serve as Governors General of Canada. I still believe this a good idea, and something that would serve to strengthen the Commonwealth connection. My recommendation to the Queen on this matter, however, came as a consequence of that sort of coincidence that alters the course of history.

In June 1959 I was honoured by the University of Montreal, whose Chancellor, Cardinal Léger, presented me with an honorary degree. While I was addressing the convocation, I noticed General Georges Vanier in the audience. I had met him only once previously but had always been impressed by him. His military record in the First World War was a most heroic one. He was a dedicated constitutional monarchist. He had had a wide and distinguished experience in the diplomatic service, from which he had recently retired. No one had suggested his name to me, but as I thought about it, I concluded he would be an ideal Governor General. When I finished speaking that afternoon, I asked the Cardinal, if he had the opportunity, to let Vanier know that I would like to see him. He came to see me in Ottawa. I told him that I could not make any promises, but that I was interested in whether he would accept the office of Governor General if he were offered the position. He asked time to think it over. Several days later he said he would be honoured to accept. When I brought his name to the attention of Cabinet, there was unanimous agreement. I recommended his appointment to the Queen in Halifax in August 1959. The occasion was a dinner given by the Premier of Nova Scotia and myself for Her Majesty and Prince Philip prior to their departure from Canada after their national tour that summer. She regarded my suggestion most favourably.

The Right Honourable Georges Vanier was a success as Governor General. He was highly regarded across the country. In my dealings with him, I found that he looked into such matters as required his attention with care. This was especially so when capital cases came up. He would read the evidence in each case, determined that any portion of it favourable to the condemned man should receive full consideration by Cabinet. In other matters, he seldom gave his views unless these were related to External Affairs, in particular Commonwealth affairs. When I sought his opinion, his wealth of experience was always available to me.

Under General Vanier, Government House functioned as it had under Mr. Massey. I mention this because I am somewhat concerned about reports in the press which indicate that, as Governor General, the Right Honourable Jules Léger can act only on the recommendations of the Prime Minister, even as to the management of his household. My wife and I have been friends with Jules and Madame Léger since our wedding trip to Mexico in 1953, and I welcomed his appointment. But I am concerned lest his office be diminished by the anti-monarchical forces at work in the present government. What is one to make of the present Prime Minister's statement that the "Queen of England" was going to open the Olympic Games in Montreal? What is the significance of removing the portraits of all but Canadian-born Governors General from the walls of Rideau Hall? These are but examples of a continuation of the senseless assault on our institutional heritage in the name of "Canadianization", which in reality is no more than a sad reflection of the personal insecurity of the Ministers of the Crown concerned. As important has been the removal from the Queen of Canada of her right to sign the Letters of Credence of all Canadian Ambassadors and Ministers abroad.

I am a Canadian, first, last, and always, and to me the monarchy remains a vital force in the Canadian constitution. Not only is it the cornerstone of our institutional life, it remains a highly functional and necessary office. The Queen, or, in her absence, the Governor General, performs those many official and social functions incumbent upon a head of state, thus relieving the Prime Minister of many incredibly time-consuming duties. More important are the prerogative powers of the Monarch to be consulted, to advise, and to warn on all matters of state. The Queen, these twenty-four years after her accession to the throne, is perhaps the most knowledgeable person in the world in the fields of Commonwealth and foreign affairs. As Prime Minister I benefited from her wisdom. The two Canadian Governors General during my period as Prime Minister were both, as I have indicated, men of long experience and wisdom. My government was immeasurably richer because of their presence and because of their diligence in the performance of their duties.

But most important are those prerogative powers assigned to the Monarch that come into play only in extreme political situations. One is the responsibility to see that Canadians shall as her subjects have a continuity of government. Our system of government cannot be disrupted by the incapacity or death of a Prime Minister. In this situation, it is the responsibility of the Governor General, at his own discretion, to call upon that man or woman whom he considers best able to form a new government. Should the Governor General be disabled, this responsibility reverts directly to the Monarch and not to the Chief Justice of Canada acting as Administrator. The other extreme situation is when a Prime Minister, through his own actions, has become so discredited by scandal or unscrupulous or illegal action as to render his advice unacceptable to the Governor General. The Governor General could then dissolve Parliament and insist that the government face the people in an election. This is a situation in which it is the responsibility of the Monarch to protect her people from a lawless government. As I have stated publicly on a number of occasions, no

Watergate could ever take place in Canada. As Her Majesty declared in her Coronation Oath: "I will to my power cause Law and Justice, in Mercy, to be executed in all my judgments."

CHAPTER THREE

✳

OUR TASK in forming a government on 21 June 1957 was to proceed with the business of the people as though we were a majority. I thought it quite possible that we might be defeated in the House when Parliament met in October, but I was in no way committed to an early election. I was prepared to leave my options open. I considered that as long as Mr. St. Laurent was Leader of the Opposition, and initially he indicated publicly a desire to stay on as Liberal leader, the Liberals would be content to oppose without obstructing.

One did not have to be Prime Minister to know that the condition of the Canadian economy was not so rosy as portrayed by Mr. St. Laurent and his colleagues during the election campaign. Unemployment was high and, if high unemployment is to be taken as an economic indicator, the writing had been on the wall since early 1954. Indeed, on 15 February 1954, the Right Honourable C. D. Howe had stated in the House of Commons, "Unemployment is running in excess of half a million persons." On 1 March 1955, it was still serious when he gave the figure as 362,000. There was some improvement in 1956, but by 1957 conditions were worsening and the St. Laurent government knew it. What is more, they not only knew it, they did nothing about it. Any suggestions from the Opposition that there were problems with the economy were simply brushed aside. Further, it was apparent that commodity prices were falling and that the dollar gap had reopened. Surplus wheat was stored in sky-high quantities. The United States economy was moving into a state of recession; capital spending in the United States in 1957 was below the level prevailing in 1956, and the projections for 1958 were lower still. As a direct result of the economic policies of the Liberals in the post-1945 period in Canada, our economy was so linked to that of the United States that it would have been impossible for our country to escape the consequences of an American recession. Yet the Liberal answer to these problems had been tight money: the pursuit of fiscal and monetary policies appropriate for restraining demand-induced inflation, when, in fact, demand pressures were easing and resources and labour were moving to excess supply. The policies of the St. Laurent administration had simply aggravated the situation in Canada. Excessive taxation and tight-money policies had increased costs at a time of declining demand. When we came into office, there were no plans ready to meet the economic situation with which we were faced.

There was proof that Mr. St. Laurent's government knew the situation. This fact notwithstanding, the only action to result from their knowledge was the decision to call the election in June, before the facts became obvious to the public. And when I say "proof", I mean irrefutable evidence. Patrick Nicholson, one of the Parliamentary Press Gallery members, came to me in early January 1958 with a document which he described as the foundation document on the state of the economy in the Department of Trade and Commerce. This document had been available to the Prime Minister and his Cabinet before the budget was brought down in early 1957. Entitled *The Canadian Economic Outlook for 1957*, and signed by

M. W. Sharp, Associate Deputy Minister of Trade and Commerce, it proved a remarkable analysis of the last stages of the post-war Canadian boom and the beginning of a period of readjustment which, it stated, could quite possibly turn into a recession leading to high levels of unemployment. Among other things, it pointed out:

Some symptoms that typically are found in the later stages of a cyclical expansion have begun to appear and such indications have tended to become more apparent since the turn of the year. More conflicting tendencies in construction and manufacturing have begun to emerge and increases in unemployment in Canada since October have been *much more* than seasonal. . . . The possibility of declines in the seasonally adjusted aggregates during the current year cannot be ruled out. . . . Careful attention to possibly conflicting tendencies and emerging trends will be appropriate in these circumstances.

These may be the typically hedged remarks of a professional economic forecaster, but their import is unmistakable. A recession was on the horizon. By rejecting the advice of its economists, the St. Laurent government made certain that what it had been warned against would happen.

When I brought this matter up in the House of Commons in January 1958, the Liberals opposite did not deny the report or their knowledge of it, but claimed my using it was an unacceptable exercise. It was, they claimed, marked "Confidential" and should never have been revealed to the public. The copy I received was not marked "Confidential", nor had I, as they pretended to believe, ripped the cover from it. In any event, in my view, "confidential" does not mean that the truth contained in a document shall be concealed from all except those who will not use it: a position that has recently received the sanction of the Supreme Court of Ontario in a precedent-setting decision. The Liberals found themselves high and dry with their spurious charges concerning the sanctity of government documents. They were but echoes in their own graveyard and their protestations had no saving effect on their political fortunes whatsoever.

Other portions of the St. Laurent legacy with which we had to contend were the heaviest tax burden in Canadian history combined with the highest expenditures, waste, and extravagance of any Canadian government we had experienced. We faced a record deficit in our commodity trade with the world, as well as an unheard-of deficit of commodity trade with the United States. A loss of markets in the United Kingdom and in all parts of the world for our agricultural products and finished goods did not help. We inherited a high cost of living, the highest interest rates in a generation, and the tightest credit conditions. We were bequeathed an impasse between the Dominion and the provincial governments on fiscal relations; municipal governments knew not where to turn in their financial plights. And, with all this, we inherited a degraded Parliament.

As I said in the House of Commons on 30 August 1958: "Our concept of a national policy is based on the belief that the national welfare demands positive action to meet the basic causes of distress and maladjustment in particular industries and regions." This was our philosophy in 1957. We set about, through positive measures, to get the Canadian economy back on its feet. We increased the Old Age Pensions to fifty-five dollars a month, and increased pensions for the blind, the disabled, and the veterans. We increased the salaries of civil servants, the armed forces, and the RCMP. We reduced taxes. The excise tax on automobiles was cut from 10 per cent to 7½ per cent. Personal income tax was cut to benefit every taxpayer in Canada. Corporation tax was reduced to benefit the small businessman. Under the National Housing Act, new monies were made available for low- and middle-income housing. As I stated in a television broadcast on 28 October 1957:

The adverse effects of sudden and precipitate credit restrictions were being widely felt long before we assumed office. The most affected area was low and middle income housing in which the credit restrictions had virtually nullified the rights of prospective home-owners under the National Housing Act. We were concerned not only with the physical inconveniences and hardships of individuals but also with the fact that it was creating unnecessary unemployment and impeding the normal development of our most precious asset, the average young Canadian family. It was for this reason that we made immediately available $150 million to stimulate home-building and we shall, of course, be dealing with the problem in a broader way as our legislative programme expands in Parliament.

We provided cash advances for farm-stored grain. I had advocated this, as had other Opposition Members, for several years. The Liberals claimed such a program would result in heavy losses in unpaid loans—all of which was nonsense, as our experience proved. The Minister of Trade and Commerce, the Honourable Gordon Churchill, explained our policy:

... this resolution is the first of a series of resolutions introducing measures which will be for the benefit of the people of Canada. This is the first item of our legislative programme, and it is designed to permit prairie farmers to receive advance payment for the grain they can expect to deliver this year. The legislation is necessary because of the large surplus of wheat which has been accumulated in recent years due to a number of factors such as larger than average crops, a reduction in exports because of the loss of former markets, increased productivity per acre, subsidized competition from other wheat exporting countries and so on.

We gave notice of legislation to ensure the enactment of permanent floor-price legislation based on a definite formula to allow for variations in production and demand for individual agricultural products; these were to be announced well in advance of the production period each year after consultation with the representative producers and agricultural organizations. We moved to protect the poultry industry against United States dumping. We aided the dairy industry. The price-support price on butter was raised from 58 cents to 63 cents, with a resulting improvement in the price of whole milk. The price-support program on butter was enlarged to cover all forms of butterfat which the Board designated. Butterfat was put under import control. This action removed the threat to the price structure of the entire dairy industry. Dry skim milk was placed under import control. The potato-starch diversion program in New Brunswick was extended to June 30, then to July 15, and finally to July 20. Freight-rate assistance on hay was provided to relieve the shortage in Nova Scotia. An agreement was concluded with the United Kingdom to make dollars available with which to purchase Canadian apples. The power to collect an equalization levy was extended to the Ontario Cheese Producers Marketing Board. Funds were provided under the Agricultural Products Marketing Act to a number of producer associations, to enable them to market their products.

By taking over one hundred thousand persons off the federal income tax rolls, by reducing the rates of taxation of the smallest incomes, by reducing the excise tax on motor cars by $20 million, by helping small corporate businesses through reducing their taxes by an additional $12 million, we lightened the tax burden borne by the Canadian people by $178 million and did it, not by a deficit, but with a surplus budget. By putting the construction industry back on its feet, by increasing the federal grants for hospital construction from $1,000 to $2,000 per bed for general hospitals and from $1,500 to $2,000 per bed for convalescent hospitals, by providing new grants for the construction of nurses' residences, by increasing seasonal unemployment insurance benefits from sixteen to twenty-four weeks and extending the benefits to married women and others, by increasing the payments to the provinces by $87 million, by embarking on a public works program calling for an expenditure of $1,185 million, we pumped hundreds of millions of dollars into an atrophying economy. The result was that the recession was short-lived (it had reversed itself by 1961). It should be noted that during the worst of it, our unemployment rate never rose to the level of that in the United States.

Nevertheless, unemployment was a serious problem for us in the 1957-58 period. On 21 December 1957, the Dominion Bureau of Statistics reported 292,000 without jobs and seeking work in November—or 4.9 per cent of the labour force. We had little doubt that unemployment would rise to the 500,000 mark by March 1958. The question at issue was not whether the government's economic policy to meet the recession was sound—it was. The question was whether the Liberals could create in the public mind the stereotype of the Conservatives as the party of unemployment. In this endeavour they enjoyed no success. As the *Financial Post* on 11 January 1958 observed:

Estimates to March, 1958, prepared by the former Liberal Government, contained a number of votes for public buildings and other works more political than practical.

Ordinarily they would not have been pushed, and so when the Conservatives took over they found no plans drawn up for them, and six months of lead time needed before action.

In other words, the much-vaunted Liberal shelf was bare, and everyone knew it. The Liberals had nothing ready to meet a recession, except for a repetition of their 1954-55 performance.

As a direct consequence of Liberal policies, Canada, when we came into office, faced a very serious trade imbalance. There had been in the post-1945 period a concentration of trade with the United States. The result was that by 1957, the United States accounted for nearly 60 per cent of our exports and 73 per cent of our imports. Furthermore, the value of our imports from the United States since 1954 had been more than twice that of her imports from us, with the result that in 1956 we had a merchandise deficit of approximately $1.2 billion. When interest payments, dividends, and other invisible items were added to this amount, we experienced for 1956 an over-all negative balance on current transactions of close to one and two-thirds billion dollars. Trade with Britain and the Commonwealth, on the other hand, had declined from its pre-war position to about 20 per cent of our exports and 12 per cent of our imports. Britain, which at one time was Canada's largest customer, now purchased from us goods less than one-third the value of those purchased by the United States.

Contrary to some popular myths, never at any time did I suggest that our trade with the United States was anything but valuable and essential for the growth and prosperity of the Canadian economy. But it would have been impossible for me to fail to recognize that annual deficits in our trade with the United States of such magnitude raised difficult and serious problems, problems that were not without political implications. To begin with, our trade deficit could be balanced only by a heavy inflow of American investment capital. The consequence was that American investments had risen from $5 billion in 1945 to $10.3 billion in 1955 and to over $12 billion in 1957. Now it is true that during the days before the First World War, Great Britain contributed a great deal to investment in Canada. But its investment was generally in mortgages or debentures and was not equity investment. In contrast, the United States was building up its industries in Canada by equity capital investment.

In specific terms, by 1957 United States residents controlled over half of all Canadian manufacturing, mining, smelting, and petroleum industries. There were obvious problems. The policies of foreign-controlled industries are determined by the interests of their parent companies; so far as they reflected a national interest, it was not Canada's. Frequently, Canadians were excluded from participating in such enterprises either through the purchase of equity stocks or, as employees, through management positions. Occasionally a United States parent company would take over export orders which had first been explored by Canadian trade officials. Sometimes American-owned industries failed to play their appropriate part in Canadian life through contributions to cultural and charitable organizations. Furthermore, these companies, given the resources of their parent companies, frequently had advantages in exploration and development over those enjoyed by their Canadian-owned competitors. More important, excessive foreign control reduced the control a Canadian government could exercise in attempting to stabilize our economy and further the process of balanced economic growth. Had the Conservative Party been content to remain hewers of wood and drawers of water as a supplier of raw materials to the United States, these problems might not have loomed so large.

One of our first problems was to make the United States understand the nature of our problems and the reasons for our policies. If they had been able to imagine their country suffering a 12- to 15-billion-dollar annual trade deficit with Canada which was being met by a massive alienation to foreign ownership and control of their industries and resources; if their external trade had consisted largely of an exchange of primary products for manufacturers, thus ensuring a permanently unfavourable balance of trade; and if their creditors followed trade and economic policies that prevented a redressing of this trade imbalance, they then might have understood our determination to alter so far as we could the existing situation.

I, for one, considered the Liberal policy of selling our birthright (the ownership and control over our resources) too high a price to pay to maintain our standard of living and our post-Second World War rate of economic growth. It was simple logic that Canada could not maintain its independence if we continued existing Liberal policies. Recognition of this implied no hostility to the United States. It was a case, as it was for so many of my government's policies, of being pro-Canadian, not anti-American. If we failed to diversify our trade, Canada would cease to belong to Canadians; we would have no destiny to fulfil.

When I made my Dominion Day address to the Canadian Club in London on 1 July 1957, I said: "We believe this, that while we will maintain trade with the United States the time has come to diversify; the time has come to extend our trade on a wider basis than ever before." When I suggested on my return from the Commonwealth Prime Ministers' Conference on 6 July that we strive to divert some of Canada's imports from the United States to Britain, I was not suggesting that my government was about to apply selective quantitative controls against United States goods or that we would adopt tariff policies designed to increase the degree of British preference in Canada. I sought simply a substantial increase in imports from Britain of goods which we were then importing from the United States, to the serious detriment of Canada's balance of trade and its future economic independence. And we insisted that these imports from Britain be competitive both in price and in quality. It was for this reason that the Honourable Gordon Churchill led a fifty-man Canadian trade mission to Britain on 21 November 1957. Composed chiefly of Canadian industrialists, this mission had as its basic purpose the stimulation of the flow of British products to Canada; in order to supply us, the British had to know how to deal with our needs.

It was to stimulate Commonwealth trade that the Commonwealth finance ministers met on my initiative and at the invitation of my government at Mont Tremblant, Quebec, on 30 September and 1 October 1957, to discuss plans for a full-scale Commonwealth Trade and Economic Conference in 1958. As to the free-trade proposal, or more properly, the free-trade suggestion, that received so much publicity at the time of the Mont Tremblant conference, this was something that could only be taken seriously, if at all, in the long term. Further, regardless of the sensationalist treatment it received in the press, the world's experience with free-trade arrangements in 1957 was severely limited. The Common Market, under the Treaty of Rome, was not to come into effect until 1 January 1958. Common sense dictated that we wait and see what happened there before going off on any experiment of our own. The Liberal Party criticism of our position as voiced by Messrs. Lester Pearson and Paul Martin was contradictory, cynical, and dishonest. On the one hand, they said that the Conservative proposal to divert some of Canada's imports from the United States to Britain was irresponsible discrimination. On the other hand, they denounced us for not accepting, as they suggested they would, the British free-trade proposal. The explicit purpose of the proposal, as the British repeatedly stated, was to legalize trade discrimination against the United States.

To return to the domestic front, we immediately entered into negotiations with the government of Saskatchewan to arrange the terms for building the South Saskatchewan Dam. I mentioned in Volume I my long advocacy of this project. Now that I was Prime Minister, I was not prepared to follow the course of my predecessors and allow a national need to be frustrated by cost-benefit bureaucratic studies.

The idea for constructing a dam on the South Saskatchewan River was not new. In 1857, the British government sent an expedition under Captain John Palliser to explore Western Canada. The following year Professor H. Y. Hind of Trinity College, Toronto, acted as geologist and naturalist for an expedition which explored the Assiniboine and Saskatchewan river valleys. Both men reported on the close relationship between the valleys of the South Saskatchewan and the Qu'Appelle rivers. Palliser suggested a water communication system connecting the two valleys; Hind, the construction of a dam across the South Saskatchewan to divert its waters down the Qu'Appelle valley. As this land was settled at the century's turn, the need for irrigation became more and more apparent. The settlers who pinned their hopes and futures on the production of grain, particularly wheat, were constantly haunted by the danger of prairie droughts which could transform the whole area of the Palliser Triangle into a dust bowl. A 1919 study by William Pearce, noted engineer and land surveyor and one-time Superintendent of Mines, centred on the possibility of diverting water from the North Saskatchewan, Clearwater, and Red Deer rivers to supply agriculture throughout the central plains of Saskatchewan and Alberta. It was not, however, until after the great depression of the 1930s when the dust-bowl nightmare became a reality that the Prairie Farm Rehabilitation Administration, established by the Bennett government on 17 April 1935, began to follow up the Pearce proposal. Its investigation into the feasibility of a South Saskatchewan River Dam got under way in 1943. Ten sites were considered along the river from Outlook to a point north of Swift Current; the one finally chosen midway between Outlook and Elbow was picked as the most suitable. The Liberals had held out this promise to the electors of Saskatchewan for years. King, Gardiner, and St. Laurent all talked about it. But this was all they did: talk!

We now set about to bring this project to fruition. Its estimated cost was $182 million. Its estimated benefit was the irrigation of 500,000 acres of farm land, and a new era for agriculture where only dry-land farming had ever been known. It would make possible a switch from an uncertain, insecure, and unbalanced wheat economy to one balanced and diversified by the addition of livestock, mixed farming, and speciality crops, where increased production would more than double gross farm revenue. The terrible days of the hungry thirties were to be banished into history. It was further estimated that after the river basin had been fully developed, sufficient water would be available to produce 475 million kilowatt hours of electricity annually. This new source of power would pave the way for a stepped-up rural electrification program. It would provide a new source of water for municipalities, and would almost certainly stimulate industrial growth in Saskatchewan. It was a project that would produce many construction jobs in the short run, and in the long run attract new industry, increase the population, produce new wealth, and ensure a more stable income for the people of Saskatchewan. In short the South Saskatchewan Dam was a project of national significance, of importance to all Canada.

We also moved to assist electric power development in the Atlantic provinces. On 15 January 1958, Parliament passed legislation authorizing the federal government to enter into agreements with any of the Atlantic provinces, to provide assistance in the building of thermo-electric power projects, and in the control and transmission of the electric energy so generated. The act also included provisions for payment of a subvention for coal used in this production. On 31 January, legislation was enacted which authorized loans up to $30 million to the government of New Brunswick so that it might complete the Beechwood Power Project, at a rate of interest not to exceed 4⅜ per cent.

I realized that in the past the Maritimes had been too often forgotten. Their population provided them with a membership in the House of Commons that was so small in proportion to the total representation in Parliament that they were ignored. Their Members might speak out, condemning the failure of governments to act, but beyond that very little ever happened. I hoped that by aiding the Atlantic provinces in this way, we might stimulate a greater industrial development there. I intended that my government be responsive to their needs.

We also set up a Royal Commission under Henry Borden to inquire into and make recommendations concerning policies which would best serve the national interest in relation to the export of energy and sources of energy from Canada. I might note in passing that our attitude to organized labour was shown by the fact that one of the members appointed to that Royal Commission was Gordon Cushing, then Executive Vice-President of the Canadian Labour Congress.

To meet unemployment, we introduced on 20 November 1957 a highly successful program to increase employment during the winter months. The Minister of Labour, the Honourable Michael Starr, told the House of Commons: "This is a specific programme, the object of which is to increase winter employment so as to alleviate the normal seasonal slump in Canada. The programme . . . aims at providing an industrial and occupational climate favourable to the planning and execution of projects in the wintertime where possible." If the reader will contrast the construction activity during the Canadian winter today with that of twenty years ago, he should be able to appreciate how important and significant this new concept, which in 1958 became known as the Winter Works Program, has been for the Canadian economy. Before 1957 the construction industry in Canada virtually closed down in the winter months.

On 17 December the Minister of Transport, the Honourable George Hees, announced that early in January his department would call for tenders for the construction of six ships, totalling in cost approximately $10 million. It was estimated that the construction of these vessels would provide 3½ million man-hours of work for Canadians. The Canadian Vessel Construction Act was amended to further stimulate the shipbuilding industry. As he explained in the House of Commons: "Shipbuilding in Canada is a more expensive undertaking than it is in European or Japanese yards. . . . For reasons of our national economy as a great trading nation it is also necessary for us to maintain the necessary shipbuilding and ship repairing facilities to meet the needs of the many ships of all nations that come to carry away our exports. The Canadian shipbuilding industry is also an important source of employment for Canadian workmen."

The programs of the Department of Northern Affairs and Natural Resources were expanded to provide for the additional employment of some nineteen hundred men in national parks and on the Mackenzie Highway. These are only some of the measures that my government took to alleviate the situation of the unemployed in Canada. By the beginning of 1958, we had plans to spend an estimated $286 million on public works projects in the first half of the year. As the Honourable Donald Fleming, the Minister of Finance, explained in the House of Commons on 21 January 1958: "We are not going to put a balanced budget above our firm determination to provide, through the agency of public works, jobs for unemployed Canadians."

In our dealings with the provinces, I believe that we were successful in creating a new atmosphere of confidence between the two senior levels of government. I convened a Dominion–Provincial Conference in Ottawa for 25-26 November 1957. Instead of following the Liberal precedent of presenting the provinces with a hard and fast federal line, I invited each of the provincial premiers to present his own proposals and suggestions. This was an invitation to which they responded readily.

We agreed at the conference that the fiscal position of the Atlantic provinces should be regarded as a special problem. My government agreed to provide a special Atlantic Provinces Adjustment Grant of $100 million to be paid to the four eastern provinces at the rate of $25 million per annum beginning 1 April 1958. We also agreed that the provinces and, through them, the municipalities required some immediate addition to their share of the tax dollar if they were to have sufficient money to fulfil their constitutional responsibilities to provide adequate schools, roads, hospitals, housing services, and other personal and family essential services. Under the former Liberal government, the provinces had been entitled to receive ten per cent of the personal income tax collected by the Dominion. My government moved immediately to increase this share to thirteen per cent, and to consider further adjustments—indeed, this was the first step towards a whole new tax-sharing arrangement. In immediate relief, the provinces received $62 million-plus that would have otherwise gone into the federal treasury. When the conference adjourned until the new year, we had a multitude of proposals brought forth by the provincial premiers to consider in formulating our own policies. H. L.

Walsh, writing in the *St. Catharines Standard* for 10 February 1958, had this to say about the effect of our financial assistance to the provinces:

In budgeting for the provincial and municipal needs that means a tremendous difference for the better. "Renew your faith in Liberalism," says Mr. Pearson now to the Canadian jury, "and we will do a better job." After twenty-two years of power, after repudiation by the Canadian jury less than nine months ago, that sort of lame appeal not only taxes the credulity but the commonsense of the intelligent citizen. The truth is, and the record shows clearly, that in constructive and remedial measures the seven-month minority government of John Diefenbaker did more for the country at large than its Liberal predecessors did in the previous seven years.

Following the June election the Liberal Party set about the business of selecting a new leader. They moved with what some considered ingratitude and indecent haste to cast off Mr. St. Laurent. Mr. St. Laurent's contribution to his party and to Canada is well known. His former colleagues, who had persuaded him to run in the first place, now, when they (more through their own actions and those of C. D. Howe) were repudiated outside of Quebec, pushed him out. I was laid up with a heavy cold during the Liberal convention and thus had the opportunity to listen to every part of it as it was carried on radio and television. I was somewhat concerned that Paul Martin might be the Liberal choice because I felt that he would be harder to meet on the stump than anyone else in the Liberal Party. I thought that Mr. Pearson did very well in his acceptance speech to the convention, but my general reaction was that despite the excitement and the hoop-la, the Liberal Party would face defeat whenever the election took place.

When I welcomed Mr. Pearson to his new role as Leader of the Opposition in the House of Commons on 20

January 1958, I had no idea of the train of events he would put in motion. If someone had come to me that morning and told me of Mr. Pearson's proposed course of action, I would have laughed him out of my office. Mr. Pearson rose from his desk that winter's afternoon to acknowledge the compliments of myself and the leaders of the other parties. He then launched into the standard Liberal criticism of my government's record, which he ended with the following motion:

... In view of the fact that, in the seven months His Excellency's advisers have been in office, Canada's total trade has ceased to expand, export markets have been threatened and proposals for freer trade have been rebuffed;

That investment has been discouraged and unemployment has risen drastically;

That farmers and other primary producers have been disillusioned and discouraged;

That relations with provincial governments have deteriorated into confusion;

That the budget is no longer in balance, revenues are declining, expenditures are rising and parliament has been denied a national accounting;

That there is growing confusion about defence and security;

That day to day expedients have been substituted for firm and steady administration;

And in view of the desirability, at this time, of having a government pledged to implement Liberal policies;

His Excellency's advisers should, in the opinion of this house, submit their resignation forthwith.

I was watching the Honourable Jack Pickersgill while Pearson was reading his motion. Jack was in a state of ecstasy. He was the only Member I've known who could strut sitting down, and that's what he did that day. He was so proud of his contribution to the production, it was obvious he wanted to be singled out as, if not the father, at least the stepfather of it all. Apparently he regarded it as the most brilliant technique ever produced in the House of Commons. I could barely believe my ears. I turned to Donald Fleming, my desk mate, and said, "This is the complete end of opposition to us." And laughing, I turned to Howard Green and said, "This is it."

Imagine! They were ready, they were willing, to take over the government of the country by a simple transfer. Simplicity itself: they were demanding that I go to the Governor General and say, "Your Excellency, I feel that the people of Canada didn't know what they were doing when they decided to turn their backs on the Liberal Party last June. I've been convinced of this by Mr. Pearson's motion. I therefore ask you to accept my resignation, and I recommend that the party which was defeated at the polls shall be the new government of the country." Yet that was the proposition which they advanced by the collective wisdom and acumen of some reputedly astute politicians. The supreme example of Liberal statesmanship was to annihilate us by a motion. But under no circumstances did they want an election. In order to understand how they perpetrated on themselves such a monstrosity, one has to go back and realize that behind it was a feeling of superiority that had become the hallmark of the leaders of Canadian Liberalism. They had departed from every liberal principle to become virtually a law unto themselves.

My speech in reply to Pearson was one so destructive to the Liberal Party that many said it virtually decided the outcome of the next election. And some say, what do speeches in Parliament do? In the days that followed the Pearson motion, the Liberal front bench made it obvious that they were moving from opposition to obstruction. Mr. St. Laurent's wise leadership and gentlemanly ways had been replaced by blatant partisanship. Little did they seem to realize the direction in which they were galloping. I remembered watching them at their convention, marching back and forth under the banner "We'll soon be back." They didn't know how far back that was.

On 30 January 1958, I went to Halifax to receive an honorary degree from St. Mary's University. I had been considering the need for an election for some days, but it was there that I decided to go to the people. On my return, I discussed the question with my Cabinet colleagues. On 1 February I proceeded to Quebec City, where the Governor General was in residence. I informed Mr. Massey of my reasons for seeking a dissolution of the House of Commons. I returned to Ottawa the same afternoon and entered the House a minute or so after six. Mr. Gardiner was speaking when I arrived. To his consternation and to the general dismay of his colleagues, I announced that Canada's twenty-third Parliament was no more. Needless to say, the reaction on the Opposition side was pretty stormy. Indeed, this was the only occasion in the history of Canada when the House of Commons went on as if it actually existed, when in fact it was completely "non est", having been already dissolved. Those who insisted on speaking were speaking as in a vacuum; they were no longer Members of Parliament.

From my point of view, it had been, with the possible exception of its last few days, a good Parliament. It had begun gloriously on 14 October 1957, when the Queen of Canada for the first time read the Speech from the Throne. As I wrote in the first volume of these memoirs, we had provided, through the medium of television, an opportunity for all Canadians to take part in this event. I had had the personal honour of being named Her Majesty's senior adviser during her visit to the United States, and had been made a member of Her Majesty's Imperial Privy Council. From a legislative point of view, we had got much of our short-term program through Parliament. We now required a mandate from the Canadian people to begin those long-range plans central to our philosophy. I saw the opportunity of giving leadership in the building of a great nation in which the population of Canada would more than double by the century's end. The basis of our future greatness lay in our ability to exploit, *in the interests of all Canadians* and not of foreign entrepreneurs, that vast treasure-house that the Almighty had provided us in the Canadian North.

I told my fellow Canadians that it would take from five to ten years just to lay the foundations for the Canada of my dreams. Sir Wilfrid Laurier had once laid claim for Canada to the entire twentieth century in his prophecy of Canada's greatness. I was not dealing in expressions of blind faith when I told Canadians of my vision of the future. It may have seemed curious to some that, in my speech opening the 1958 election campaign in Winnipeg on 12 February, the first point of the National Development Program that I announced dealt with our road program in the Yukon and Northwest Territories. It was obvious that our first priority had to be that of establishing the extent of our resources. Sixty to seventy-five per cent of Canada's resources were believed to be in the north and were almost completely unknown. "Roads to Resources" was more than just a catch phrase: the first step of any planned development program was roads to open up the land masses hitherto virtually unexplored. We did have geological maps of most of the regions in Canada, and for some regions good maps, showing gravity meter, magnetometer, and seismic surveys. But even here there were great gaps in our information. When the Honourable Alvin Hamilton, Minister of Northern Affairs and Natural Resources, asked the officials of Mines and Technical Surveys how long it would take, at their present rate of operation, to complete a hydrographic survey of the coast of Canada, the reply was *250 years*. When we took office, the geological survey was moving at the same pace as in the 1920s. We needed northern roads, airfields, weather stations, and improved marine transportation into many otherwise inaccessible areas. We had to find out exactly what our resources consisted of before we could realize our destiny. The Liberals under Pearson dismissed our Roads to Resources as wasting the public purse building roads from igloo to igloo. Many years before, they had dismissed Sir John Macdonald's transcontinental railway as proceeding from teepee to teepee. Macdonald had brought Canada into being. I wanted to extend that vision. So did the people of Canada, for on 31 March 1958, my government was returned to office with the largest majority in the entire history of our nation.

CHAPTER FOUR

✳

IN OCTOBER 1958, I left Ottawa on a world tour that would take me to New York, London, Paris, Brussels, Bonn, Rome, Karachi, New Delhi, Colombo, Kuala Lumpur, Singapore, Djakarta, Canberra, and, finally, Wellington before returning home some six weeks later. It was a tour that provided me with the opportunity of discussing many of the world's problems with political leaders whose perspectives differed from my own. It was also an opportunity to see for myself something of what was happening in a world made ever smaller by technological advances.

It would be well to remember that 1958 was not a year noted for détente. The Cold War was still a harsh reality; nuclear weapons and sophisticated delivery systems had created a psychology of nuclear terror among the peoples of the world, Canadians included. (The resultant effect on popular values accounts for much of the social upheaval in the 1960s.) It was certainly a time when a political leader required all the experience and wisdom he could muster if he were to guide his ship of state successfully through the troubled waters of international affairs.

On 29 October I met with the Secretary General of the United Nations, Dag Hammarskjöld, in New York City. In a conversation that lasted for three-quarters of an hour or so, we talked about developments in the Middle East, disarmament, China, and the United Nations Peace Forces. I was particularly interested in Hammarskjöld's views on the question of recognizing Communist China. As he saw it, the Western world would sooner or later have to accept Communist China, since there was no prospect of its de-Communization. He had no doubt that it would have been better to have recognized Peking three years before rather than now; similarly, he considered that it would be better to do it immediately than three years hence. He thought we should get what advantages there were from prompt recognition, while accepting and doing our best to minimize the disadvantages. When I asked him the question that was central to my thinking on this issue: what the effect of recognition would be on Southeast Asia, he responded that most Asian governments would be relieved if recognition of China became more general. He cited Burma as the principal example to support his argument, but admitted that the Philippines, South Vietnam, and Formosa were exceptions. My principal impression of Dag Hammarskjöld was of a man of high principle and dedication, if a bit inclined to the employment of oblique phrases, but determined to maintain the independence of his office against both East and West. This is why I came so vigorously to his defence when the Soviets advanced their troika proposals in September 1960 (see Chapter Five).

Prime Minister Macmillan, with whom I met in official discussion the following Monday, 3 November, was preoccupied with France and the North Atlantic Treaty Organization, and with France and the European Economic Community. It would be much more accurate if for the word France I were to substitute the word de Gaulle. Before coming into power in France, General de Gaulle had expressed privately strong reservations about the Atlantic Alliance. Prior to my visit, he had sent a note to both

President Eisenhower and Prime Minister Macmillan expressing his dissatisfaction with the organization of the Atlantic Alliance, in that "It does not answer the essential security requirements of the Free World as a whole." What de Gaulle suggested was the setting up of a new directorate within NATO composed of the United States, Britain, and France with responsibility for "taking joint decisions on all political matters affecting world security and for drawing up and, if necessary, putting into action strategic plans, especially those involving the use of nuclear weapons." Prime Minister Macmillan made it very clear that Britain was strongly opposed to any idea of a political directorate. Canada was equally opposed. From our own point of view, we were very concerned that the range and frequency of consultations within the North Atlantic Council be improved. The French proposal, if implemented, would serve to exclude Canada completely from many of the Alliance's more important political considerations. In other words, this would improve things for France and for no other nation. I told Prime Minister Macmillan that I had already decided to take a strong stand against any French attempt to achieve this reorganization, and that I would tell General de Gaulle exactly where Canada stood on this question.

With regard to the European Common Market, the Treaty of Rome had only come into effect on 1 January 1958. Thus, most of Mr. Macmillan's concerns were yet to be confirmed. The other items on our agenda covered such things as the export of arms to Israel, the situation in Algeria, the Law of the Sea, the Baghdad Pact, Cyprus, civil air agreements between Canada and Britain, and the state of trade relations between Canada and Britain (a subject that will be discussed in detail, along with other aspects of our relations, in another chapter). All in all, our discussions proved, as they most often did, quite satisfactory.

On 6 November I met with General de Gaulle for a hour and a quarter before lunch at the Hôtel Matignon in Paris. The General invited me to begin the discussion. I began by noting that there were a few things that made rather difficult relations between France and Canada; one in particular was the General's proposal for a reorganization of NATO. I suggested that if he was proposing a closer consultation within NATO, then Canada was in full agreement, but that if he was, in fact, proposing the creation of a triumvirate which would take decisions without consulting the other members of the Alliance, and under which members of the Alliance would have to behave like automatons, then Canada was opposed.

General de Gaulle replied by pointing out that there was a considerable difference between the circumstances surrounding NATO's birth in 1948 and 1949 and the situation ten years later. The Soviet Union had in those years posed a direct military threat, as demonstrated by the *coup d'état* in Prague. In 1958, however, he considered we could be certain that neither the United States nor the Soviet Union intended to go to war deliberately against each other. While he felt that NATO must remain as an Alliance, ready to defend the common interests of its members, there were particular problems which had not existed in 1949. The reality of 1958 was that the political decisions concerning NATO were, in fact, taken by the United States, the strategic plans of NATO were carried out by an Anglo-American high command, and the West was in the process of being integrated under United States leadership. The result was that problems in East–West relations were broached as though they were United States–Soviet Union problems alone (for example, the Middle East or the China off-shore islands). The General did not believe that this method of attacking problems could bring useful results. What was needed was a new *modus vivendi* between East and West. He felt that

France, and perhaps other countries, had a legitimate role to play in East–West relations. Certainly, France's position had changed since 1949. France had a useful role to play in world affairs and considered it quite inconceivable that she should be committed to war without consultation.

General de Gaulle pointed out that in his talks with Harold Macmillan and John Foster Dulles in Paris early in the summer of 1958, he had been told by both that neither country intended to land troops in the Middle East. Yet the United States had subsequently landed troops in Lebanon, as Britain had in Jordan. In neither case had France been consulted. Had either case resulted in a general war, France would have found herself committed to bear the consequences of policies that she had not even known about until two hours before the actual landings. France, the General said, was not prepared to accept such a situation. I could only point out that from Canada's point of view a political triumvirate was not the answer, but that we would certainly support increased consultation within the Alliance. I did not tell him that President Eisenhower had consulted me by telephone about the landing of two United States Marine battalions in Lebanon on 14 July 1958, a day in advance of the event. I had considered that the urgent appeal from President Chamoun of Lebanon justified the United States intervention.

The General was equally frank in his criticism of the integrated forces and command structure within NATO. These were not suited to France's present needs. France could not continue to accept an Anglo-American organization; thus, some transformation must take place. I could fully appreciate (and said so) his stated desire to change the post-war psychology of France so that the French people would realize that they had in the first instance to depend upon themselves for defence, and not merely to think that some other country would do it for them. During President de Gaulle's visit to Ottawa in April 1960, Canada's Secretary of State for External Affairs, the Honourable Howard Green, had the opportunity of carrying this topic further in conversations with his French counterpart, M. Couve de Murville. The question concerned United States policy on nuclear weapons in NATO countries. Both Canada and France considered this a most difficult problem. The French Foreign Minister thought that the duality of General Norstad's responsibilities as the NATO Commander-in-Chief and as an American general was a stumbling block to solution of nuclear stockpiling and the use of nuclear weapons. When Mr. Green inquired whether France would accept the "double key" for controlling the use of atomic weapons, Couve de Murville answered that even that formula meant United States control, and this France could not accept on her territory.

To return to my 1958 conversation with General de Gaulle: when the General asked for my views on the question of the Common Market, I replied that Canada was glad to see any action taken to draw Europe closer together, both economically and politically, but that Canada hoped that it would not be drawn together behind a protective tariff barrier. I said that for our part we did not want to be denied traditional markets in Europe and that we hoped any arrangements made under the Common Market would not exclude our agricultural products. I was concerned, as I have elsewhere explained, that we have the opportunity to expand our markets, and so far as possible counter our overwhelming economic dependence on the United States. In this context, the loss of the "inner six" to Canadian agriculture was relatively important. If one contemplated the addition of Britain and the other West European nations to the Common Market, the consequences for Canadian agriculture could be serious indeed. However, when I said we stood in favour of ex-

panded trade among countries, the General rejoined that
if we were committed to pursuing freer trade, what then
did I have to say about the trade restrictions established
by the Commonwealth at its recent conference in Montreal? I explained that the preferences were no longer of
their former importance; that in 1932, restrictions had
been made at a time when we were facing a depression,
but that most of the restrictions in the 1932 agreements
were now gone; that the most important element had
more of a sentimental character. General de Gaulle replied: "We are still back in 1932. We do not move as fast as
your new country, but perhaps in twenty-six years we
will reach the point where you are now." With that, he
broke into laughter and proposed that we adjourn for
lunch and continue our talks afterward.

During the luncheon, de Gaulle suggested we might
talk that afternoon with only our interpreter present. In
private, we talked about Algeria, his principal preoccupation. He displayed none of the calm confidence of his
public image. Indeed, he was beset with worries and repeatedly said that at least ten years would be required
before real order could be established in Algeria, and that
he feared he was too old to see it through. As I recall our
conversation on Britain and the Common Market, he said
he didn't know why I was so concerned about Britain's
entry, because they were not going to get in. They will not
get in, "Ils ne passeront pas," he said. I asked him to repeat his statement, and he did. I recall saying, "The way
you speak is reminiscent of General Pétain at Verdun."
He replied, "It's just as certain." I suggested that I let
Prime Minister Macmillan know. He demurred. I said, "I
can't do otherwise." After a short discussion, he said that
if I felt that strongly, he would agree. I so advised Macmillan, whose attitude was that I must have misunderstood the General. If I may anticipate my discussion of
the Commonwealth Prime Ministers' Conference of Sep-

tember 1962, when I suggested that Britain was not going to gain entry into the Common Market, despite the apparent success of her negotiations at Brussels, it was obvious that my fellow Prime Ministers thought there was something wrong with me. Four months later de Gaulle said, "No."

I considered the General a remarkable man. I was fascinated that day in 1958 by his account of his first meeting a few weeks earlier with Chancellor Adenauer, although I was not to have a full account of what took place until I later talked with Adenauer. When I asked de Gaulle about their discussions, he said he believed Adenauer to be a sincere and responsible man, and that as a result of their meeting the age-long antagonism between France and Germany could be ended. I expressed surprise that this could be achieved in one meeting. He replied that so long as he remained alive and so long as Adenauer's principles were followed in Germany, he would do everything to bring about a rapprochement between their two countries. This did not commit him to support necessarily the principle of German reunification. This was a subject that we discussed when he visited Ottawa. I recall his saying that some hoped German reunification might some day be accomplished; not everyone did—not many in France in any event. He felt sure I would understand why. The Russians, for their part, would never give up Prussia and Saxony. It would not be realistic, he suggested, to say that everything should be done to achieve reunification, but at the same time reunification should not be condemned and it should not be said that it would never be achieved. At the present time, he considered that reunification would bring dissatisfaction on both sides. Germany, as a reunited country, might not be in a position to retain its close links with Western Europe, and it was essential, in his opinion, that Germany remain in the Western camp.

I was very much impressed with de Gaulle's wisdom and with the fullness of his dedication to the service of France. In truth, he was the soul of France. My experience with him belied his public reputation as a cold and arrogant man. Our reception in Paris was unbelievable in its warmth. The pomp and circumstance stemming from the days of Louis XIV were there in full. Of all the official visits that I made during my period of office, none exceeded in splendour General de Gaulle's reception in honour of Canada. But more important, the relationship that developed between de Gaulle and me was most friendly and frank, and continued so. Indeed, while I was in Paris, he did me the high honour of asking me if I could be present at Verdun on Armistice Day, 11 November, to take the salute. I told him it was impossible, since I was to be in Bonn on that day. I asked him why he did not take the salute himself. He replied that he had been wounded near Verdun and had memories he did not want to recall. He was so anxious that I should accept that I finally changed my plans. It was a most moving occasion. Some 800,000 German and French soldiers made the supreme sacrifice in and about Verdun during the First World War, a vast memorial to the courage of men and the folly of nations.

It may be that the warm feelings that existed between us went back to the message that I sent him following his move to power in June 1958, when he again became Premier of France (he did not become President until several weeks after my visit):

Monsieur le président du conseil,

J'ai suivi, avec la solicitude et l'attention qu'on pouvait attendre du gouvernement et du peuple canadiens, les évènements qui ont eu pour résultat la formation d'un nouveau gouvernement sous votre direction. Les Canadiens honorent tout spécialement les grandes traditions françaises, où ils ont tant puisé

1. A confident party leader speaks to a Toronto press conference just before his 1957 election campaign is officially launched.

2 & 3. *(Above)* The enthusiastic meeting at Massey Hall in Toronto on 25 April that opened the Progressive Conservative Party's 1957 electoral campaign. *(Right)* Shortly after Mr. Diefenbaker's election as party leader Allister Grosart accepted the position of National Director of the Progressive Conservative Party and played a key role in organizing the 1957 campaign.

4 & 5. (*Above*) From the beginning of the campaign Premier
Leslie Frost of Ontario predicted, "We're going to win."
(*Left*) On the morning after the
election that toppled the Liberals from power after twenty-two
years, John Diefenbaker and a
few friends went fishing at Lac
La Ronge—with continued success.

6 & 7. *(Opposite page, above)* The new Cabinet with Governor General Vincent Massey outside Rideau Hall after the swearing-in ceremony, 21 June 1957. *(Below)* In July 1957 Mr. and Mrs. Diefenbaker flew to London to attend the Commonwealth Prime Ministers' Conference.

8 & 9. The equality of every Canadian regardless of race, creed, colour, or ethnic origin is a proud and essential part of Mr. Diefenbaker's concept of "One Canada". *(Below)* Mr. and Mrs. Diefenbaker with Happy I.

10. *(Above left)* Her Majesty Queen Elizabeth and Prince Philip with the Canadian Cabinet, October 1957.

11. *(Left)* Chatting with Premier Leslie Frost and Premier Maurice Duplessis during a break in the official proceedings at the Dominion–Provincial Conference, November 1957.

12. *(Above)* On 14 October 1957, Queen Elizabeth opened Canada's Parliament, the first time in the nation's history that a reigning monarch had done so.

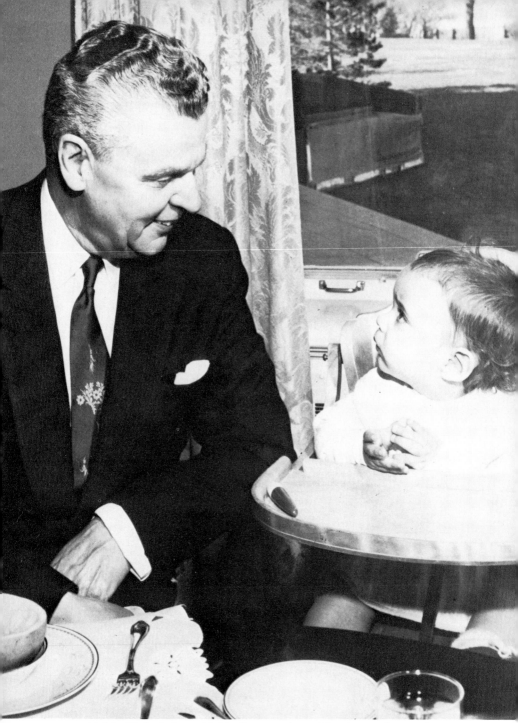

13. Mr. Diefenbaker with his first grandson, John Weir, who was born only a few days before the 1957 election. Newspapers ran this photograph with the caption: "What about an increase in the baby bonus!"

par le passé, et se réjouissent de l'amitié qui unit nos deux pays depuis si longtemps. J'espère que l'avenir nous réservera de nouvelles occasions d'affermir ces liens dans le cadre de la communauté nord-atlantique.

Je vous félicite de votre accession à la présidence du conseil de la République Française et vous exprime mes voeux de succès les plus sincères dans la solution des problèmes difficiles auxquels vous devez faire face. Soyez assuré de mon entière collaboration, si vous jugiez que mon gouvernement pouvait vous aider de quelque façon dans la poursuite de cette tâche.

Bien que les devoirs de votre charge doivent retenir toute votre attention, j'espère qu'avant longtemps il vous sera possible de venir au Canada. Non seulement votre visite serait accueillie avec joie par le peuple canadien, mais elle soulignerait le rôle important que la France joue dans le monde occidental, aussi bien en Amérique du Nord qu'en Europe.

Dans la conjoncture présente, j'ai le sentiment que les qualités d'initiative dont la France a traditionnellement fait preuve, peuvent affermir les bases d'une politique concertée entre l'Europe et l'Amérique du Nord que je tiens pour essentielle à la solution des grands problèmes de l'heure.

Ce sera pour moi un plaisir et un honneur de faire votre connaissance et de discuter avec vous certains de ces problèmes. Dans l'intervalle, je tiens à vous réitérer mes meilleurs voeux et ceux du gouvernement et du peuple canadiens à l'occasion de votre accession à la présidence du conseil de la république.

Veuillez agréer, monsieur le président du conseil, les assurances de ma plus haute considération.

His reply (carried by Reuters at the time) read:

Mr. Prime Minister,

I have very much appreciated the message which you have sent me. You have been able to evoke, in terms that will have touched the heart of all Frenchmen, the friendship that unites our two countries and the spiritual heritage inspiring them. I trust, like yourself, that our governments will find the opportunity to tighten still further ties so useful to a better understanding of the peoples of Europe and North America in the face of the problems which they both must confront in common. I am in no doubt that the noble Canadian nation will be pleased to see France playing fully the role that is quite naturally her own in the world and, more particularly, in the Western community within which Canada, for her own part, realizes so happily and so effectively the vocation to which she is called.

I thank you for your kind invitation to come to Canada where I was, during hours of trial but also of glory, given a reception the recollection of which remains so alive in my memory. I deeply hope that the tasks which I must assume will leave me, some day in the near future, time to visit you.

Please accept, Mr. Prime Minister, assurances of my very high consideration.

On the practical side, the economic side, we made considerable progress. The year 1959, for example, witnessed important changes in our trading relations with France. As a result of the truly remarkable success of the French economic stabilization program introduced by M. Antoine Pinay, de Gaulle's Finance Minister, in December 1958, with the devaluation of the franc and the institution of convertibility for non-resident accounts, the French government proceeded to remove many of the quota restrictions and controls which had impeded the sale of dollar goods to that country since the end of the war. These moves virtually eliminated discrimination against the dollar area and placed France on a par with other European countries in the degree of trade liberalization achieved. The effects of these developments on Canadian exports to France began to make themselves felt. France in 1959 ranked twelfth as an export market for Canadian goods.

The reader may be left to contrast the message by the President of the Republic of France on his arrival at Ottawa on Monday, 18 April 1960, with his message in Montreal seven years later. In 1960 he said:

How delighted and honoured I am to find myself on Canadian soil. Many are the reasons for this: first of all, our deeply rooted past—numerous indeed are the links which bound us, and which, indeed, still bind us—and then there is the more recent past. I recall the two World Wars in which your country and mine joined forces in the battle for the freedom of the world; and then again I am delighted at having been able to accept the invitation of the Prime Minister and the Government of Canada because it gives me an opportunity to renew my friendship with Governor-General Vanier, whom I have so long—and for so many reasons—held in profound and warm esteem.

And, there is also the fact that at this juncture which is so important—and, I add, so dangerous—for the entire globe, I considered it essential that I should come here to meet with the government and people of this dear, strong and vigorous Canada. This, after having been in England, and on the eve of my visit to the United States. In this we see a kind of chain linking the free peoples, and nobody, today, is unaware of the capital importance of their solidarity.

I am therefore pleased to be back on your soil, and to renew my many friendships, and to greet you in the name of France.

Long live Canada,
Long live France,
Long live the free peoples.

President de Gaulle endured a great deal of criticism over his "Long Live Free Quebec" statement in 1967. It was Prime Minister Pearson, however, who advocated the two-nations theory of Confederation. Perhaps the General simply accepted as factual the Pearson philosophy.

To return once more to my 1958 world tour: in Brussels I had rather lengthy conversations with Paul-Henri Spaak, Secretary General of NATO, and with General Lauris Norstad, Supreme Allied Commander Europe. These centred mainly on the whole problem of consultation within the Alliance and on the question of the possible benefit to be derived from a discussion of this question at the December Council meeting, at least in terms of defining what the Alliance could not be expected to do. I was particularly interested in Norstad's explanation of changing concepts of strategy within the Alliance and its implication for a greater dependence upon conventional weaponry. Basically, Norstad's exposition went along these lines: in 1950 we had no new weapons; in 1954 we began to plan on the full use of nuclear weapons as part of our NATO defence strategy, and also developed the forward strategy concept. In 1958, we began to implement this planning and to carry our forward strategy a little farther. We were trying to get fully effective modern weapons into NATO Europe and were defending the closest line to the Iron Curtain which was militarily defensible. The objective of this strategy was to make the deterrent sensitive and to make it fully effective as a deterrent. Any accidental incursion or deliberate movement would be brought up at once against forces equipped to oppose it with the strength and type of weapons necessary; at the same time, because these forces were linked to the retaliatory deterrent, the extent of the risk was evident to the potential enemy. The latter was thus faced with a choice between not fighting or fighting with all its consequences. Norstad felt that the presence of the forces on the forward line made possible a pause in which the potential aggressor could consider this situation. I was thus very much aware from the beginning that strategies within NATO were very much subject to change and that an increasing emphasis on conventional forces might be part of future planning.

On 7 November, Olive and I arrived in Bonn. We were met at the airport by Chancellor Konrad Adenauer. His pictures show him with a stern face that never seemed relaxed. Nothing, however, could be farther from the truth. His skin had a parchment-like quality, and his face seemed to crinkle when he laughed. He and Olive got along famously. He had been Lord Mayor of Cologne until he was dismissed and jailed by the Nazis.

On the way in from the airport I asked him about his meeting with General de Gaulle. He told me in detail what had happened. Close to Adenauer's heart was the establishment of close bonds with France and the use of these as a basis for a united Germany. He had taken steps unpopular in Germany in order to promote reconciliation and had been most apprehensive lest the rise of de Gaulle destroy the fruits of his labour. Adenauer told me that his fears on this score had been lessened by the General's conduct in office and particularly by their convincing heart-to-heart talk at the General's château at Colombey-les-Deux-Eglises on 14 September. The Chancellor's description was very dramatic. Before General de Gaulle would permit him to enter his country residence, he told Adenauer he had always hated everything German, because of the Franco-Prussian War of 1870, the First World War, and the Second World War. De Gaulle told him that when the Second World War ended he had decided to spend the rest of his life doing everything he could to destroy all things German—thus his move towards an alliance between France and the USSR. His general idea was that Germany would then be in the position of a nut in a nutcracker, the USSR being one of the heads and France the other. He said that he had been wrong in this and on the division of Germany, and that from that point on there would be a new chapter in Franco-German relations. De Gaulle then invited Adenauer to cross his threshold; Adenauer accepted and the new chapter began.

I asked the Chancellor, "What did you think?" He replied, "I believe him." He went on to note that no one could say there would never be war again, since history does not permit the use of the word "never". How wise he was, especially when one thinks of Japan and Germany today and the change that has taken place in the thinking of their peoples towards us and in ours towards them. It was one of the experiences of my life to have been present so soon after the historic meeting of de Gaulle and Adenauer and to hear from each of them, in the absence of and without the knowledge of the other, the same magnificent message, a message of peace.

Much of my conversation centred on the development of the European Economic Community and on its rivalry with the British-led European Free Trade Association, the outer group of nations. Chancellor Adenauer seemed quite worried over the possible unfortunate political effects which this economic rivalry in Europe might provoke. He noted that there was already within NATO a dispute between the United Kingdom and Iceland, and a three-way dispute over Cyprus between the United Kingdom, Greece, and Turkey, and that the addition of economic tensions might be more than the Alliance could bear. He felt that if General de Gaulle had a weakness, it was in the realm of economic affairs, where he seemed badly out of touch with the developments of the preceding twelve years.

One of the interesting contrasts between de Gaulle and Chancellor Adenauer was that the Chancellor placed great emphasis on the importance of continued United States leadership and co-operation; he felt that without the United States, Europe, including Britain, would soon be lost to the Soviet Union. Indeed, the Chancellor thought Mr. Dulles a man who acted consistently on principle, although not always wise in the phrasing or tone of his remarks. However, the Chancellor believed it a good thing for all of us that Mr. Dulles was there. The Chancellor was most concerned that the United States remain firmly bound to NATO, to which West Germany had been admitted in 1955. I was certainly prepared to agree on the importance of NATO and, further, that every effort had to be made to prevent the United States from slipping back into isolationism. At one point, he laughingly observed: "Adenauer, Eisenhower, and Diefenbaker—what a threesome!"

During some of our more informal conversations, Adenauer spoke at some length on his talk with Khrushchev in Moscow in 1955. Khrushchev kept reverting to his concern about China with its expanding population, all of whom were workers, and with its ability, unlike other great powers, to survive a nuclear war. Khrushchev had even asked Adenauer what he thought might be done to lessen the dangers to Russia and other countries of the threat of this growing power. The Chancellor believed that Khrushchev had recently stirred up the Chinese to precipitate a crisis with the United States over the islands of Quemoy and Matsu, apparently in the hope that this would weaken both. He told me that he had come to believe that the best way to negotiate with the Russians was with a club.

It was of course difficult in 1958 to know whether a serious Sino-Soviet rivalry would develop. I recall a conversation in Ottawa on 26 June 1961 with Prime Minister Ikeda of Japan, who commented—I thought with considerable perception—that although it was still difficult to estimate the extent of Sino-Soviet disagreement, there was no long, close, historical relationship between the two countries; the differences in tradition and temperament of the two peoples would not lend themselves to a long continuation of the alliance. Generally speaking, their alliance had been based on ideology alone. He suggested that when China developed an atomic weapon, which it would, he thought, within two or three years, the split between the two Communist giants might become permanent.

On 11 and 12 November I had talks with Prime Minister Fanfani in Rome. In a short private conversation we exchanged opinions on recent developments in NATO and found ourselves in general agreement regarding the controversy aroused by General de Gaulle's triumvirate proposal. With our officials present, we discussed the probable relationship between the European Economic Community and the European Free Trade Association, and the relative difficulties of both France and Britain. In the Middle East, Prime Minister Fanfani thought that the Americans had made a colossal mistake by not going through with the Aswan Dam project in 1956. After the Suez crisis, in which they had dissociated themselves from British and French policy, they had failed completely to take advantage of the favourable position which they had won for themselves. Mr. Fanfani pointed to the way in which the West had treated Tito, catering to him so that he would not fall back into the Soviet camp. This, he thought, was a policy which ought to be followed towards Nasser.

While in Rome, Olive and I visited the Vatican for an audience with His Holiness Pope John XXIII. Our visit came shortly after his election by the College of Cardinals, and I was the first leader of a foreign country to have an audience with him. I was most impressed by his deep religious humility and his lively sense of humour. He was approaching his seventy-seventh birthday and was regarded by many as occupying an interregnum. Our conversation began with his asking whether we were Catholic. I replied that we were not, but were Protestant, belonging to the Baptist denomination. His reply was: "It does not matter; we all are going to the same place." It was a reply that in retrospect seems significant, for early in 1959 he surprised everyone by calling an ecumenical council. Our conversation had proceeded in a spirit of such general good humour that I asked him: "How does it feel to be Pope anyhow?" He laughed heartily and replied: "Well, here I am near the end of the road and on top of the heap." Before we left, he blessed a rosary for Olive's grandson, John. I was concerned that following our audience a popular news magazine reported at length on the views expressed to us by Pope John. To no one did either Olive or I make any statements, and I can only ascribe the detail in the article to the interpreter.

On 15 November, a few weeks after he took power in Pakistan, I met with President Ayub Khan in Karachi. A British Sandhurst graduate, he was a soldier of distinction and a statesman who knew what he wanted to achieve for his country. I came to admire Ayub Khan very much. I was disturbed by the extent to which a dictatorship could have been so easily established. I said so. He had been head of the army. He had simply said to the Prime Minister, "You're out," and the Prime Minister agreed. After a few weeks as Prime Minister, he declared himself President and took over completely. In a restricted session which followed my main meeting with most of his Cabinet, the President said that he wished to say a few words about his decision to assume the reins of government. He considered that he had been obliged to take supreme power himself, although he made it clear that he had done this only with reluctance and as a last resort. He said it had been clear for some years that the politicians who had been running the country had failed to make democracy work. The required standards of integrity and leadership had not been forthcoming, and Pakistan, surrounded as it was by enemies and plagued by economic weakness, had declined to a desperate state of demoralization; the army itself had been affected.

In response to my question on what had provoked his decision to act on 7 October, Ayub Khan said that his action had been taken not in response to any particular provocation, but rather as a means of forestalling bloodshed. There had been growing signs of disintegration: violence in the Parliament of East Pakistan, the openness and prevalence of corruption, the increasing clamour of the neutralists, and talk of bloody revolution. All these factors had had their place as a climax was reached. The President spoke as if he himself had been from the beginning the effective force behind the plan to put an end to the old régime. He considered that elections were not needed. Efficiency was the need. The great mass of the people had no land. The overlords had. He said, "We're putting an end to this. We're going to see that the people have a share in the land so that each will be able to own his own, however small." He understood what he called "basic democracy" in Pakistan. He said, "We'll not do anything improper or unjust." Ayub Khan regarded his position as that of trustee, not only for the present generation but also for those who would follow. "How long is this going to continue?" I asked. He replied, "My plan is that within two years I'll bring about elections and establish constitutional government." As is so often the case with prophecies, his was many years out. But he loved the common people and they loved him. He did much for his country.

On the question of Kashmir, the President said that opinion in Pakistan was "really burning" over the unreasonableness of the Indian attitude, and that unless some progress were made, it might be difficult for the government to hold the people of Pakistan in check. If war came, it would be total war: Pakistan would either destroy India or destroy itself. Such a war, he suggested, would open the door to communism, with incalculable consequences in Asia, Africa, and the Middle East. His remarks carried the tone of anxious concern lest failure to move towards a solution might bring on an outbreak of violence. In speaking of the Indian attitude, the President expressed the interesting view that as soon as Nehru's hold was loosened, it was not impossible that India might "break up". When I questioned him on this point, the President professed to believe that India's problems with the caste system and with regional rivalries were such as to threaten India's survival as a unified state. When I asked what he thought the Commonwealth might do to assist in finding a solution to the Kashmir dispute, the President said he thought that the Commonwealth countries should exert pressure by saying to Nehru: "You are playing with fire!"

On 18 November, before leaving for India, we drove from Peshawar to the Khyber Pass. It was one place I had always wanted to see. I walked to within a few feet of the Afghanistan border and looked north along the route that had seen the armies of Alexander the Great and the legions of Tamerlane. In later years the famous Khyber Rifles had fought to hold the vitally strategic northwest frontier to protect the British Empire's claim to the subcontinent.

When I met with Prime Minister Nehru in New Delhi on the morning of 19 November, the major item in the press that day concerned the *coup d'état* in the Sudan. Nehru, however, was clearly more interested in securing my views on the régime in Pakistan than on anything else. He did not believe that Ayub Khan was behind the military take-over; Ayub, he said, had never been accused of too much intelligence and there must have been someone else behind it. While he admitted that the coup had been "in a sense, popular", he did not see how the new government of Pakistan would lift themselves out of the emergency. They were faced with almost insuperable economic problems, and from a constitutional point of view he could see no hope of elections taking place. There was not much that I could say except to express my faith in Ayub Khan's good intentions, since I did not feel I could pass on the information I had gathered in Pakistan to Mr. Nehru.

I will always think of Pandit Nehru as a transplanted Englishman who, while living in something of a metaphysical world, nevertheless was one of the great realists, capable of achieving his objectives with courage and determination, a Harrovian to the end. Imprisoned for his revolutionary activities, he used the time to develop his political philosophy. He never developed a hatred for the British people, and retained an admiration for British justice that stayed with him throughout his life. He often spoke of this, and of what Britain had done in providing India with a trained civil service. You might talk with him at length on almost any subject; he was a man of catholic tastes. Yet, when you expressed a view with which he disagreed, he would suddenly place himself in a kind of oriental box. It was the most peculiar thing. There he was, saying nothing and giving the appearance that he was completely detached if not entirely removed from you.

Nehru's views in favour of the recognition of Red China were well established. Thus, I was somewhat surprised in discussing the Dulles policy with regard to Communist China to hear him voice the opinion that this policy suited the Communist Chinese perfectly. He felt that the Peking government attached more value to building up an inner strength within their country than to taking the offshore islands of Quemoy and Matsu, or even Formosa. American policy enabled them to push their people to work harder. Nor did he feel that the Communist Chinese would in the near future attack Formosa and thereby precipitate a war with the United States. The Chinese had an infinite capacity for patience, he said. The Peking government expected that eventually Formosa would fall into their hands like an over-ripe apple. He saw no danger that Red China could become aggressive in her relations with neighbouring states. He was quite bitter in 1962 when China invaded his country; his letters to me indicate this. But when I asked him at the Commonwealth Prime Ministers' Meeting in London that year what had happened to bring about the invasion, he retreated into his defensive vacuum and said nothing.

On disarmament, Nehru was worried that international talks always seemed to lag behind developments in armament. I agreed and cited our experience with the AVRO "Arrow" as a case in point. Nehru thought that the Soviet Union's possession of short- and middle-range missiles further illustrated the change in the nature of the disarmament problem, and that it was important to avoid a disarmament agreement which would be bogus (involving meaningless concessions by one side or the other, i.e., agreement to give up weapons which nobody wanted). As he saw it, a new psychological approach to the problem of disarmament was required. The basis of the arms race, the urge to arm, was the fear of others. If we could lessen that fear, the urge to arm would itself lessen. No country could afford to take a major risk by disarming unilaterally (it would be politically foolish), but the arms race itself was a major risk. I could not but agree that this was a fundamental dilemma, and asked Nehru how it could be circumvented and whether a continuing hostile attitude was a necessary concomitant of a strong military position. He instanced Khrushchev's unpleasant remarks regarding Britain in Burma and said that he had asked Khrushchev, in reply to the latter's question as to how he could improve the Soviet Union's relations with the United States and Britain, why it was that he spoke in these hostile terms. Khrushchev had admitted that there was something in what Nehru had said but justified himself by adding that the Soviet Union had lived for forty years in a state of siege and encirclement, and that this caused Russians, including himself, to react rapidly to what they believed to be interference. Thus, statements made in the United States created anger and fear in the USSR. Nehru concluded that if, while maintaining their armaments, nations could make a deliberate attempt not to curse one another, this would perhaps have a psychological impact on the disarmament problem. He then added that, in his opinion, the Soviet people were in any case more afraid of a rearmed Germany than of the United States.

When I asked him about the size of India's defence budget, Nehru said that he thought it was some 22 to 23 per cent of the national budget. In relation to revenue, this was not very large, he said, especially when one considered the size of the country and the length of the frontier. India's whole policy was a policy of defence. It could not afford the latest types of arms; it relied on second-rate arms that could be made in India. Nor did India attempt to get long-distance offensive weapons such as bombers. If this has changed with time, a constant in the Indian position has been its unwillingness to settle the Kashmir question with Pakistan. That problem could not be settled under Nehru as long as he was Prime Minister, because he was born in Kashmir, as were his forebears, and there was no argument that could be advanced which was acceptable to him that would in any way threaten a cleavage of Kashmir from India. In both India and Pakistan, both privately and publicly, I over and over again pressed for the acceptance of one principle as basic to the concept of our Commonwealth: that war between members must not take place. And in both countries the reaction was favourable; more than that, it was enthusiastic. It was clear, however, that in both countries there was a deep determination that if war was necessary in order to preserve the *status quo* on Kashmir or to change it, war would come.

On the question of American foreign aid, Nehru stated

that two years previously he had told President Eisenhower frankly that the effect of pouring out American treasure was not what the United States intended it to be. When I agreed that the attachment of strings to aid was always suspect, Nehru said that it was more than that; too frequently, help failed to reach the people to any important degree. An equally important failing in aid programs, as he saw it (and this applied to Britain as well as to the United States), was that help was given to the government of the day, so that if that government happened to be unpopular or reactionary, the donor country inevitably lost credit.

I told him that I had spoken in similar terms to President Eisenhower and had commended the idea of creating greater liquidity through the International Bank. I felt that this was the kind of channel through which the Americans might give aid without strings. To this Nehru rejoined that people didn't like to be bossed by large numbers of foreigners, no matter how generous. This, in turn, led to a short discussion about the balance which had to be observed in the implementation of economic aid projects between the use on the one hand of indigenous employees and on the other of experts from outside. Nehru pointed to the Bhakra Dam as an example of what he had in mind, where some two to three thousand Indian engineers were employed as compared with only some fifteen Americans.

While in India, I went on a Bengal tiger hunt with the Maharajah of Kotah along the banks of the Chambal River. I was quite happy to bag nothing; it was a most relaxing day without official duties or the need to dress in anything more stylish than old fishing clothes and a crumpled straw hat. At the University of Punjab, I was given an honorary degree. The Chancellor of the university, in his remarks to the convocation, said that I was a graduate of the University of Saskatchewan. The word

"Saskatchewan" gave him some difficulty. In my response, I told the story of the two English ladies who were crossing Canada by train. At Saskatoon, where there was a brief stop, one of the ladies asked a man standing on the platform the name of the city. When he replied, "Saskatoon, Saskatchewan," she commented to her companion, "Well, it's obvious they don't speak English here."

Our next port of call was Colombo, the capital of Ceylon, where Olive and I were the guests of the Governor General, Sir Oliver Goonetilleke. I had always been interested in Ceylon. I had met previously several of the great tribunes of freedom in that country, Sir John Kotalawala among others. Sir John, formerly Prime Minister and leader of the United National Party, had suffered defeat in the election of 1956. A strong anti-Communist, he had been a very able Prime Minister. During our visit, I met frequently with the then Prime Minister, Mr. Solomon W. R. D. Bandaranaike. He was a man who had given good service to his country. His principal preoccupation in our conversations was the stabilization of commodity prices throughout the world. A semi-intellectual leftist, he believed that Ceylon would achieve its greatest destiny if it sat in the neutralist camp and did not become too closely allied with Britain and the Commonwealth. So far as the policies of the USSR were concerned, he considered it the course of reason to adopt an attitude of benevolence in all his judgments.

Our reception in Ceylon was unequalled anywhere in Asia. It was my distinct impression that the people had been made aware of Canada's contribution to the elevation of the Ceylonese standard of living through such projects as the modernization of their fishing industry, and were further aware that under my administration there was to be a large increase in the amount of Colombo Plan assistance from Canada. I believe that our first consideration in external aid programs should be to raise the living standards within the Commonwealth, for I consider the Commonwealth the greatest instrument for freedom that the world has ever seen. Nevertheless, the degree of public awareness in Ceylon was unusual. I have often found that countries receiving the most assistance are the fastest to forget. I think of the Warsak dam in Pakistan which I declared open during my visit. It was to bring untold benefits in flood control, irrigation, and hydro-electric power. Yet the people in the area in which it was located had no idea that Canada had provided the funds for its construction. To me Canadian officialdom had failed in its responsibility: these people should have known of the advantages that accrued to them because they were a Commonwealth country.

The warmth of the people of Ceylon had its finest example at Kandy, that oasis among oases, that other Eden, demi-paradise. There I rode my first elephant; and Olive, always popular, not only with the people of Ceylon but wherever we went, had named in her honour the Olive Diefenbaker orchid. You might think that an insignificant matter. Nothing of the kind! To me, always knowing her to have been orchidaceous, it was simple fact translated into effective action.

On 28 November 1958, I met with the Malayan Prime Minister, Tunku Abdul Rahman, in Kuala Lumpur. We became fast friends. In our conversation, the Tunku spoke at some length about the nature and operations of Communist Chinese subversion and infiltration in Malaya. It was impossible, he said, to prevent the infiltration of terrorists and Communist Chinese agents who could enter either across the Thai border or at many points along the Malayan coastline, or again through Singapore, where the immigration regulations were not such as to discourage seriously their entry. The Tunku also spoke of the emergency regulations in force and illustrated on a wall map the progress made in anti-terrorist operations, a subject covered in much broader detail the next day when I received a briefing from Lieutenant-General Cassels, the brilliant Director of Operations.

When I inquired about the effect of Communist Chinese trade activity in Malaya, the Tunku explained that the inroads made by the Peking government in introducing low-priced textiles into Malaya had represented a serious menace to Malayan producers. His government had, therefore, imposed a ban on the import of textiles from Communist China. In retaliation, the Communist Chinese had themselves prohibited all exports to Malaya. As it had turned out, however, the Communist Chinese had acted too hastily, since their action had given the Malayan government an opportunity to forbid the Bank of China to continue its operations in Malaya. The Tunku explained that his government had taken this drastic action against the advice of its legal and financial experts. He was, however, convinced that as a means of forestalling economic penetration and to preclude the Bank of China from providing financial assistance to subversive groups, the action taken had been fully justified and would indeed have a beneficial effect.

I asked the Tunku whether the trend toward the establishment of military or semi-military governments in other countries of Asia and Southeast Asia was having any appreciable effect on the political situation of Malaya. The Tunku did not think so, but he made it clear that military *coups d'état* such as had occurred recently in Burma, Pakistan, and Sudan naturally made Malaya feel uncomfortably conspicuous in its efforts to preserve a genuinely democratic government. The Tunku had no liking for military governments, however sound the reasons for their establishment. He hoped in particular that the new régime in Pakistan would soon restore representative institutions.

When I asked him to explain Malaya's abstention from membership in SEATO (South East Asia Treaty Organization), the Tunku's explanation was twofold. From a domestic political point of view, the government would be criticized if so soon after securing independence it accepted an association which placed it, so to speak, under the protection of the United States. He stated that the government could not ignore the sentiments of the people on this question. Second, the Tunku said that the Malayan government was satisfied with the assistance and commitments which it enjoyed by virtue of its Bilateral Defence Agreement with Britain. By providing a base for Commonwealth Far East strategic reserves, Malaya had an assurance of effective support in case of need not only from Britain but also from Australia and New Zealand.

I then asked the Tunku to outline the Malayan viewpoint with regard to Quemoy and Matsu. The Tunku said that in strict logic these islands should belong to mainland China. In terms of international politics, however, to surrender Quemoy and Matsu would be to encourage the Peking government in its campaign to achieve a single China. The Tunku believed that it was to be expected that the Communist Chinese would eventually try to take the islands by force if they were not evacuated. Nevertheless, the Malayan government agreed with the firm position which the United States had adopted. Malaya could not look favourably on any move which opened the way for further expansion by the Peking régime. He was a strong opponent of any suggestion to broaden the diplomatic recognition of Communist China. And he made it clear that the war against Communist infiltration which had been waged so successfully in Malaya would be weakened were Canada to accord official recognition to Peking. Those who stood against Communism would see this as approval of Red China's expansionist policies.

Needless to say, I was very much impressed by the Malayan government's desire to acquire a position of strength and self-sufficiency so as to forestall conditions in which Communism might flourish. Foreign aid had been effectively used for the improvement of Port Swettenham and for the installation of the Cameron Highlands hydro-electric project. When I asked about the efforts to convince the average citizen of the value and virtue of democracy, the Tunku referred to the system of Leadership Scholarships established in consultation with the United States government and also to the progress being made in other forms of education. When the Tunku emphasized the difficulty which his government was experiencing in retaining teaching personnel for post-secondary levels and below, and indicated that this was a field in which Canadian assistance would be welcome, I was most sympathetic. Indeed, one of my official acts in Malaya was to make a presentation of books to the university. I was also anxious to meet his request concerning the secondment of senior treasury advisers. I was more than pleased to be able to announce our decision to make available to Malaya the sum of $1.5 million in Canadian Colombo Plan aid.

En route to Australia, we stopped briefly in Singapore and at Djakarta. In Singapore, I had useful conversations with Sir William Goode and Sir Robert Scott, respectively the Governor of Singapore and the British Commissioner General for South East Asia. Our visit to Djakarta on 2 December, as our visits elsewhere, received extensive and favourable press coverage. In my discussions with the Indonesian Prime Minister, Dr. Djuanda, I stressed the non-expansionist basis of Western policy in Asia and cautioned him against permitting Communist parties controlled from abroad to subvert democratic institutions. He outlined the current political and economic situation in Indonesia and explained President Sukarno's "guided democracy" program. Curiously, he said very little about Indonesia's dispute with Australia over West New Guinea or about Colombo Plan aid from Canada, which at that time amounted to about $600,000. I did not meet President Sukarno during my brief stopover; he was at Bali convalescing from an illness. I might note that I was obliged to travel to my meeting with Dr. Djuanda in a gun carriage.

Prior to my visits to Karachi, New Delhi, Colombo, Kuala Lumpur, Singapore, and Djakarta, I had not been entirely convinced of the soundness of the "Dulles concept" on the matter of recognizing Communist China. I was now in a position to conclude that the United Nations Secretary General, Dag Hammarskjöld, had been rather optimistic in his assertion that Asians would sleep better at night if Communist China were recognized and allowed to take its seat at the United Nations. It appeared to me that Pakistan, Malaya, Singapore, Thailand, South Vietnam, the Philippines, and Formosa would have greater difficulty in sleeping at night if recognition of Peking were forthcoming. If it was true that official recognition would be construed as the acceptance and welcome of Communism in Asia, then Canada's responsibility was to avoid recognition of the Peking régime, at least until the achievement of a greater economic and political stabilization in non-Communist Asia. Certainly, I was well aware that six hundred million people could not be ignored forever. In one sense, it was unfortunate that this question of recognition had not been settled in the early 1950s, since the longer it was delayed the more anomalous our position became. We were now obliged to wait until we could be reasonably certain that by this act the Canadian government would not damage our Commonwealth sister nations and other friends in Asia.

I might note that where I could, I advanced specific Canadian interests during my tour. For example, in Pakistan, India, and Ceylon, all countries that were importers of foodstuffs, I emphasized that public opinion in Canada would not understand if they continued to buy their wheat from the United States while Canada, with a large wheat surplus, contributed other forms of aid under the Colombo Plan. It seemed to me that given the $15 million increase in Canadian Colombo Plan aid in 1958, the governments in question ought to be aware of Canada's surplus grain problems and should view with favour taking Canadian wheat as part of Canada's Colombo Plan contribution.

Whenever I travelled or received official visitors, I tried to advance Canadian commercial interests. During my conversations with President Lopez Mateos in Mexico in April 1960, I was successful in promoting the sale of Canadian manufactured steel rails to the Mexican State Railways. Canada was not in a position to match the terms which might be extended by such a country as the United States on a commercial transaction of this size, but I was able to convince the President that the successful consummation of this transaction would do more than anything else to strengthen the commercial relations between our two countries. Occasionally, one may be aided by the unexpected. One evening during the visit of Prime Minister Ikeda of Japan to Canada in June of 1961, we were discussing trade questions over dinner. I was anxious to expand the Canadian market for wheat in Japan. Prime Minister Ikeda was explaining Japan's economic policies when one of those seemingly insignificant things happened that sometimes change events. He had been studying the plate before him while he was talking. On the corner of each plate was a sheaf of wheat in gold. He commented about the strange coincidence, given the nature of our conversation. He picked up the plate, turned it over to read: "Made in Japan". The effect was unbelievable. At first he was offended. I assured him that I had never seen the dinner service before. His attitude changed. Whether he considered that fate had entered into our discussions I do not know, but from that moment it was very clear that he had become enthusiastic about finding a Canadian market for wheat in Japan.

The second-to-last stop on our 1958 trip was Australia. Australia's post-war defence, immigration, and foreign policies had been shaped by the emergence of a dozen independent Asian nations, and by the emergence of Communist China as potentially the dominant military and political power in Asia. In this highly explosive post-colonial world, Australia was increasingly an outpost of Western civilization. Thousands of miles away from her natural allies, Australia was by 1958 dependent upon the United States for its defence. As the Foreign Minister, the Right Honourable Richard Casey (afterwards Lord Casey), told me in our conversations on 4 December, Australia was in the position of having to depend on United States goodwill for its ultimate survival. He thought it essential that Australia keep the United States intimately interested in Asia, and to see that United States bases in Asia were maintained. The most far-reaching danger to Australia, he contended, was the growth of Communist China's influence in Southeast Asia and particularly in Indonesia; the containment of Communism was vital. Should Indonesia go Communist, to cite his example, Australia would find its sea- and air-ways to Singapore barred. Australia had entered into the ANZUS treaty with New Zealand and the United States and into SEATO with the principal Western powers and their Asian allies; and had further collaborated with Britain and New Zealand in the defence of the ANZAM area, including Malaya.

On the economic front, Australia had recently entered into trade agreements with Japan, Malaya, and Ceylon in an attempt to expand friendly economic relations with its Asian neighbours. She had taken a leading part in the establishment of the Colombo Plan, and by 1958 had committed some $60 million in capital aid and technical assistance to it. However, Australia's principal preoccupation was to increase its population and to establish economic self-sufficiency. Its immigration policy was designed to populate Australia with people of European origin who would provide the human material with which its economy could be expanded and diversified.

Canada and Australia are the two oldest sister Dominions of the Commonwealth. Our countries are bound together in countless ways; the patterns of our association, whether national or individual, are myriad. I had visited Australia previously in 1950 for the meetings of the Commonwealth Parliamentary Association and had known many of Australia's leading political and legal figures for years. It was in an atmosphere of family informality that I met with that remarkable statesman the Australian Prime Minister, the Right Honourable Robert Menzies, the members of his Cabinet, and the Leader of the Opposition, the Right Honourable Dr. Herbert Evatt. Our conversations covered many of the things I had seen and heard on my tour, and the major international problems of the day, as well as matters relating specifically to Canada–Australia relations.

My visit to New Zealand gave me an opportunity for long discussions on Commonwealth and international affairs, and on trade matters, with the New Zealand Prime Minister, the Right Honourable Walter Nash. Prime Minister Nash was a socialist, but one who didn't try to shove his socialism down your throat. He considered the recognition of Communist China both "inevitable and sensible", but was not prepared to move in that direction "if it would do harm". Mr. Nash, at seventy-six years of age, was a most energetic man, possessing a capacity for work considered by many as phenomenal. He was devoted to the Commonwealth and welcomed its developing multi-racial character. Like Australia, however, New Zealand was increasingly dependent on the United States in matters of defence, a fact that drew Australia and New Zealand ever more closely together despite the different political philosophies of their two governments. I must note that I still regard highly the honour accorded me by the Maori people of New Zealand when they made me an honorary chief.

Forty-eight days and fourteen countries later, I returned to Ottawa. From the point of view of goodwill and Canadian prestige, the tour had been a success. More important was the furthering of international understanding that resulted. Visits between national leaders have a considerable potential for international good. The personal relationships that result often allow a Prime Minister the opportunity of giving his opposite number a full, first-person account of a specific policy point of view. This may prove to be an important factor in the success or failure of a conference or a bilateral negotiation. As I said over the CBC's national television network on 21 December 1958:

I have come back more convinced than ever of the importance of these personal meetings with national leaders. The more we know each other, the more likely we are to find amicable solutions of our differences; to understand the viewpoints and problems of others; and to appreciate the basic goodness and goodwill in the hearts of human beings. This is something that can never be communicated through third parties, or by correspondence or diplomatic exchanges. . . .

There is another vital reason for the importance of these talks with world leaders. The normal diplomatic channels are still of the utmost importance, but there are times when direct communication between those in high authority, often by long distance telephone, becomes desirable and indeed essential. I need only mention the fact that there is a world of difference between speaking to someone, under such circumstances, whom you have never met, and the kind of frankness and understanding that is possible with one whom you know personally.

Also, one has the opportunity to see and learn. For example, I came away from Southeast Asia in 1958 very much impressed with the value of student exchanges, particularly as established between Australia and her neighbours. Here was an avenue of aid to the third world which Canada might successfully pursue. Finally, I consider the symbolic value of these visits to be important. They are worth the time, the effort, and the upsets of digestion they sometimes include. Olive and I marked our fifth wedding anniversary flying home some twelve thousand feet above the Pacific Ocean.

CHAPTER FIVE

※

AS I LOOK BACK over my period as Prime Minister of Canada, I consider my most important single statement on Canadian external relations to have been my address before the United Nations General Assembly on 26 September 1960. The Fifteenth Session of the General Assembly of the United Nations opened on 20 September in the midst of serious deterioration in international relations, marked by a disturbing resort to extreme language, irritability, and rocket-rattling on the part of some countries. The Summit Meeting in Paris had collapsed on 18 May, and the international tension which followed seemed likely to result in a grave challenge to the prestige and authority of the United Nations. Therefore, the Canadian delegation was instructed by the government to seize every opportunity to encourage an improvement in the conduct of relations between Eastern and Western countries and to promote understanding between the latter and the countries of Asia and Africa.

On 23 September 1957, when I spoke to the UN General Assembly for the first time, I made it clear that my government regarded Canada's commitment to the United Nations as the cornerstone of our foreign policy. Of course I was aware of the extent to which that world organization had been undermined through the Soviets' employment of the veto in the Security Council. I was aware also that had the Soviets not been granted this veto power there would have been no United Nations in 1945. More important was the possibility that the Assembly would be distorted and stultified by bloc politics as its membership expanded by the inclusion of many new small states. I said in my 1957 speech: "I believe that if the United Nations is to maintain its capacity to exercise an ameliorating influence on the problems of mankind, it must be a flexible instrument. The United Nations must not become frozen by the creation of hostile blocs. . . . "

By 1960, my government was even more determined that none of Canada's other international associations would prevent us from judging the issues before the UN on the basis of their merits, and as we saw them. Small powers and middle powers such as Canada, acting in consultation with other friendly nations, in my view had the opportunity to exert through the agency of the United Nations an international influence far stronger than would ever otherwise be possible. I was prepared, therefore, to give strong support to the United Nations despite its imperfections; there was nothing better in sight for maintaining peace and advancing the social and economic welfare of mankind.

The major goal of the Canadian government at the UN throughout the course of my prime-ministership was the elimination of nuclear weapons. In the years following the Second World War, our anxiety over the consequences of the widespread possession of nuclear weapons increased as first one and then two further countries were added to the once exclusively United States "nuclear club". These fears were sharpened during the period of my government by the realization that it was possible for almost any state possessing the advanced technology to devise "cheap" methods of constructing nuclear weapons. Although these fears were offset to a certain extent by the enormous cost and complexity of the effective delivery systems required for full nuclear capability, none the less it was increasingly imperative that the spread of nuclear weapons be halted and that some comprehensive disarmament agreement be reached. Maintaining a nuclear balance of terror was not an acceptable alternative. I might say in this context that I have often thought, and still think, that the Honourable Howard Green, who became Canada's Secretary of State for External Affairs on 4 June 1959, should have received the Nobel Peace Prize for his efforts to make the world safe for future generations.

I might note also that our quest for disarmament sometimes had a complicating effect on other aspects of our foreign and defence policies. For example, a resolution sponsored by Ireland and adopted at the Fifteenth Session of the General Assembly called upon all states to make every effort to "achieve permanent agreement" on the prevention of the wider dissemination of nuclear weapons, and in addition, "as a temporary and voluntary measure", for states possessing such weapons to refrain from "relinquishing control" over them to states not possessing them, or from giving such states information necessary for their manufacture. This resolution also called for states not possessing such weapons to refrain, on a similar temporary basis, from manufacturing them "and from otherwise attempting to acquire them". Canadian defence planning called for the stationing of nuclear weapons on Canadian territory and for the supplying of these weapons to Canadian forces in Europe. (The whole question of Canadian defence planning and the political issues related thereto will receive chapter-length treatment in Volume III of these memoirs.) It was possible to argue that if nuclear weapons were stationed in Canada, we would not have "acquired" them because they would continue to be owned by the United States. However, in my view this line of reasoning was not persuasive, since in all but a legalistic and very narrow interpretation, it was clear that a state which permitted nuclear weapons to be stationed on its territory under joint control and supplied these weapons to its forces was in a very real sense "acquiring" such weapons. To accept these weapons under strictly American control was, in my view and that of Cabinet, not acceptable to the conditions of Canadian sovereignty. Rejecting nuclear weapons entirely placed Canada in some difficulty in regard to defence planning in NORAD and NATO, whereas a rejection of the Irish resolution might have forced Canada into a paradoxical, even an intolerable, position.

In seeking a disarmament agreement, we had no interest in unsubstantiated declarations, whatever their source, but sought an acceptable means of inspection adequate to guarantee any disarmament undertaking that could be devised. This I explained in a letter to President Kennedy on 30 October 1962, in response to his letter indicating personal "distress" over my government's intention to support a UN resolution calling for a moratorium on nuclear weapon testing:

I am sure that you would wish to have a clear indication of the main considerations underlying the Canadian position as it has been for the past three years on this important matter.

To begin with, I would state unequivocally that Canadian policy on this question involves no endorsement of an uncontrolled moratorium on nuclear testing. In the 18-nation committee and at the United Nations we have reasserted our long-standing support for an international agreement to end tests, and our representatives have at all times been instructed to give equal emphasis in their public statements as well as in private consultations to the need for both a cessation of testing and a multilateral agreement containing adequate safeguards.

The Western nuclear powers and the Soviet Union are in

agreement that nuclear tests in the atmosphere, outer space and under water can be discontinued without any special system of international control. The only stumbling block to complete agreement now relates to the means of controlling a narrow range of underground nuclear explosions. I am fully aware, Mr. President, that there remains a risk that low yield underground tests could be carried out in secret. Such a risk should not be judged in isolation, and should be weighed against the graver dangers which will continue to exist as long as an agreement is not reached and the tests go on.

In the opinion of the Government of Canada, the resolution of the non-aligned nations represents a genuine effort to achieve a compromise position on the question of nuclear tests. It recommends an end to testing by January 1, 1963, not an uncontrolled moratorium; it also indicates a commitment to an international agreement, which clearly is intended to cover underground as well as above ground tests; and it calls for urgent negotiations to this end, and a report to the General Assembly by December 10, 1962. These points have been repeatedly endorsed by Canada. . . .

In September 1960, I hoped that the presence at the United Nations General Assembly of the Soviet Union's Nikita Khrushchev signified some desire on the part of the USSR to forward in meaningful fashion the establishment of international peace and security. I suspected, however, that in the normal course of things, he would make a slashing attack on the West. As Prime Minister Harold Macmillan had written to me on 15 September: "What one doesn't know is whether that is all he has in mind or whether he is prepared for something more constructive." As it turned out, there was surprisingly little positive content in Khrushchev's UN speech. Despite the fact that he had insisted that disarmament was the number one question for the General Assembly, he had no new proposals to make. Some two-thirds of his speech was devoted to a Marxist analysis of emerging colonial nations and to a vociferous but puerile assault on the record of the Western democracies in this connection. He made it evident that he was prepared to sacrifice the United Nations to the imperial ambitions of the Soviet Union. His vicious and bizarre attack on the UN Secretary General, Dag Hammarskjöld, and the proposal of the USSR that the office of Secretary General be replaced by a triumvirate, an executive of three, one of whom would be a Soviet representative, was a desperate attempt to salvage Soviet objectives in the newly independent Congo.

The United Nations operation in the Congo (ONUC), initiated at the request of the Prime Minister of that country, Patrice Lumumba, and directed by Dag Hammarskjöld, had in Khrushchev's eyes operated in a partisan way; that is to say, against Soviet interests. The Soviets seemed surprised to discover the remarkably wide powers of the UN Secretary General once he had been given general authority to act. They now sought to impose a Soviet veto on his office. The effect of their proposal would have been to have made the secretary-generalship an instrument of indecision and impotence, powerless to proceed effectively and promptly in the event of international emergencies. Khrushchev went so far as to make the resumption of disarmament negotiations contingent on the acceptance of his triumvirate demand. President Eisenhower, in a constructive speech, had opened the door to international conciliation. Premier Khrushchev had attempted to slam that door shut.

My government was concerned and did its part to ensure that the African continent should not become the focus of the East–West struggle. The Soviet Union had discovered that the most potent tools of diplomacy in dealing with under-developed countries were hypocritical solicitude, aid, and trade. These were most effective in detaching under-developed areas from Western influence and of increasing the prestige of the Soviet bloc. Substantial credits were provided to a number of countries, and particularly important was the announcement of Chairman Khrushchev in October 1958 that the USSR had agreed to grant to the United Arab Republic a credit of up to $100 million for equipment to be used in the first stage of the Aswan High Dam project. When the former Belgian territory of the Congo gained its independence on 30 June 1960, the Soviet Union attempted to draw this new government into its orbit. The result was devastating.

Canada's interests in that part of Africa had been limited to missionary activities. Indeed, at the time, Canada had diplomatic representation in only three African countries: Egypt, Ghana, and the Union of South Africa. We did not even have an African Division in the Department of External Affairs. When Congolese independence resulted in rebellion, civil war, and political chaos, and a request for United Nations help, I agreed with Dag Hammarskjöld that the bulk of any proposed UN peacekeeping force should come from independent African states. Initially, Canada contributed emergency food supplies and air transportation. On 30 July, however, I agreed, subject to parliamentary approval, to a UN request for a signals unit. On 6 August, the Soviets charged that the dispatch of Canadian signallers constituted NATO aggression in the Congo: as ridiculous a charge as I have ever heard. The record of our troops in the Congo is one in which every Canadian can take pride. In December 1960, Cabinet approved an instruction to our delegation at the United Nations to indicate Canada's willingness to contribute $600,000 to the cost of the Congo airlift.

We considered that should the Congo operation fail, the future effectiveness of the United Nations in dealing with emergency situations involving peace and security would be jeopardized. Any loss of confidence in the United Nations' ability to fulfil one of its primary functions would inevitably be reflected in other areas of United Nations activities. The cumulative effect could be that the United Nations might then become totally discredited as a body dedicated to co-operative international action. When in May 1961 President Kwame Nkrumah of Ghana requested my support for his plan to move for a solution of the Congo crisis outside the confines of the United Nations organization, I replied:

I confess to doubts that consultation on the Congo elsewhere than in the UN would be likely to contribute to an improvement of the present situation. I recall that when the Congo situation was reviewed at our [Commonwealth Prime Ministers'] meeting last March in London, you stressed your belief that the UN provided the best hope for peace and security in the Congo, as indeed for the world as a whole. I agreed with you when you said this in London and I must say that more recent developments have reinforced me in this conviction.

I might add the footnote that my understanding of the Congo situation was not particularly helped by the visit of Prime Minister Lumumba to Ottawa in the fall of 1960. It was apparent he had no clear idea as to what was required to turn the former Belgian colony into a viable nation state. The only definite request he made of the Canadian government was for assistance in the establishment of a national radio service in the Congo. It is reported that he based his judgment of Canada and of Canadian attitudes on the failure of Howard Green and the officials of the Department of External Affairs to provide him with female companions during his visit.

It is my general view that peacekeeping forces have their uses in preventing brush-fire wars from becoming widespread conflicts. But they are at best a stopgap measure. Political questions can only be settled politically, and often peacekeeping forces work against political settlement in that they alleviate the urgency to find solutions to the problems that necessitated the creation of the peacekeeping force in the first place. Cyprus I would consider a classic example of this problem. As Prime Minister, I believed that Canada should take an appropriate part in United Nations peacekeeping activities. But I never thought that this should be automatic; I think the idea ridiculous that Canada should perforce participate in every United Nations peacekeeping activity.

I was the first leader from any major Western State to speak in the UN Assembly after Khrushchev had delivered his diatribe. I decided I would give a frank, direct answer to his 140-minute tirade. The External Affairs officials were disturbed when I gave them a general outline of what I wanted to say. I asked that a draft speech be prepared along the lines I had indicated. They wrote and they re-wrote, and each time a draft was brought to me, it failed to contain the things I had told them I wanted to speak about. Finally, about seven p.m. on the evening of 25 September, I simply said: "This is what I'm going to say. I am not going to accept your version of what I should or should not say. Now get to work. I do not want any more of the pussyfooting or dilly-dallying that has characterized Canadian external affairs in recent years. You will prepare what I want."

I remember reading in one of the British illustrated weeklies an article in 1945 in which someone had written about the dropping of the Iron Curtain on Eastern Europe. This struck me immediately, and I made a note of it. On 5 March 1946 that phrase became Churchill's patent right when he used it in his speech at Westminster College in Fulton, Missouri: "An Iron Curtain has descended across the continent." The London *Times* pointed out that the expression "Iron Curtain" was originally coined by Lutz Shwerin von Krosigk, Hitler's Minister of Finance. Actually, Ethel Snowden had used it first in her 1920 book, *Through Bolshevik Russia*. The point of this small digression is simply that I've all my life had a small fascination with the way in which striking phrases or descriptive words fathered by one person find their way into another's credit column. This is to take nothing away from Churchill, who through the employment of the Iron Curtain phrase aroused Western public opinion to an awareness of the dangers of the Communist advance.

The USSR had given undertakings in treaties or agreements, only to break them at the first opportunity in the consolidation of its empire over hundreds of thousands of square miles of territory in Eastern and Central Europe and more than ninety millions of people. Only the signing of the North Atlantic Treaty in 1949 and the creation of an effective North Atlantic Treaty Organization following the outbreak of the Korean War in 1950 brought a halt, however temporary, to the Soviet advance. I emphasize the word "temporary". Today the USSR has achieved goals beyond even the dreams of Catherine the Great. The USSR has the largest navy on earth. Her fleet is in the Mediterranean. Her fleet is in the Indian Ocean. The Black Sea is but a puddle in her backyard. It is not the Soviet economy that is put in peril when the Arab oil lords are stirred up. The Soviet Union moves forward because the West is in retreat. This is no longer a Cold War, it is an obvious war.

Yet people persist in believing that the USSR is going to exchange its aggression for love and affection. When the Helsinki Conference on Security and Cooperation in Europe was first mooted, I was alone in parliamentary circles in opposing any agreement which would result in the USSR's acquiring Western approval of boundaries established by force and subjugation. I shake my head in wonder when I think of the part played by Canada in the Helsinki Treaty of 1975. There this country signed an agreement destroying forever the hopes of all those who, since the Second World War, have worked and prayed that freedom might one day be returned to the enslaved colonial peoples of the Soviet Union. Canada does not have to go to war with Russia to speak out on behalf of the self-determination of the people of the Ukraine, Estonia, Latvia, Lithuania, or Byelorussia. Talk of raising rebellion in the Ukraine or the Baltic States, or of the Western world's going to war in order to force Russia to end its enslavement of these captive peoples, is at best thoughtless—a perilous notion in this era of hydrogen bombs. "There is, however, a limit at which forbearance ceases to be a virtue," to quote Edmund Burke. He also said: "All that is necessary for the triumph of evil is that good men do nothing."

"Me too"-ism may achieve some form of international amity, but it will never constitute a declaration of national greatness. I have never understood the reluctance of Canadian External Affairs officials, or indeed of some Canadian politicians, to criticize the Soviet Union. Why are these people loath even to speak out against the diabolical cruelties perpetrated by the USSR against captive peoples who have committed no offence, even under Soviet law? There are more than a million people in slave camps today in the Soviet Union. What has been done in the last two years about the tyrannical treatment of Valentyn Moroz? His alleged offence is that he dares to believe in his right of freedom of speech and to ask the right of self-determination for his people. Moroz is but one of hundreds of thousands who today are in prisons or mental institutions, many of them in solitary confinement. Aleksandr Solzhenitsyn, in his *The Gulag Archipelago*, reveals, in all the starkness of personal knowledge, a record of cruelty beyond anything that anyone could have believed possible. How can we maintain a silent voice against wrong-doings so terrible as to deny description in ordinary words? Why has there been no national protest?

The Ukrainian Canadian Committee and the World

Committee on Ukrainian Freedom have asked for action. They have been met by evasiveness and pretence. Canada could take a stand, but it refuses to do so. The apologists for the government claim that Canada has no right to speak out on matters of an internal nature in the Soviet Union. It is not an internal matter when the actions of a government deny every principle of the United Nations Charter and Universal Declaration of Human Rights. Liberal Party supporters have claimed that the Pearson and Trudeau governments have spoken quietly to the representatives of the USSR. They must have spoken so quietly that nobody heard them!

When I spoke at the United Nations on 26 September 1960, my message was not misunderstood. Khrushchev had bitterly attacked Western colonialism. My reply was: "Physician, heal thyself;" I said:

I now turn to a subject dealt with at great length by the Chairman of the Council of Ministers of the USSR, the subject of colonialism. He asked for and advocated a declaration at this session for, "the complete and final elimination of colonial régimes". I think it would be generally agreed that, whatever the experience of the past, there can no longer be a relationship of master and servant anywhere in the world. He has spoken of colonial bondage, of exploitation and of foreign yokes. Those views, uttered by the master of the major colonial power in the world today followed the admission of fourteen new members to the United Nations—all of them former colonies. It seems that he forgot what had occurred on the opening day.

Since the last war seventeen colonial areas and territories comprising more than forty million people have been brought to complete freedom by France. In the same period fourteen colonies and territories, comprising half a billion people, have achieved complete freedom within the Commonwealth. Taken together, some six hundred million peoples in more than thirty countries, most of them now represented in this Assembly, have attained their freedom—this with the approval, the encouragement and the guidance of the United Nations, the Commonwealth and France. There are few here that can speak with the authority of Canada on the subject of colonialism, for Canada was once a colony of both France and the United Kingdom. We were the first country which evolved by constitutional processes from colonial status to independence without severing family connections.

The Commonwealth now embraces ten nations, including the United Kingdom, all of them free and voluntary members from all the continents, comprising one-fifth of the world's population and representing virtually every race, colour, and creed. We are united not by the sword, but by the spirit of cooperation and by common aspirations; and the process is a continuing one. Within the next week another country, Nigeria, the most populous in Africa, will attain its independence and remain in the Commonwealth family.

Indeed, in this Assembly the membership is composed in a very considerable measure of the graduates of empires, mandates and trusteeships of the United Kingdom, the Commonwealth and other nations. I pause to ask this question: How many human beings have been liberated by the USSR? Do we forget how one of the postwar colonies of the USSR sought to liberate itself four years ago, and with what results? I say that because these facts of history in the Commonwealth and other countries invite comparison with the domination over peoples and territories, sometimes gained under the guise of liberation, and always accompanied by the loss of political freedom. How are we to reconcile the tragedy of the Hungarian uprising of 1956 with Chairman Khrushchev's confident assertion of a few days ago in this Assembly? Mr. Khrushchev said: "It has been and always will be our stand that the peoples of Africa, like those of other continents striving for their liberation from the colonial yoke, should establish orders in their countries of their own will and choice." That I accept—and I hope that those words mean a change of attitude for the future on the part of those he represents.

What of Lithuania, Estonia, Latvia? What of the freedom-loving Ukrainians and many other East European peoples? Mr. Khrushchev went further and said: "Complete and final elimination of colonial régimes in all its forms and manifestations has been prompted by the entire course of world history in the last decades. . . . "

There can be no double standard in international affairs. I ask the Chairman of the Council of Ministers of the USSR to give to those nations under his domination the right to free elections—to give them the opportunity to determine the kind of government they want under genuinely free conditions. If those conclusions were what his words meant, for they must apply universally, then indeed will there be new action to carry out the obligations of the United Nations Charter; then indeed will there be new hope for all mankind.

When I saw President Eisenhower in his suite at the Waldorf Astoria the next afternoon, he and his Secretary of State, Mr. Herter, were warm in their appreciation of my remarks. Prime Minister Harold Macmillan's comments were glowing. The Soviets, on the other hand, were enraged. I was attacked on Radio Moscow and in *Izvestia* and *Pravda*. Gomulka of Poland rose in the Assembly on 27 September to denounce my remarks and to make the preposterous argument that Canada had a vested interest in the perpetuation of colonialism. The climax, however, did not come until some days later in the Assembly debate when Senator Sumulong of the Philippines, in recapitulating my arguments, said that the declaration proposed by the USSR should cover the inalienable right to independence of all peoples, including those of Eastern Europe and elsewhere, who had been deprived of the free exercise of their civil and political rights. It was here that Khrushchev totally destroyed his credibility by waving his clenched fist and taking off his shoe and slamming it on his desk. Earlier in the Assembly debates, Macmillan, with that pawkish humour that so enriched his character, asked for a translation of a similar outburst. I too experienced Khrushchev's odd behaviour. When he passed me in the corridor following my speech, he stepped sideways and nearly knocked me down with his shoulder. I am reminded of the story about the Russian peasant who paraded up and down before the walls of the Kremlin shouting "Khrushchev is a fool. Khrushchev is a fool." He was arrested and brought to trial. His sentence: six months for disorderly conduct and an additional nineteen and one-half years for revealing a state secret.

In response to those who claim speeches such as mine can do no good, Archbishop Major Joseph Cardinal Slipyj of the Ukraine, who was himself in prison for eighteen years under the Soviets, much of it in solitary confinement, stands as evidence to the contrary. I met with the Cardinal at the invitation of Monsignor Kushnir at St. Vladimir and Olga Cathedral in Winnipeg on 27 April 1973. Dr. S. J. Kalba, who was then Director of the Ukrainian Canadian Committee, has provided me with the following account of this meeting, the details of which he confirmed with Metropolitan Hermaniuk and Monsignor Kushnir who were also present:

After having extended his affectionate greetings to you, Cardinal Slipyj said he was waiting for this happy moment to personally thank you for the courageous stand you have taken as the Prime Minister of Canada at the United Nations in 1960 in defending the right for independence of Ukrainians and other peoples enslaved by Soviet Russia. The news of your historic speech was received in the Soviet prison camps shortly after it had been delivered at the United Nations in New York.

Your speech, Cardinal Slipyj said, was the greatest moral support ever received by political prisoners in Soviet Russia, and at the same time it had a very great influence on Soviet authorities who attach a great importance to the opinion of other countries and their leaders. As you know, Cardinal Slipyj was imprisoned as the head of the Ukrainian Catholic Church by the Soviets for 18 years and was permitted to leave Soviet Russia in 1963 on personal intervention of Pope John XXIII. Cardinal Slipyj believes that your historic speech addressed to the United Nations was helpful in achieving his release from Soviet Russia.

On 19 November 1967 in New York, Ukrainians gathered from all over the world to present me with the Shevchenko Freedom Award. It is among my proudest possessions, as is their Princess Olga medal. It was the Ukrainian Canadian Committee who presented me with the bust of myself which now sits in the foyer of the Saskatchewan Legislature. I had twice tried to get into the Legislature in the flesh (in the elections of 1929 and 1938) and ended up doing so in bronze.

It is significant that India's Krishna Menon described my 1960 United Nations speech as a continuation of the Cold War. There was more in this than Menon's rather special talent for being obnoxious. Third-world countries have yet to show an interest in the enslavement of any people that does not belong to their grouping. The colonization of a European people seems beyond the grasp of most Asians and Africans. Formal approaches, made with my approval in the fall of 1962, indicated that Canada would never be able to secure the support necessary for a UN resolution against Soviet imperialism.

As to Krishna Menon himself, he had the externals of a Mephistopheles. He could be counted on to be nasty; he barely had to try to succeed. Laden with communism, he hated Britain, disliked, suspected, and feared the United States, and had no use for the Commonwealth. Olive and I once arranged a dinner for him in New York, an experience not to be repeated. Brilliant, a great orator, but a spoilt, bad boy!

To the Canada–Israel Friendship Dinner in Toronto on 24 January 1961, I explained the basis of our external policy:

Canadians must stand firm on the structure of alliances that give us strength to preserve our values at the same time as we proffer to the new nations a helping hand that asks no commitment in return. The helping hand is often spurned, often misunderstood, because it is of the West, now under attack for its so-called "colonial" past. It will require patience, tact and wise exposition to acquaint new states and their leaders with the connection between their future security and ours. We need never apologize for our insistence upon strength for not only our independence but that of our new friends of Asia and Africa would be lost without it.

Canadian defence and foreign policy are based on the realization that an equilibrium of power is essential to the preservation of peace. Commitments under NATO have become the measure of our stake in the defence of the whole Atlantic community and are part of the effort to achieve a balance in the world. Canada stations in Western Europe an army brigade and an air division. The Royal Canadian Air Force has also an important role in the air defence of North America in cooperation with the United States. Over a part of the sea lanes a watch has been assigned to the Royal Canadian Navy.

There are those who clamour for Canada to renounce its defence agreements with the United States, to withdraw from NORAD, wholly or effectually, even to withdraw from NATO. We should not be wise to act on such advice. We are a part of the Atlantic community. Our past and future make us that. When the Atlantic community is threatened, so is Canada. Proof of this overriding truth was two World Wars in which so many Canadians gave their all.

Neutrality may be expedient for some countries. It is not for us. Canada's geographical position denies it. Furthermore, those who would have Canada separate itself from its closest friends forget that the capacity of nations to exert a beneficial influence in the world is in direct relation to the esteem in which they are held by other nations, and especially by their traditional friends. Canada's interests are promoted by staying in the circle to which it belongs; by contributing to the strength and wisdom of that circle. Membership of the Western alliance does not limit our freedom of action.

It is not in individual power but in combined strength and resolution that the rights of free men are safeguarded. To escape the devastating consequences of World War Three, that war must be prevented. We must bring potential enemies to an equal realization of that truth. The NATO alliance has stood the test of eleven dangerous years. The peace has been preserved. The 1960s may require us to redefine the defence and political objectives which must be attained if NATO's purposes are to be fulfilled.

... Twentieth century man, with all the accomplishments of civilization to inherit and to protect, lives under the shadow of nuclear war. Just as there is no alternative to maintaining the strength of our defences, so there must be no shrinking from the search for disarmament. Mankind craves the freedom to disarm, to reduce the onerous burdens of armament now resting so heavily on the conscience and on the economies of nations everywhere.

On the question of disarmament, I devoted a part of my 1960 UN speech to a proposal for breaking the impasse in the ten-nation disarmament talks. The Soviet Union had frequently expressed the view that Canada was using its northland in co-operation with the United States to prepare for an American attack on Russia. Although there was not one grain of truth in this, I accepted their fears at face value, and was prepared to provide the means to alleviate those fears. Canada advanced proposals that were neither pretentious nor quixotic. I said to Mr. Khrushchev: "If you will open your areas, we will open ours." I had in the past frequently urged the end to nuclear weapons, the systematic control of missile delivery systems, the designation and inspection of missile-launching sites, the abolition of biological and chemical weapons, the outlawing of outer space for military purposes, the end to the production of fissionable materials for weapons, the conversion of existing weapons stocks for peaceful purposes, and an end to nuclear testing. I had long felt that by opening our Arctic spaces to Soviet inspection, Canada might be able to advance the cause of humanity where others had failed. For a period of seven months beginning in December 1957, I had taken part, as had the heads of government of other NATO countries, in an exchange of letters with the leaders of the Soviet Union. The final exchange in May 1958 dealt largely with disarmament topics, notably suspension of nuclear tests and prevention of surprise attacks, and revealed Premier Khrushchev's refusal (or inability) to understand the intentions of the Canadian government in supporting the proposals originally made in the Security Council for a system of control in the Arctic regions for purposes of prevention of surprise attack. His response, however, had not been entirely negative, and I welcomed the opportunity to attempt once again in public to clear away his misapprehensions about Canadian policy. Again I offered to open all or part of Canadian territory to aerial and ground inspection under a plan which would include comparable areas of the Soviet Union.

Although the Canadian Cabinet had approved this plan as early as 11 July 1957, it now seemed more relevant than ever. The Soviets had shot down two United States intelligence-gathering aircraft, one in Soviet air space, the other over international waters. When the United States gave its final answer to the Soviet charge in May 1960 in consequence of the U-2 incident, it emphasized that the reason for these flights was that the United States feared a nuclear surprise attack. President Eisenhower announced his intention to put forward a plan for "open skies" aerial surveillance under United Nations auspices as a means of removing that fear. When the Security Council met on 23 May 1960 to consider the Soviet item relating to the U-2 affairs, the United States countered that the USSR maintained a vast espionage network to perform the same work, and suggested that implementation of the open-skies plan would obviate the necessity of such measures of self-defence. In September 1960, I repeated our offer; this was the sixth time. It was spurned by the Kremlin.

I had proposed a World Food Bank at the NATO Heads of Government Meeting in December of 1957. In doing so, I remembered the words of my father when I was a boy. He had been concerned that there was no machinery to ensure the use of surplus foods to meet the demands of people suffering starvation, for he believed that each of us was his brother's keeper. He often had recalled to me the Old Testament story of Joseph, who made provision during the days of surplus for the years of drought. More than once in the 1930s, when wheat was piled in unsaleable hundreds of millions of bushels, I suggested the establishment under the League of Nations of a World Food Bank to meet such a contingency. I had advocated this as a private Member before I became Leader of the Conservative Party. The proposal I brought before the NATO meeting in 1957 was twofold. I proposed the establishment of a Food Bank to store surpluses against the probability of crop shortages or failures in the future. The Bank would be a storehouse for the assistance of those countries which found themselves short of necessary food. I also proposed at the time the creation of strategic food reserves in NATO countries. This proposal for a strategic

Food Bank would solve the problems of supply in Europe in the event of a Soviet attack. Another aspect of a World Food Bank was that food assistance was frequently as important, and sometimes more important in furthering the economic development of under-developed nations, as capital or technical assistance. In building up the sub-structure of an industrial economy in third-world countries (i.e., the building of dams, roads, bridges, power communications, and transportation), a substantial portion of the capital outlay was for labour-intensive projects. Thus wages were the biggest factor in building roads in India, wages that went directly into the purchase of food. If India were food deficient, this meant either a substantial increase in food imports or uncontrolled inflation in domestic food prices. In these circumstances, it was not difficult to reconcile the objectives of my proposals for a World Food Bank with the protection of commercial interests.

This idea was one of the many I put forward which encountered negative responses from the officials in the Department of External Affairs. In December 1957, they advised me not to touch this issue. Their general attitude was that the only course worth following internationally had already been established. Most of the personalities in External Affairs fit Churchill's description: "There but for the grace of God goes God." There were exceptions, of course; and Basil Robinson, now Under-Secretary of State for External Affairs, then the Department's liaison officer in the PMO, was one whose contribution to international relations was always eminently wise and forward-looking. He was not frozen into the pattern followed by External Affairs under St. Laurent and Pearson. I brought up the question of a World Food Bank at the NATO meeting; I didn't go into details. I put this forward as an idea. It wasn't received in a way that would indicate any commanding support; only Norway was enthusiastic about it.

The major country in the North Atlantic Treaty Organization in 1957 did not want it. President Eisenhower was not seriously opposed to it, but his Secretary of State, John Foster Dulles, was. By 1960, Dulles was gone; Christian Herter, who succeeded him, and the President were now prepared to publicly support the idea. However, when I met Eisenhower on 27 September 1960 and queried his progress in planning his Food for Peace program, he admitted that he had not got very far. He had, however, at least progressed to the point where he was advocating the need for such a plan "among the surplus producing countries under the aegis of the United Nations". There was no question but that I would support the President's Food for Peace proposals. Among other things, Canada had since 1945 provided wheat and flour under gifts and loans to Colombo Plan countries and international agencies to an aggregate amount of $111 million.

By 1960, most of Canada's economic aid to less-developed countries of the world was provided through bilateral assistance programs, the largest of which was the Colombo Plan. Under the Canada–West Indies Aid Program, Canada undertook to provide assistance to the value of $10 million over a five-year period beginning in the fiscal year 1958-59. This included the construction of two inter-island passenger–cargo vessels for the proposed West Indies Federation, the *Federal Palm* and the *Federal Maple* (one of which has since mysteriously disappeared). In my address to the General Assembly in September 1960, I announced Canada's intention, subject to parliamentary approval, to support the newly established special Commonwealth African Aid Program by a contribution of $10.5 million over a three-year period. This program was to include technical assistance and aid to education, as well as capital assistance. In addition, we provided for technical assistance to .Commonwealth countries not eligible for assistance under the Colombo Plan, the Canada–West Indies Aid Program or the special Commonwealth African Aid Program. A sum of $120,000 was specially included in the 1961-62 estimates so that we might offer some technical assistance to British Guiana, Hong Kong, and British Honduras. At the opening of the Commonwealth Economic Conference in 1958, I announced that we had approved the launching of a Commonwealth education program. Appropriately, given his background in education, the Honourable Sidney Smith, Canada's Secretary of State for External Affairs, set out our Commonwealth Scholarship and Fellowship Plan in detail. It began in 1960-61, and by 1961-62 required a million dollars a year for its continuation. It was, of course, a multilateral exchange rather than a bilateral aid program.

We further participated in various multilateral economic aid programs to which Canada had contributed some $31.58 million by the 1961-62 fiscal year. These included the United Nations Expanded Program of Technical Assistance, the United Nations Special Fund, the United Nations Children's Emergency Fund, and the operational program of the International Atomic Energy Agency. We also made special contributions to the Malaria Eradication Program of the World Health Organization, the United Nations Technical Assistance Centre in British Columbia, and the Freedom from Hunger campaign of the Food and Agriculture Organization. In addition to membership in the International Bank for Reconstruction and Development, the International Monetary Fund, and the International Finance Corporation, to which Canada subscribed capital in earlier years, Canada in 1960 joined the newly established International Development Association. The share of the Canadian subscription to the capital of IDA to be paid in 1961-62 amounted to $7.19 million. Furthermore, Canada contributed on a voluntary basis to a number of United Nations aid programs designed to deal with such problems as the care and settlement of refugees. Canada also made contributions which dealt with such emergencies as famine and floods. The estimates for 1961-62 included $900,000 for contributions of this nature.

Yet my government was subject to some domestic and international criticism because Canada was not doing enough! Donald Fleming, the Minister of Finance, sent me the following memorandum on "Canadian aid as a percentage of GNP" on 21 April 1961:

There is no agreed definition of aid. If export credits and private capital are included, a very different picture emerges from that given by comparison of long-term loans and gifts by governments.

Two percentages are set out below—one based on our normal grant aid programmes only, and the other based on these combined with the export financing programme. (Military aid is excluded from these figures.)

Grant Aid Programmes

During the current year we are providing grant aid in the amount of $62.13 million.

In addition, we will be required to make a payment to the International Development Association of $7.19 million. Although this payment will show in the Public Accounts among Loans and Advances, the purposes of the Association and its methods of operation make the probability of repayment in dollars unlikely and I believe that we might consider this payment as part of our foreign aid programme. Adding this amount to our grant aid programmes referred to above, total Canadian aid will amount to $69.32 million in 1961-62.

The Canadian GNP for 1960 is estimated at $36 billion so that our aid programmes represent .19% of this figure. It would be necessary to increase our aid to a total of $360 million annually to meet the 1% target.

Long-Term Export Financing

We will also be providing for our long-term export financing. It is estimated that at the outside our *cash* requirements under this programme will only be $25 million this year. If we add this amount to our grant aid programmes we obtain a total figure of $94.32 million representing .26% of our GNP.

The above figures are based on the current year only. It is also possible to assemble figures for our aid over the fifteen years since the war and relate them to our GNP for that period. Our economic (grant) aid has been increasing over the years, since 1950, and the percentage of GNP we would derive would undoubtedly be lower than those set out above. If military aid were to be included the picture would, of course, be quite different; we would show, for the early 1950's, a higher percentage of GNP and the percentage would decline fairly persistently through the decade. And if we went right back to the end of the war, and included our post-war (concessional) loans to the U.K. and other countries, our proportions would appear very sizeable indeed.

I could only agree with Mr. Fleming when he suggested that in view of our 1961-62 budgetary position and other needs any commitment even to consider raising our aid programs to one per cent of our GNP could not be considered. The Canadian economy was just emerging from the recession which my government had inherited from the Liberals, and, in the opinion of the Cabinet, the Canadian people would not look favourably on a government that appeared to be more concerned over economic conditions abroad than those at home. We were already doing more in the field of Commonwealth and foreign aid than any Canadian government in history.

In my concluding remarks to the Assembly in 1960, I summarized my philosophy on Canada's international position:

I have spoken for Canada. We are, as I have said, a middle power, large enough to bear responsibility but not so large as to have traditions of national power or aspirations which arouse fears and suspicions. As a nation of North America, we have our deep roots in two European cultures—the British and the French—and also in the cultures of all the other races of men who have come to us.

By the accident of geography and history we find ourselves squarely between the two greatest powers on earth. We have no fortresses facing either. We want to live at peace with our northern neighbours, as we have lived so long in peace with our southern neighbours.

In a world passing through two great human experiences—the thrust of technology and the thrust of political and social change—new perspectives have been given for a better life. Must we admit that we cannot control these revolutions of science and society? Or shall we rather harness them for the common good, do it now and prevent them from upsetting the all too fragile foundations on which peace rests today? That is our task. We hear voices that speak of victories for propaganda. We are not here in this Assembly to win wars of propaganda. We are here to win victories for peace. If I understand correctly the thinking of the average man and woman today throughout the world, they have had enough of propaganda, of confusion and fears and doubts. They are asking us for the truth. We are not mustered here under the direction and domination of any nation. We are mustered not for any race or creed or ideology. We are here for the hosts of humanity everywhere in the world. Peoples and nations are waiting upon us. Man's hopes call upon us to say what we can do. My hope is that we shall not leave this place without having done something for mankind so that we shall be able to say to the peoples of the world that death's pale flag shall not again be raised in war, that fear shall be lifted from the hearts and souls of men.

Needless to add, those hopes have not been attained.

As I looked ahead into the 1960s, the major problems seemed to be: one, how to work out effective international agreements to reduce the dangers resulting from the development of methods of mass destruction; two, how to minimize the dangers to the free world created by the rise of China to the rank of a first-class power; three, how to maintain an effective balance of military power with the Russo-Chinese bloc; four, how to reduce the dangers created by the division of Europe into a Soviet zone and a Western zone, particularly the division of Germany and Berlin; five, how to organize effective help to India to speed up its economic development; six, how to prevent independent Africa south of the Sahara from relapsing into chaos and how to facilitate the orderly progress of the remaining dependent territories in Africa (including Angola and Mozambique) to independence; seven, how to deal with the population explosion; and eight, how to work out equitable international arrangements under which the Western industrialized countries would each accept its fair share of a rapidly increasing flow of low-priced manufactured goods from the underdeveloped countries. I considered that if the United Nations was to be preserved as a useful international instrument as distinct from a forum for sterile propaganda, firm and wise leadership would have to be exerted by the leading states in the various power groupings, and a serious effort would have to be made to reach accommodation among them. Above all, the notion that the majority of members could impose their will on the minority would have to be dismissed. The United Nations was not and is not the Parliament of Man, and it could serve the needs of its members only if they were prepared to seek solutions through negotiation and agreement. The experience of the Fifteenth Session of the United Nations General Assembly suggested that this was a lesson that all power groups at the UN had yet to learn; certainly the Afro-Asian group was showing a discouraging disposition to use their voting strength irresponsibly. If the

United Nations was to play a useful role in the future, each of its members, East, West, and Neutral, would have to do its share of accommodating. The ultimate test of the usefulness and effectiveness of the United Nations would continue to be the extent to which it was able to serve the cause of reconciling the interests of its member governments.

CHAPTER SIX

※

IN MY FIRST PUBLIC ADDRESS in the United States after I
became Prime Minister, at Dartmouth College in Han-
over, New Hampshire, on 7 September 1957, I took the
opportunity to establish the position of my government
on Canada–United States relations. I spoke for the heart
of Canada. I spoke in the interests of the strongest and
closest relations between Canada and the United States
when I suggested a need to view each other's problems
with "common sense, frankness, absolute confidence, and
mutual trust". I noted that the United States Secretary of
State, the Honourable John Foster Dulles, had recently
stated before a congressional hearing that the purpose of
the State Department was "to look out for the interests of
the United States". I said, "The responsibility of the Canadian government, in like measure, is to consider Canadian interests first." I then emphasized what I was to reit-
erate over and over again as Prime Minister, that this
"should not be misinterpreted as being anti-American."

I proceeded to indicate the major areas of Canadian
concern in our relations. In particular, I told them that
the concentration of Canadian trade with the United
States "makes the Canadian economy altogether too vulnerable to sudden changes in trading policy at Washington. Canadians do not wish to have their economic, any

more than their political, affairs determined outside Canada." I did not speak in a spirit of truculence or of petition, but attempted to place our problems in perspective. I explained that I fully recognized it was only natural that Canada–United States trade problems should not make the same claim on the attention and consideration of the United States as they did on Canada. I dealt with the United States' agricultural disposal program as it related to wheat and wheat flour. The surplus-disposal legislation of the United States had made it difficult, if not impossible, for Canada to maintain its fair share of the world market. I explained that "Canada cannot compete for agricultural markets against the dominant economic power of the United States, with its export subsidies, barter deals and sales for foreign currency." I indicated a sense of disquiet in Canada over the political implications of large-scale and continuing external ownership and control of Canadian industries. I stated that the question was frequently asked whether a country could have a meaningful independent existence in a situation where non-residents owned an important part of that country's basic resources and industry and were, therefore, in a position to make important decisions affecting the operation and development of the country's economy. I said, "Canadians ask that American companies investing in Canada should not regard Canada as an extension of the American market; that they should be incorporated as Canadian companies making available equity stock to Canadians. That there is cause for questioning seems clear when I tell you that it is estimated that of American-controlled firms operating in Canada not more than one in four offers stock to Canadians." The message I tried to convey to my audience was epitomized by President Eisenhower when he spoke to the Canadian House of Commons on 13 November 1953:

More than friendship and partnership is signified in the relations between our countries. These relations that today enrich our peoples justify the faith of our fathers that men, given self-government, can dwell at peace among themselves, progressive in the development of their material wealth, quick to join in the defence of their spiritual community, ready to arbitrate differences that may rise to divide them.

I should add that contrary to the foreboding and dire expectations of some officials in the Department of External Affairs, my speech did not annoy the United States. Canada is not a country that can be taken for granted or a country that follows whatever the United States does, regardless of whether it is beneficial to Canada or not. And I might add, for the benefit of those who claim that Canada–United States problems should never have a public airing, that there was, very quickly, a marked improvement in United States agricultural dumping practices. I subsequently discussed this question at length with President Eisenhower. The outcome, at the 1958 meeting of the United States–Canadian Joint Committee, was that the United States gave assurances that in all surplus-disposal activities they would endeavour to avoid, so far as possible, interfering with normal commercial marketings. It was affirmed that their barter contracts would have to result in a net increase in exports of the agricultural commodity involved. This proved not only to our advantage but to theirs as well.

The American Presidents during the course of my prime-ministership were Dwight D. Eisenhower and John F. Kennedy. Successful in two presidential elections against Governor Adlai Stevenson, Eisenhower had been President for over four years when I formed my government in June of 1957. Unlike his successor, he did not regard the United States presidency as a glittering jewel; he saw it as a job to be done. I found Eisenhower a warm and engaging person, and we became the best of friends. He had an appreciation of Canada and Canadians. No doubt his feelings about Canada were based in part on his relations with Canadian officers and troops during the Second World War. Unlike his Secretary of State, John Foster Dulles, Eisenhower was a man that one could talk to. He had a temper, and we disagreed from time to time, but he was prepared to listen to my point of view, except in one matter.

I recall the occasion of his visit to Ottawa at my invitation in July 1958. The President, Mr. Dulles, Sidney Smith, and I were sitting in my office in the East Block. We were chatting about matters in general and not really agreeing on anything, as Dulles was in a rather obstructive mood. Without warning, Sidney Smith suggested that public opinion in Canada was getting more and more interested in some form of normalization in our relations with Communist China, particularly in the field of trade. He went on to suggest that perhaps the time had come to accord the Peking régime formal recognition and to admit China to her seat in the United Nations. This put President Eisenhower into a temper and he replied that public opinion in the United States was so dead set against this, he could not see the day when recognition would become possible. He stated categorically that he did not think "the United Nations could hold together" if Communist China were admitted. This would lead the Senate and the House of Representatives to call for an immediate United States withdrawal from the United Nations and the departure of the UN from American soil. Later on in our discussion the President admitted that China was somewhat of "an obsession". He said he would have more difficulty in supporting Canada in this matter than in any other.

Among the reasons he advanced in defence of United States policy concerning Communist China were its aggression in Korea, detention of United States prisoners, and aggression in Vietnam. Drawing on his own experience in the Far East, the President also referred to the importance of retaining the loyalty of the overseas (as opposed to mainland) Chinese; if they had no alternative but to look to Communist China as their "homeland", he considered that they would all become Communists. Throughout our discussions, he emphasized that he considered the admission of Communist China to the United Nations a much more serious problem than recognition.

Mr. Dulles added that the recognition of Communist China would be a very serious setback for the Free World. In his view, the United States was carrying ninety per cent of the responsibility of the defence of the Free World in the Pacific. If recognition were extended, most if not all pro-Western countries in the Far East would come within the Communist orbit and American forces would then be obliged to withdraw to Hawaii. Under such conditions, the defence of the Pacific would become next to impossible. The United States therefore needed the co-operation of its friends. He thought that recognition should only be extended when it was in the national interest to do so. At the present time, the national interest was to make sure that Communism was to remain as far as possible from American and, for that matter, from Canadian shores. Dulles went on to refer to his conversation with General de Gaulle on this subject, and added that for their own reasons the French had decided, after an extensive review of the matter, not to extend recognition.

When I observed there was a strong feeling that the present situation could not go on much longer, and that for Canada it was complicated by the need to sell Canadian agricultural surpluses, President Eisenhower said that, while he personally felt there were too many barriers in the way of world trade and that restrictions against trade with the Communists might indeed have spurred those nations to even greater economic progress than would otherwise have been the case, he nevertheless considered that recognition of Communist China would not open up important avenues for trade. He did not think they could buy much, and on the whole believed that the hopes of those who expected to expand trade with Communist China were not well founded. Mr. Dulles added that the United States was not asking its friends not to trade with Communist China. Their policy was designed to prevent Communist infiltration through trade in weaker economies, such as the Philippines. They knew that such penetration would not take place were trade with China expanded in countries such as the United States or Canada.

In answer, I raised strong objection that Canadian subsidiaries of American companies were prevented from accepting sales orders from the Red Chinese. At issue was the action of the Ford Motor Company in Detroit in applying American laws imposing an embargo on United States trade with Red China to its Canadian subsidiary. A firm order had not been turned down but the approach of the Communist Chinese government, through a Vancouver auto dealer, for the purchase of Canadian Ford cars had been discouraged. President Eisenhower agreed that there would be no interference thereafter with Canadian subsidiaries in making contracts with other countries on non-strategic goods. To members of my Cabinet, Mr. Dulles suggested an announcement that would render unlikely a repetition of this incident. "The Canadian and United States governments have given consideration to situations where the export policies and laws of the two countries may not be in complete harmony. It has been agreed that in these cases there will be full consultation between the two governments with a view to finding through licensing procedures satisfactory solutions to concrete problems as they arise." Mr. Dulles stated that the United States would be prepared to grant permits to United States parent companies which would enable subsidiaries in Canada to engage in a transaction when doing so would have an appreciable effect on the Canadian company and the Canadian economy. However, while he did not think United States laws should operate to the disadvantage of a Canadian company, nevertheless, he did not want to open the door wide in regard to subsidiaries of United States parent companies around the world, nor, he thought, would Canada wish this to be done.

In answer to a question from Mr. Smith about the possibility of attempting to lure Peking away from Moscow through more flexible policies, Mr. Dulles replied that this question was related to the very nature of Communism, and that the United States could not yet come to the conclusion that there was such a thing as "national Communism". So long as the Soviet Union and Communist China were in the hands of strong Communist parties, it was impossible to think that anything could be done in attempting to separate Moscow from Peking.

I was generally pleased with the Eisenhower–Dulles visit. Unlike the visit of Prime Minister St. Laurent and Mr. Pearson to White Sulphur Springs in March of 1956, we had an agenda, and Canada was not treated as a forty-ninth state composed of Mounted Police, Eskimos, and summer vacationers. There were significant discussions of commodity arrangements, the World Food Bank, immigration and travel restrictions, United States trade policy, American tariffs on Canadian base metals, the export of Canadian petroleum, cattle, and feed grains to the United States, and the Columbia River project.

On the Columbia River issue, President Eisenhower suggested that the time had come for the two of us to put some pressure on the different agencies then considering the problem so as to make sure that something was being done. He indicated that he was under the impression that the experts, and particularly General A. G. L. McNaughton, were busy finding obstacles rather than solutions. And while he had no solution himself to offer, he thought that the two Foreign Secretaries should consult so that some progress could be made. The United States, he said, was prepared to make as many concessions as Canada to get things under way. Without going into great detail, since the subject comes up again in a later chapter, studies to "determine whether a greater use than is now being made of the waters of the Columbia River system would be feasible and advantageous" had begun in the early 1940s. Where our predecessors had engaged in talk, my government was prepared to act; and our intention was stated by Her Majesty in the Speech from the Throne on 14 October 1957. We put forth a tremendous effort to obtain an agreement that would be fair to Canada and at the same time would develop the great power potential of the Columbia. We had to negotiate not only with the United States, but with Premier W. A. C. Bennett's government in British Columbia, and with General A. G. L. McNaughton, Canadian Chairman of the International Joint Commission, who sometimes acted so imperiously that one might have assumed that he was the Canadian government. Finally an agreement was reached. We considered that the benefits to Canada far outweighed those to the United States. With Mr. Fulton, I journeyed to Washington to sign the Columbia River Treaty with President Eisenhower on 17 January 1961, three days before the end of his term of office. The fact that British Columbia finally determined to sell its birthright, and in the process delayed any implementation of the treaty until we were out of office, does not diminish in my eyes the accomplishment of the treaty's negotiation or the principle of down-stream benefits which it established.

Another example of Canadian–American co-operation

was the opening of the St. Lawrence Seaway on 26 June 1959 by Her Majesty and President Eisenhower. It was indeed a happy occasion. The opening of the Seaway had been a dream for generations, and for this the St. Laurent government deserves great credit. There was a recognition by all that in bringing it about, the relations between our countries were bound to be greatly strengthened, and to our mutual benefit. For subservience is not an essential in the co-operation of Canada and the United States. I might add that President Eisenhower and I were from our first meeting on an "Ike–John" basis, and that we were as close as the nearest telephone. For example, he wrote me on the eve of his world tour on 1 December 1959:

THE WHITE HOUSE

WASHINGTON

December 1, 1959

PERSONAL

Dear John:

Before leaving on my forthcoming tour to Europe, the Mediterranean and the Near East, I have found it desirable to write the various Presidents of the Latin American Republics to try to afford them some perspective regarding my plans and objectives in these various visits. I know that very little explanation is necessary in your case, but I do desire to drop you one more line of correspondence before leaving.

My visit will take me to Rome, Ankara, Karachi, Kabul, New Delhi, Tehran, Athens, Tunis, Paris, Madrid, and Casablanca. In each country I will of course have an opportunity to visit with the head of government and exchange views, as well as to participate in ceremonial occasions. Accordingly, I have every hope that at least some good may come from this undertaking.

Whenever one undertakes a project of this sort, there is the danger that his motives and objectives will be widely misinterpreted. Most prevalent, of course, is the concern held by many that I will be attempting to negotiate on this trip, to represent the views of other members of the North Atlantic Alliance, and possibly even to further the cause of the interests of the United States in some parts of the world, as against those of our friends. I need not assure you that nothing could be further from the truth. My purpose in making these visits is simply to do what I can to strengthen the ties which bind the nations of the Free World together. You and I have found from experience that there is no substitute for personal contact in furthering understanding and good will.

I think it is desirable also to take all possible steps to allay the fears of those in underdeveloped countries regarding the objectives and ambitions of the West, and the United States in particular. I am especially anxious to convince our friends that the vast military power, including the nuclear deterrent which is maintained by the West, serves, in our view, one purpose only—a defensive purpose to deter aggression.

The tour will be fatiguing, to say the least, and when we couple this with commitments for a Summit meeting and a return visit to Moscow, my schedule would appear full indeed for my remaining time in office. I still count, however, on the opportunity of seeing you in the months ahead.

I leave Thursday evening. That time is almost upon us, but if you would want to suggest anything to me before departure, I would, as always, welcome a phone call from you.

With warm personal regard,

Sincerely,
Ike

The Right Honorable
John G. Diefenbaker, Q.C., M.P.
Prime Minister of Canada
Ottawa

PERSONAL

In June of 1960, I visited Washington on the invitation

14 & 15. The fine art of "main-streeting" received a warm and enthusiastic response from the people of Canada in the 1958 election campaign.

16 & 17. *(Right)* Typical of gatherings throughout the campaign is this one in Dauphin, Manitoba. *(Below)* The news of a stunning victory is mirrored in the happy faces at Conservative headquarters in Saskatoon on election night, 31 March 1958.

18 & 19. *(Above)* The Prime Minister greets Governor General Massey at the opening of Parliament in May 1958. *(Left)* One of the country's keenest fisherman displays a fine trout caught at Kathleen Lake in the Yukon Territory, September 1958.

20. The Cabinet, 1958.

21, 22, & 23. In July 1958 President and Mrs. Dwight D. Eisenhower paid an official visit to Ottawa. *(Above)* With the President came Secretary of State John Foster Dulles. *(Above right)* It was not all formality—a lighter moment on the lawn at Sussex Drive. *(Right)* President Eisenhower addresses the Canadian Parliament.

24. Mr. and Mrs. Diefenbaker on the grounds of the Prime Minister's official residence, Sussex Drive, Ottawa.

of the President. In our talks, the President informed me that he was still against the recognition of Communist China, but that even if he were in favour, he personally could not do this because the attitude of the American people had not changed. Indeed, he still thought that it would wreck the United Nations, at least in so far as the United States was concerned, in the event that Communist China was admitted. When I asked him whether the United States expected any aggressive action by China in Formosa or elsewhere in the East, he replied by saying that he differed with his Secretary of State, Mr. Herter, in regard to expressing views in public on this matter. Mr. Herter had previously singled out Formosa as a possible next trouble spot. The President judged it not desirable to pinpoint places where the Communist bloc might cause trouble. He was in favour of the public stand that they would look for places to probe wherever they thought they could achieve some effect. But he did not believe that the Chinese or other members of the Communist bloc would attempt any real blow in the near future.

Pursuing this point, I inquired whether he expected any challenge to the freedom of access to Berlin. The President said that he did not expect such action by Mr. Khrushchev, not simply because he had said they would not do it, but because he had referred to this forcefully on various occasions and was concerned about his own reputation. Rather, he thought, the Soviets might get the East Germans to annoy Western countries over access to Berlin. At that point, Secretary of State Herter read a press report of the answer Khrushchev had given to a question on this matter that morning saying that if it appeared after another six or eight months that the West was not interested in a Summit Meeting, then Russia would sign a peace treaty with East Germany which would put an end to the right of access to Berlin of those countries which did not sign a treaty with East Germany; and if they tried to get to Berlin without signing such a treaty, then the Soviets would stop them. Mr. Herter emphasized the significance of the fact that the Russians in this statement implied that they, rather than the East Germans, would enforce the ban. President Eisenhower responded by saying that he did not think the Soviets intended deliberately to provoke the West to war in the near future. He thought that if Russia reached the level of two or three thousand missiles, they might then start some target practice, but that this would not happen soon.

Throughout my period as Prime Minister, the centre of the Soviet political offensive against the West was West Berlin. I was reminded of my conversation in February 1959 with West Berlin's Mayor Brandt. The Soviets had begun another in the series of Berlin crises the previous November. In diplomatic notes to the United States, Britain, and France on 27 November 1958, Khrushchev challenged the right of these countries to maintain troops in the city. He claimed the wartime agreements underlying the Berlin situation were no longer applicable. He offered to negotiate the establishment of West Berlin as a free city, and said that if there were no results in six months the Soviet Union would turn over its responsibilities in Berlin to the German Democratic Republic. The Berlin problem had been discussed at length at the NATO ministerial meeting in mid-December. In the communiqué on these discussions, the NATO Council associated itself with a policy of firmness in maintaining allied rights in Berlin and in rejecting the Soviet Union's unilateral repudiation of the Berlin agreements. Herr Brandt had considered that Khrushchev's motives were twofold. One, he wanted to disturb the internal stability and economic growth of West Berlin. Second, West Berlin was a handy pawn in the Soviet's international power game, with Berlin itself or some other East–West issue as the possible prize. Khrushchev raised the ante in 1960 by wrecking the Summit Meeting over the West's refusal to yield on Berlin.

I had had high hopes for this meeting. As I explained to President de Gaulle during his visit to Ottawa, I hoped that the Summit Meeting might make some progress in obtaining at least temporary agreement on Berlin. I believed the maintenance of Berlin as an entity independent of the USSR and East Germany to be absolutely necessary. If this independence could be assured, then to some degree it would be possible to effect a reduction in the number of troops in Berlin without in any way encouraging the desire of the USSR that Berlin become part of East Germany. I added that I hoped that it would be at least possible to agree on a declaration setting out the position of Western countries on German reunification. President de Gaulle said that while he shared my views in general, it would be difficult in eight days to settle any problems effectively. He added: "Ce sera un succès si ce n'est pas un débôc."

When Khrushchev met the new American President, John F. Kennedy, in Vienna on 3-4 June 1961, Berlin was at the centre of their divergent views, as were their personalities. Internationally, small and trivial matters sometimes determine attitudes. For example, Kennedy was bitterly offended by the fact that Khrushchev continually referred to him as "the boy". On 15 June, Khrushchev issued another ultimatum: the Soviet Union planned to conclude a separate peace treaty with East Germany by the end of the year. On 8 July, the Soviets announced that they were increasing defence expenditures by one-third. On 13 August 1961 the East German régime began the building of the Berlin Wall. Kennedy decided to meet force with force and on 25 July called for a build-up of NATO forces. He said, "We cannot and will not permit the Communists to drive us out of Berlin, either gradually or by force." Canada stood firmly beside its NATO allies throughout the many phases of the Berlin crisis. A major problem was to inject an element of flexibility into the broad Cold War front. The Western allies were agreed that nuclear war would not be a satisfactory answer when there were other options, short of surrender, open to us.

On the question of the Organization of American States, President Eisenhower asked me when Canada was going to join. I replied that I had discussed the matter with the President of Mexico and several Latin-American ambassadors some weeks earlier. Generally, they were of the view expressed by Señor Manuel Tello, the Mexican Foreign Minister. When I asked him what would be the advantages to the OAS of Canada's membership, Señor Tello observed that as a member of the American community, Canada could not dissociate itself from its neighbours; in the economic field, the OAS would benefit from Canada's wisdom, experience, and high degree of achievement; politically, Canada would provide a new element of stabilization. I wondered whether Canada's admission to the OAS would not be a source of embarrassment to Mexico, in view of the joint defence arrangements between Canada and the United States. Señor Tello replied that Mexico was represented on the Latin-American Defence Board, and that Canada's representation on that board would not entail additional commitments.

Previously, Canada had thought it inappropriate because of her position as a constitutional monarchy to join an organization of republics, and did not wish to be a member of any organization if it appeared to clash with our position in the Commonwealth. This argument, as I explained to President Eisenhower, was not so strong as in the past. Given the large-scale development going on south of the Rio Grande and the growth in the population and importance of Latin-American countries, my government was prepared to reconsider its attitude on this question. President Eisenhower noted that the United States was a member of various alliances and organizations; he considered the inter-connections important. For example, he had advised Harold Macmillan that Britain should get into Europe as effectively as possible. I indicated that we might send an observer to the OAS meeting the next spring, and that I regarded this as a step forward and not simply procrastination.

To return for a moment to the question of a World Food Bank, this subject had come up briefly during the Eisenhower–Dulles visit to Ottawa in 1958. Mr. Dulles, as I have earlier mentioned, was very strong in his opposition to this; he considered the costs of international storage prohibitive. In consequence, our discussions did not proceed very far. During my talks with President Eisenhower in June 1960, he observed that there were a great many hungry people in the world who could not afford to buy food, whereas we in North America had tremendous surpluses. He wondered what we could do about it. He felt that people around the world were wondering where we stood as a group of civilized Christian countries on this humanitarian question. When we compared the costs of holding stocks of wheat in Canada and the United States with the cost of international storage, we were able to agree that we should pursue the question to see whether there were not some form of joint or parallel action that could be taken by our two countries, and possibly with others, on the most useful disposition of surplus stocks. I earlier mentioned the President's "Food for Peace" proposals, and their lack of progress. On 26 October 1960, a UN resolution sponsored by Canada and the United States, among others, and unanimously adopted, invited the UN's Food and Agriculture Organization to study "the feasibility and acceptability of additional arrangements . . . having as their objective the mobilization of available surplus foodstuffs and their distribution in areas of greatest need, particularly in the economically less developed countries." This was an idea that would come of age; and I believe that with the conference in Rome in November 1974 it finally did so.

On the question of NATO, I suggested to Mr. Eisenhower that something should be done on a high level to reassess the position of the Alliance, looking ahead some ten years. I observed that in general the press in Canada did not agree with me when I contended that the Alliance had been knit more closely as a consequence of the Summit collapse. The President agreed that it was important to re-examine NATO in the light of recent problems. I referred to the 1957 NATO meeting and said I felt there had not been enough preparation for it, and that none of the heads of government present seemed to reflect in their speeches a knowledge of where NATO was going. We had been rather like a newly elected village council. I felt we needed another NATO meeting of heads of government for the purpose of strengthening and projecting the Alliance. At this juncture, Mr. Herter mentioned that the United States had set up a task force of their own officials in Washington to work on a study of the future of NATO. The President said he was prepared to go along with a review, but that the staff work should be thoroughly done before the top people sat solemnly around a table to pontificate on the subject. From the Canadian point of view, I suggested there were five principal areas of concern:

1) *Responsibilities of the Alliances*—An estimate as to how they would develop over the next decade. Whether NATO should attempt to develop a global outlook which directly or indirectly might mean some widening of the responsibilities of all its members. How French demands for tripartite co-ordination with the United States and the United Kingdom on matters of global policy and strategy could be reconciled with the principle of equality of all members of the Alliance.

2) *Political Consultation*—The need for improving the process of consultation with special reference to the obligation of the larger and more powerful members of NATO to make a reality of consultation and to reconcile the responsibility of leadership with those of true partnership.

3) *Military Requirements*—An estimate of NATO's changing military requirements and ensuring that they would be co-ordinated with and yet not submerge the political aims and objectives of the Alliance.

4) *Non-Military Co-operation*—What more could be done to minimize economic or political rivalries which weakened NATO solidarity and its collective defence effort.

5) *Information*—How NATO's purposes could be explained to the uncommitted nations in a way which would reduce suspicion and misunderstanding.

The President and I also discussed the possible exchange of United States F-101B fighters for Canadian CL-44 transports, the President's open-skies proposal, the perennial question of United States wheat-surplus-disposal policies, Canadian participation in seismic research, and operation "Sky Shield", as well as reviewing the progress of the Columbia River Treaty negotiations.

Nineteen-sixty was, of course, a presidential election year in the United States. One of the topics of conversation which arose in my talks with Eisenhower had to do with the proposed debate between the two candidates, Richard Nixon and John Kennedy. As a matter of fact, he and I had some argument about this. I contended that such a debate should never take place. I pointed out that Nixon, because he was Vice-President, had to stand on the record of the administration. There was nothing he could say that Kennedy couldn't better. The only effect of such a debate would be to augment Kennedy's stature. There was no advertising value in it for Nixon. As Vice-

President, he was nationally known. Kennedy was well known only in his own state of Massachusetts. The debate would give Kennedy the publicity he lacked. Eisenhower was known to be a poker player. I had a modest knowledge of the game, and I used it to illustrate my point: "Supposing you were in a poker game where every time you bet, other players bumped you and you were not able to call. How many pots do you think you could win?" He agreed that, to use his expression, he would be "cleaned up". He nevertheless pinned his hopes on Nixon's special knowledge of domestic and international affairs. He felt Nixon was more than a match for any arguments advanced by his opponent. Of course, when the debates took place, Nixon was the all-round loser. He never regained the initiative against Kennedy, who proved to be a much more effective TV speaker. Given the small margin of Nixon's defeat in 1960, there can be little doubt that had the debates not taken place he would have won the election. I might add that when I saw the President on the morning after the first debate, which took place on 26 September, I told him that the rest of the debates should be cancelled. He did not agree. Had the debates been called off, the United States public would have forgotten the whole thing in three or four days. What the general consequences of a Nixon presidency in 1960 would have been for American politics, I cannot say; I do know that the course of Canada–United States relations would have been a happier one.

Prime Minister Harold Macmillan was also on a first-name basis with the President. He had served as the British Minister with Eisenhower's Headquarters in North Africa during the Second World War. I recall an amusing occasion during a state dinner given by the President of France in honour of all the NATO heads of government in 1957. I was sitting next to Macmillan. The President of France rose to propose a toast to the United States, and in the course of that toast he said in effect that France owed everything to the United States; that freedom would not have survived but for the United States in two world wars; that the United States was the saviour of freedom and civilization. President Eisenhower responded saying that Western civilization would not have survived but for France. He called forth the contribution of Lafayette in saving freedom when George Washington was in deep difficulties during the Revolutionary War. Both seemed to forget that Britain and Canada had each made tremendous contributions to freedom, or that Macmillan and I were present. Macmillan, with characteristic wit, turned to me and said: "I think, if you will second it, I should move a toast to the glorious memory of George III; then this performance will be complete."

In January 1961, I travelled to Washington, the first leader of a foreign government to visit Kennedy after he became President. He was youthful in appearance, charming, and proud of the office he had attained. "Just imagine," he said, "here I am, President of the United States." When he remarked that it had taken him a long time to achieve his office, I replied that if he wanted to know what a long time really was, he might think about the time it had taken to bring about a Conservative government in Canada. At one point he asked me: "How am I doing?" I indicated that so far as I could tell everything seemed to be going well with his new administration, but that I could not understand why he would appoint his brother Robert Attorney General; he was not a practising lawyer and would know nothing about it. He laughed and said: "Can you tell me how he could learn law faster?" Learning that I had never walked all the way around the White House, he suggested we do so. We went outside without our coats. When I remarked that it was colder that day in Washington than in Ottawa, he went quickly in through the press door and came out with my raincoat.

His favourite expression in describing those who opposed him, several outstanding Americans, was "sons of bitches". Beyond that, I never heard him use foul language. Nor did he ever comment on the subject of women in my presence. We did talk about fishing, however. He said he was a most enthusiastic fisherman, and mounted on one of the office walls was a large sailfish. He asked: "Have you ever caught anything better?" I told him about the 140-pound blue marlin I had recently caught off the coast of Jamaica. He said he had spent thousands of dollars to catch one. Friends had taken me out, and my catch did not cost me anything. I told him it was being mounted for my office wall. I knew that he would want to see it, although Howard Green thought otherwise. We got it back from the taxidermist just in time for his visit to Ottawa in May.

Many changes had taken place in the decor of the Oval Office and the adjoining office since President Eisenhower's departure. Steel engravings of United States naval engagements adorned the walls. I noted that there were some from the War of 1812. I asked: "Where are the pictures of the British victories?" He rejoined that his reading of history did not indicate there had been any. I told him about the encounter of the *Shannon* with the *Chesapeake*, in which the American ship was defeated and taken to Halifax. He remarked: "If I had that picture I would put it up." I had inquiries made in various countries for a steel engraving of the battle; a short time before the tragedy of his assassination I secured one, too late to send it to him.

My first visit with Kennedy was short, and a pleasant occasion. My program for the day called for me to leave Ottawa at approximately nine in the morning, arrive at Washington airport at eleven, and proceed straight to the White House for a conversation lasting from eleven-thirty until lunch. After a working lunch with the President, I departed for the airport, left Washington at three o'clock, and arrived back in Ottawa by five. We reviewed defence and security problems, reaffirmed our purpose to work together for peace and freedom in the world, and reviewed bilateral questions of interest to our two countries, with emphasis upon the various consultative arrangements of a formal and informal character which have been developed between us over the years. It is important to note that, in the course of our discussions, we reached agreement on the question of the conditions under which nuclear warheads for Canadian forces in Canada and Europe would be stockpiled. We agreed that detailed arrangements on all aspects of this matter should be worked out and embodied in agreements ready for immediate execution *when conditions made it necessary.* So far as I was able to judge, based on my conversation with the President, on his special message to Congress on 28 March 1961, and on a statement by the United States Permanent Representative to the North Atlantic Council on 26 April 1961, the new administration's policies on defence were not going to be fundamentally different from those of its predecessor.

In May 1961 President and Mrs. Kennedy visited Ottawa at my invitation: his first visit to a foreign land as President. In our discussions, the President noted two areas of particular concern to the United States: Cuba and Southeast Asia. He was obviously still agitated by the humiliation of the Bay of Pigs fiasco, although he claimed the United States government had learned certain lessons from it. He said his administration had been faced with a difficult decision as to what to do with thirteen hundred highly trained Cuban volunteers in Guatemala and Nicaragua. The point had been reached where it would have been necessary either to break them up or to use them in active operations, and he had decided that they would be better in Cuba than out. He claimed that the part played by the émigré groups around Miami had been exaggerated. The Cubans were compulsive talkers and the volume of press comment from Cuban sources in the Miami area had certainly made it much more difficult to mount the operation, with the result that what had been intended in the first place as a covert operation had become extremely overt. He placed no blame on the Central Intelligence Agency for what had happened. Indeed, in the chats I had with him, he showed none of his predecessor's concern with the growing authority and capacity of the CIA. On the contrary, he seemed quite proud of it. Kennedy said that he had hoped to keep the United States removed from direct involvement in the Bay of Pigs invasion. As it had turned out, however, the United States had become engaged. He had no doubt that had he authorized air cover for the assault force, this would have turned the balance. The Castro government had succeeded with the five MiGs at their disposal in causing heavy losses early in the landing, from which the attacking force was never able to recover. In particular, an ammunition ship was hit, and after only one day in action the attackers ran out of ammunition.

It was apparent from talks which I had with both Democrats and Republicans that it was going to take the President a long time to recover from his Cuban misadventure. I made it clear that I was sceptical of his campaign to persuade Western countries to disengage themselves diplomatically and economically from Cuba. Nor did he exactly reassure me when he explained that the United States did not plan to intervene again militarily unless (a) there was serious provocation, (b) the administration thought that intervention would be the only way to prevent the Castro Communist revolutionary infection from spreading throughout Latin America, or (c) the Soviet Union "cut us seriously in Berlin". He assured me: "We would talk with you before doing anything." It is always important to know the difference between consultation on the one hand, and on the other the presentation of something which is, or which is about to become, a *fait accompli*. When the crisis came in October 1962, it would have required a considerable credulity to consider the notice we received of the impending United States action as either "talk" or consultation.

Over and over again, he pressed me that Canada consider carefully the common need and to take a long look at Latin America. It was the weakest area socially and politically, "more dangerous than any other place we are facing in the world". In his view, Southeast Asia was a long way off, but Latin America was of immediate concern to the United States and Canada. He wanted Canada to help him by using its influence more broadly in the hemisphere. Canada was without the disadvantage of the United States in its dealings with Latin America, and he hoped that Canada would seriously consider joining the Organization of American States. I told him that in my opinion Canada was now further removed from joining the OAS than it had been even a year earlier. Membership might create difficulties for us: if we disagreed with the United States it would be detrimental to good relations between our countries, or, if we agreed, it might be contended by the Latin-American member countries that we were being dictated to by the United States and we would be accused of subservience. I suggested that we might exert a better influence by remaining detached. My arguments did not impress him. Having decided that he wanted Canada (he pronounced it "Canader") as a member of the OAS, he wanted it done right now. I was not about to have Canada bullied into any course of action. This was the first of a number of occasions on which I had to explain to President Kennedy that Canada was not Massachusetts, or even Boston.

I became increasingly aware that President Kennedy

had no knowledge of Canada whatsoever. More important, he was activated by the belief that Canada owed so great a debt to the United States that nothing but continuing subservience could repay it. He could not believe it when I told him that in the First World War, Canada's contribution in men killed in action had been larger than that of the United States, or that on a percentage basis, our casualties in the Second World War had been about equal to those of the United States. He was consumed with the belief that when the United States gave assistance to any country, that country must realize that it must bow to its will. (This was his concept of aid to under-developed countries.) He seemed surprised when I told him that Canada and the United States were the only two nations that had never accepted anything in assistance for which they had not paid. Kennedy saw the United States striding the world like a colossus, whatever leadership it gave to be followed by every free nation. He hated Britain, and did not conceal his attitude, which was not dissimilar to that of his father, Joe Kennedy, United States Ambassador to Britain before his recall by President Roosevelt in the early 1940s for his belief that Britain should capitulate to Hitler's Germany before she was overwhelmed.

As to the question of our falling in line with Kennedy's embargo of Cuba, Canada's official ties with this largest of the Caribbean islands were of fairly long standing. In 1903 Cuba had opened its first Consulate in Canada, at Yarmouth, Nova Scotia. In 1909, we opened a Trade Office in Havana. We had thus carried on normal trade relations with Cuba for over fifty years before the advent of Fidel Castro. Diplomatic relations between Canada and Cuba were established in 1945, and our behaviour towards the Republic was governed by the accepted rules of intercourse between sovereign states. Following the downfall of the Batista régime on 1 January 1959, the Secretary of State for External Affairs, the Honourable Sidney Smith, had recommended, and I had approved, the immediate formal recognition of the provisional government of Fidel Castro. Instructions to this end were sent to our Embassy in Havana on 8 January 1959. I regarded the act of recognizing the new Cuban government as no different from that of our recognizing the new governments in Venezuela and Iraq in 1958, or the new government in Syria in 1961, or those in Argentina and Peru in 1962. The accordance of diplomatic recognition to a new régime was, of course, the responsibility of myself as Prime Minister, in consultation with the Secretary of State for External Affairs. Our attitude towards the Castro régime was governed by the following considerations:

1) It was Canada's duty to maintain with Cuba the cordial relations customary with the recognized government of another country.

2) It was an accepted rule of international conduct that differences in philosophical outlook in political systems do not justify a refusal to maintain normal intercourse with another government. We might disapprove of various régimes but it had long been Canada's practice to carry on normal relations with countries or governments whose philosophies were at variance with our own.

3) It was also an accepted principle that nations were free to choose their own form of government and to determine their own policies. Under this practice, outside interference with a view to changing internal conditions or external policies was unjustified.

4) The United States' interpretation of the Monroe Doctrine was not recognized by international law and was not binding on Canada. In fact, we regarded the Monroe Doctrine and its extension by the OAS Caracas resolution of 1954 as an unacceptable unilateral decision on spheres of influence and types of governments in the

Western Hemisphere.

5) There were no grounds on which Canada's departure from normal diplomatic conduct could be justified, from either a legal or any other point of view.

6) To the extent that discriminatory action vis-à-vis Cuba might have been justified (for example, an embargo on arms and strategic goods in prohibited areas), Canada could hardly be expected to take more drastic action than that taken by the Latin-American members of the OAS.

7) The diplomatic ostracizing of Cuba by the Western powers could serve only to eliminate her options and drive her into the Soviet orbit. By maintaining normal diplomatic relations with Cuba, Canada might have little opportunity to influence the course of Cuban events; by breaking diplomatic relations with Cuba, Canada would have no opportunity to influence these events at all. We had a window on an otherwise darkened courtyard.

8) Finally, and not at all least important, Canadian policy towards Cuba had the overwhelming support of Canadian public opinion and of Canada's press.

It was also a fact that we had no serious grounds of complaint in our bilateral relations with Cuba. The two Canadian banks operating in Cuba were permitted to continue in business after all other foreign banks had been nationalized. When these banks were finally nationalized, the Government of Canada received no complaint from either over the settlement reached with the Castro government. Canadian insurance companies were at the time negotiating with the Castro authorities, and we had no indication that a satisfactory settlement would not be reached. We had no indication that Canadian citizens in Cuba were subject to discrimination; where individual difficulties had arisen, our Embassy was able to straighten things out without too much difficulty. The forty-odd Canadian missionaries who elected to remain in Cuba seemed to be well treated. I noted in the opening paragraph of this chapter that the responsibility of the Canadian government was to consider Canadian interests first. I would have been hard-pressed to find any justification for yielding to the American demands for an embargo against Cuba. It is also important to remember that when Kennedy took his case against Castro before his Latin-American allies at the Punta del Este conference in 1961, the four countries that refused to go along with his economic sanctions proposals (Brazil, Mexico, Chile, and Ecuador) represented between them more than half the population of Latin America. If the majority of Latin Americans were not prepared to act on this question, I could see no good reason for Canada's taking a lead. Castroism was at worst a symptom and the most radical manifestation of the social and economic tensions existing in Latin America. One treats an illness by getting rid of its causes, not by erasing its symptoms. If economic, social, political, and administrative reforms were not effected throughout Latin America, then misery and discontent would continue with whatever explosive results. I was prepared to wait and see whether Kennedy's much vaunted Alliance for Progress program would effect a single fundamental change.

Although the position of my government was continually misinterpreted and misrepresented in the United States, I considered our actions consistent with our obligations as the ally of the United States in NORAD and NATO. In my statement in the House of Commons on 12 December 1960, I made it clear that there was no basis for the fear then being expressed in United States quarters that Canada would allow the American embargo against Cuba to be circumvented by a trans-shipment of American goods through Canada. United States goods could not be re-exported from Canada to Cuba without individual export permits, and these permits were issued only for such goods as were still being exported directly from the United States to Cuba. Further, our trade with Cuba was only in non-strategic items. Our general policy was that of refraining from exporting military or strategic material to any area of tension in the world. These regulations already applied to the entire Caribbean area. We would not have exported them to the Batista government, let alone the Castro government. As I said in the House of Commons on 12 December 1960: "We respect the views of other nations in their relations with Cuba, just as we expect that they respect our views in our relations." Or, as I said in my press release on 23 December 1960: "In answer to those well-intentioned people who feel that Canada should follow the course taken by the United States, I would emphasize that no other country, including each and all of the NATO allies of the United States, such as the United Kingdom, France, West Germany, Belgium, Norway, and other member nations, has taken any action to impose a similar trade embargo to that of the United States."

When Kennedy's Secretary of State, Dean Rusk, remarked on 1 February 1962 that the Cuban earnings in exports would be used "to promote Communist subversion in neighbouring countries", he could hardly have had Canada in mind. For the first nine months in 1961 our exports to Cuba amounted to $21.5 million, whereas our imports amounted to only $4.6 million. When I visited Kennedy in Washington in February 1961, I had pointed out to him that United States exports to Cuba were greater for the period since the imposition of the American embargo than were Canada's. He disagreed. He sent for the figures, only to discover that what I said was true. When he visited Ottawa in May, he noted that the United States' trade with Cuba for the first quarter of 1961 had been reduced to $9 million; this was still greater than

Canada's trade. In order to make total the United States' embargo, he said that he would have to invoke the Trading with the Enemy Act and that, unless further provoked, he was unwilling to do so.

It became rather tiresome repeating over and over that we were protecting United States interests, and that our motives in trading with Cuba were not simply economic opportunism. I suspect that the Cuban government was at least reasonably pleased with the state of its relations with Canada. I recall that some time in 1961, the Cuban Ambassador presented me with a box of the very best Cuban cigars, unfortunately accompanied by a note worded in such political terms that I felt obliged to return the gift.

When the subject of China came up during our May 1961 talks, I remarked to the President that when I had seen him in February, I had detected no indication that the new administration was prepared to adopt any changed attitude to the recognition of the Peking government. I wondered if there had been any change, because during the recent Commonwealth Prime Ministers' Conference in London, the Australian Prime Minister, Mr. Menzies, indicated that he had gained the opposite impression in his talk with the President. I suggested that so far as Canada was concerned, public opinion was against recognition and that I did not think that the mistake of not recognizing the mainland government before the Korean War could be rectified now without ill effects on all our friends in Asia. President Kennedy agreed. He said that his administration had not altered the United States' position on recognition. In fact, his country had been under bitter verbal attack from Peking; the Chinese Communists, unlike the Russians, had given him no period of grace after the inauguration. The plain fact was that the Senate would never confirm an Ambassador to Peking. We did agree that it was just a matter of time before

China took its place in the United Nations. The important thing was to find a solution that would keep Taiwan in.

If we had no basis for disagreement on the political aspects of Communist China, the question of Canada's trade with Peking provided quite another issue. In 1953 Canada's exports to Communist China had been nil. In 1957 they were a mere $1.4 million. Actually we imported $5.3 million worth of goods from China in 1957, leaving us with a trade deficit of $3.9 million. Our best estimates suggested that Western trade with China in the immediate future was not likely to rise in export terms much above the annual level of $450 to $500 million, of which we expected to obtain a $10 to $15 million share. In actual terms, our exports in 1958 totalled $12 million; in 1959, $11 million.

Early in 1960, however, prospects for increased trade began to improve tremendously. Nineteen-sixty was the second successive year of large-scale natural calamities in China which affected approximately half of their arable land. Our Trade Commissioner in Hong Kong, Mr. C. M. Forsyth-Smith, was invited to visit mainland China in May of 1960. To make a complicated story of negotiations short, on 2 February 1961 we were able to announce in the House the sale of 12.1 million bushels of No. 1 feed barley and 28 million bushels of average-quality wheat to China. On 22 April 1961 the head of the Canadian Wheat Board, Mr. MacNamara, signed a long-term agreement with the Chinese authorities in Peking for the purchase from Canada of between 3 and 5 million tons of wheat and between 600 thousand and 1 million tons of barley prior to the end of 1963. Mainland China quickly became Canada's second-largest market for wheat; our exports in 1962 were worth $137.3 million. These sales helped to restore our prairie economy to its rightful place in the Canadian scheme of things.

The initial problem was to arrange acceptable terms of

credit. Cash deals for the quantities of wheat that I have mentioned were not possible. Yet, if credit were arranged, loans guaranteed, etc., and if the Peking government did not pay by the due date (and we had no experience with them on which to base any sort of judgment), my government would be in an impossible position. I consulted a number of experts, and, as usual, wound up with as many opinions as there were experts. The responsibility had ultimately to rest with me. Finally, I came to a decision in a very simple way. I recalled two British Prime Ministers who had remarked that the most difficult of problems, if brought down to the denominator of the ordinary man or woman, could often be solved. During my time at the bar I had acted for a number of Chinese Canadians. My experience was that when a Chinese gave his word, it was as good as his bond, apparently because of an adherence to the teachings of Confucius and Tao. I doubted that Communism had eradicated these traditional philosophic approaches to life on mainland China. Thus, I accepted the responsibility for authorizing the necessary credit arrangements.

It was at this juncture that difficulties began to arise with the United States. The Chinese had chartered a number of Norwegian and British ships to transport the grain. Shortly before I visited Washington in February 1961, my officials received indications from the Imperial Oil Company that it might have difficulty selling bunker oil to the ships in question unless a clearance could be obtained under the United States Foreign Assets Control Regulations by its American parent company. The Foreign Assets Control Regulations were based on the United States' Trading with the Enemy Act, and under these regulations it was illegal for any United States citizen or any enterprise owned by United States citizens to trade with mainland China. I found this intolerable. I would not consider having the Canadian government request an exemption under United States regulations for the sale of Canadian oil by a Canadian company in order to carry out the export of Canadian grain. I so informed President Kennedy. A variety of suggestions were put forward by the State Department, none of which was acceptable to me. In March 1961 our Ambassador to Washington, Arnold Heeney, was instructed to so inform the United States government and to add that any effort made by United States authorities to intervene in these important and essentially Canadian transactions would have serious consequences. Finally, the United States government simply exempted Canadian subsidiaries from its Foreign Assets Control Regulations. I was pleased with that solution and so advised President Kennedy when he visited Ottawa.

The matter that gained public attention, however, was that of the American-manufactured grain unloaders, or vacuators. Because the Chinese authorities had chartered a number of oil tankers to be used in carrying the grain, they required special unloading equipment, namely suction devices called vacuators. This equipment had been ordered from a United States firm by the shipowners. On 5 June 1961, the agents for two of the vessels in question telephoned the Department of Trade and Commerce to say that delivery of the vacuators was being held up on instructions of the United States Treasury on the basis of Foreign Assets Control Regulations. This equipment had already been delivered to the Canadian port, consigned to the manufacturer, whose agent was to take delivery and assist in its installation. The manufacturer's representative was now ordered by the United States Treasury to send the equipment back to the United States.

In order to overcome this extreme application of FAC Regulations, I had to make personal representations to President Kennedy. I considered this hardly the kind of situation designed to produce amity between our governments and our countries. I had to tell him that unless he released the unloading equipment, I would go on national television and radio to tell the Canadian people that he was attempting to run our country, and that he would have to think again if he thought this United States action acceptable. When he told me that he considered ours a personal conversation, I rejoined that there was nothing personal about it: that he was not going to prevent our carrying out Canadian policies because Washington didn't think those policies right or appropriate. The grain unloaders were released, but that was the end of any friendly personal relationship between President Kennedy and myself.

As a footnote, I might add that those Canadian officials responsible for making certain no repetition of this situation could occur were not exactly helpful. More vacuators were required, but no one followed through to find a Canadian source of supply. On 25 August, when I discovered the situation, I personally had to give the order that every effort be made to make certain that vacuators be supplied from Canadian sources.

In January 1962 an even more unsavoury aspect was added to our relations with the United States over these sales to Communist China. United States Under-Secretary of State George Ball in effect suggested to a joint ministerial meeting that we turn our ploughshares into swords. He explained that in President Kennedy's view the situation in South Vietnam was even more critical and potentially dangerous than that in Berlin. United States intelligence, he said, had made it evident beyond doubt that Communist China was behind the aggressive and subversive activities of North Vietnam. The United States had increased assistance to South Vietnam, including extensive military equipment and United States military personnel (the latter as yet in a non-combat role). He suggested that the United States might have to commit combat troops and that this might mean general war. They believed that if South Vietnam fell, the whole of Southeast Asia, including Australia and New Zealand, would be in dire peril. In these grave circumstances, he wondered whether advantage could not be taken of the current contacts between the Canadian government and the Chinese Communist authorities. It had occurred to the United States authorities that it might be intimated to the Chinese that deliveries of food from free world sources could not be continued unless the Chinese Communists were willing to stop their support of subversion and aggression in Vietnam. Needless to say, the response of my government to these proposals was less than warm. Fortunately, a newspaper report from Washington on 7 February 1962 speculating on Kennedy's interest in using the famine in China and the sale of Canadian wheat to extract political concessions brought an end to these United States overtures.

The Sino-Indian dispute of 1962 added another strange dimension to Sino-Canadian trade. As a consequence of the border war, my Cabinet decided on 23 October 1962 to cut off all exports to China except wheat. On 27 November 1962, the Indian High Commissioner, Mr. Jha, called on Howard Green. He informed him that he had been instructed to raise the question of Canadian sales of wheat to China. The implication of his remarks was that we should halt all wheat sales to China as long as the Chinese posed any threat to Indian claims along the McMahon Line separating the two countries. Among other things, Mr. Green pointed out that since India had not broken diplomatic relations with China, it was unlikely that Canada would break trade relations with her.

To return to President Kennedy: his memorandum on his objectives in visiting Ottawa in May 1961 came into my possession because the President apparently dropped it into my wastepaper basket at the end of our meeting.

Regulations require that the Prime Minister's basket be checked at the end of each day to make certain no secret documents have found their way into it. This memorandum, prepared by the United States State Department's Policy Planning Director, Walter Rostow, read:

SECRET

May 16, 1961

"What We Want from Ottawa Trip"

1. To push the Canadians towards an increased commitment to the Alliance for Progress. Concretely, we would like them to have at least an observer at the July IA-ECOSOC.
2. To push them towards a decision to join the OAS.
3. To push them towards a larger contribution for the India consortium and for foreign aid generally. The figures are these: they have offered $36 million for India's Third-Year Plan, we would like $70 million from them. Over-all their aid now comes to $69 million a year; if they did 1% of GNP the figure would be $360 million. Like the rest of us, they have their political problems with foreign aid; but we might be able to push them in the right direction.
4. We want their active support at Geneva and beyond for a more effective monitoring of the borders of Laos and Vietnam.

SECRET

The stories about there being a marginal comment on it referring to me as an s.o.b. are not true. To the best of my knowledge, that story was a Liberal invention designed to provide a context for the Kennedy joke that he hadn't known I was one until that meeting. I subsequently brought this memorandum to the attention of the United States Ambassador to Canada, Livingston Merchant. I told him that I could not understand the President of the United States coming to Ottawa "to push" us into anything. An ally of Mr. Pearson, Merchant said that I threatened to make the Kennedy memorandum public.

I found it revealing that in the Opposition, Pearson and Martin began saying that we should immediately join the Organization of American States; that they would do so if they were in power. That the Liberal Party has been in office now since 1963 and that Canada has not joined the OAS is an indication of the bonafides of their contention.

By his own criteria, Kennedy's mission to Ottawa was a failure. We did not "shape up". We made no commitment to the Alliance for Progress. We were not about to join the OAS. Our position on foreign aid did not change: the explanation I gave in Chapter Five was essentially the position that I put to President Kennedy. On his fourth point, we were prepared to do all we could to make the International Control Commission in Vietnam more effective. As things turned out, there was very little we could do. The only question not previously mentioned on which he took an unexpectedly hard line during our discussions was over Canada's acquisition of nuclear weapons. He did not get his way here either. (As my readers will discover in the next volume of these memoirs, our independence was not without price.) During his visit, Kennedy engaged in a tree-planting ceremony on the grounds of Rideau Hall. He had injured his back during the Second World War, but there was no suggestion during his visit that he had injured it again during the tree-planting. I was amazed some weeks later when this story came out.

To end this chapter on a more pleasant note, when I was in New York in September of 1960, President Eisenhower asked me whether I had ever met President Hoover. Hoover was a man for whom I had always had admiration. In the days of the First World War, he headed the Belgian and Russian Relief Commission. After the war, he served in the Cabinet of Presidents Harding and Coolidge before he was elected President in 1928. I do not hold it against him that he was recognized as one of the finest fly fishermen in all the world. In August 1976, with my host Mitchell Franklin, I fished so successfully as to kill a nineteen-pound salmon in the Salmon River not far from Saint John, N.B., where Hoover used to fish from time to time. President Eisenhower arranged an appointment and we had a lengthy chat. I found him a most interesting personality. His defeat by Franklin Roosevelt in the 1932 election had not soured him. He had been condemned as being the cause rather than the victim of the depression; in that he shared the fate of the Right Honourable R. B. Bennett of Canada. He accepted without a murmur the contumely heaped upon him.

When I saw him, he was writing on the relations between East and West. He remarked that he did not have a large staff, only eight secretaries. President Hoover freely expressed opinions concerning United States Presidents, past and present, some of which I will never record. I did ask him why he, a Republican, had written on the life of Woodrow Wilson. He replied that Wilson had been a great President and that he had decided to retrieve his reputation from his detractors.

When I asked him about the Hoover Commission, he said that one day in 1946, the Speaker of the House of Representatives had called him to say that he would never get the bill establishing the Commission on the Organization of the Executive Branch of the Government through unless Hoover were prepared to accept the chairmanship. Hoover agreed. He immediately went to work by telephone. He told me that he called 352 leading representatives of business around the country and that he had 350 acceptances. He said he had always found businessmen willing to accept the challenge of public service, if you could assure them that they would not have to give up their businesses to do it. He organized his volunteers into forty-eight task forces, and of the 350 men involved, only two did not pull their weight. After the necessary information had all been gathered, they put their report together in a month. He considered they had saved the United States a minimum of $10 billion, but wryly remarked that it had probably all gone into the Defence Budget in the end.

President Hoover told me of a recent visit to Philadelphia where, much to his amusement, he had managed to lose his Secret Service guards. He had come back to New York by himself on the late-afternoon train. When he disembarked, no one except a newsboy recognized him. The newsboy approached him and asked for his autograph. Hoover was delighted that at least one person there knew him. He told me: "I said to him, 'My boy, when you're my age you'll be able to tell the story of how you were the only one among thousands to recognize a former President of the United States.' " He went on to ask the boy why he wanted his autograph. The newsboy replied, "Mr. President, it takes ten Hoovers to get one Jack Dempsey, and until now I only had nine."

Stories like this tend to become legendary. A similar one is told about me. A lad of about seven or eight years of age tried to get through the crowd at the Simpson's store in Toronto where I was autographing the first volume of my memoirs. I arranged that he be allowed through. He didn't have a book, just a piece of paper for me to autograph. I signed it; he thanked me and left. Apparently, a member of the press stopped him to ask what he was up to. He replied that it took five John Diefenbakers to get one Bobby Hull, and he had only had four!

CHAPTER SEVEN

✳

THROUGHOUT MY LIFE, I have had a deep and abiding emotional attachment to the Commonwealth. I have always been proud of the fact that Canada contributed so much to the evolution from the British Empire to an association of free and sovereign states bound by neither seal nor sword. When I became Prime Minister in 1957, the Commonwealth was about to enter a third important stage in its evolution. I saw the Commonwealth as a tremendous force for good in the world: for peace, progress, and stability in a world fraught with tension and on the brink of nuclear cataclysm. The problem was whether we could rise to meet the challenges and the opportunities that this new stage of Commonwealth development presented.

Prior to the Second World War, the Commonwealth had had but six self-governing members: Great Britain, Canada, the Union of South Africa, Australia, New Zealand, and Ireland. White, Western, and Christian, each had inherited a common parliamentary system and a similar system of judicial procedures based on those of Britain. Each was united by a common allegiance to the Empire's Crown. The Commonwealth was very much a family affair.

The second stage in the development of the Commonwealth began when India and Pakistan achieved independence and were admitted to the Commonwealth with Dominion status on 15 August 1947. At the Commonwealth Prime Ministers' Conference in April 1949, it was agreed that India might continue her membership in the Commonwealth as a republic. India became a republic in January 1950. When the Prime Ministers agreed in February 1955 to Pakistan's continued membership in the Commonwealth as a republic, the important principle was established that when a Dominion decided to adopt a republican constitution it had no automatic right to remain within the Commonwealth. Also, it was agreed that it was preferable to discuss questions of re-admission at a Prime Ministers' meeting rather than by correspondence. When Prime Minister Bandaranaike of Ceylon stated his government's intention to introduce a republican constitution and its hope to remain a member of the Commonwealth, the other Prime Ministers discussed this question at their meeting in July 1956. (Although the Prime Ministers agreed to Ceylon's remaining in the Commonwealth as a republic, Ceylon did not adopt a republican constitution until 22 May 1972.) Just prior to my becoming Prime Minister, Ghana achieved her independence and was admitted to the Commonwealth through of an exchange of correspondence. Thus, when I attended my first Prime Ministers' meeting in July 1957, the Commonwealth had completed a progression to something of an imperial "old boys' " club, its membership restricted to those who had graduated from British tutelage.

One aspect of the Commonwealth that in particular distressed me was that Ireland had left our association in 1949. Ireland had adopted a republican constitution. The impossible became possible a few weeks later when a solution was found whereby it was sufficient that a Commonwealth member simply recognize the Monarch as Head of the Commonwealth. Nothing would have pleased me more than Ireland's re-entry into the Commonwealth of Nations. I canvassed this possibility, but it was not practicable so long as the six Ulster Counties remained an outstanding issue in her relations with Britain. The general reaction in Ireland was that rejoining the Commonwealth would immediately be taken by the Ulsterites as capitulation. Yet the problems of Ireland were the problems of the Commonwealth.

When Olive and I visited Ireland in March 1961, I had discussions with Prime Minister Lemass about Ireland's relations with the European Common Market and the European Free Trade Association. He remarked that Ireland's problem was not so much with the Inner Six or the Outer Seven but with what Britain's relations with the two would finally be. Ireland's economy was basically agricultural, and her most important export market was Britain. Like Canada, Ireland enjoyed some advantage in the British market because of the Ottawa Agreements of 1932 (as renewed in 1938 and 1948). Some two-thirds to three-quarters of Ireland's trade, both import and export, was with Great Britain. Naturally, Prime Minister Lemass did not like the suggestion that the British might go into the Common Market under terms that discriminated against Irish agriculture. He considered that this might be the worst possible outcome for Ireland. Certainly, I was encouraged in my determination to pursue a Commonwealth economic alternative to Europe by Mr. Lemass's view that the British approach to the EEC was "half-hearted", and not likely to succeed at this time. Without getting too far ahead of myself on this topic, I had to agree when he suggested that Prime Minister Macmillan's approach to the European Common Market was with a view to the future when Adenauer and de Gaulle would no longer be there.

Ireland and Canada were natural allies; our interests

and cultures coincided. Canada had derived much benefit
from its Irish heritage. In 1961, we had in Canada a Governor General (General Vanier's mother was a Maloney),
a Chief Justice of the Supreme Court of Canada, and several Cabinet Ministers who were of Irish heritage. While I
was in Ireland I presented Prime Minister Lemass with
two plaques, one in the Irish language and one in English,
commemorating the great Canadian orator and statesman
Thomas D'Arcy McGee, one of the Fathers of Confederation, who had been born in Carlingford, County Louth, in
1825. And I was delighted when Mr. Lemass presented me
with two volumes of D'Arcy McGee's works, his *History
of Ireland* and a collection of his poems. In international
affairs, Ireland had been among the best and most reliable of Canada's friends. Mr. Frederick Boland, Permanent Representative of Ireland at the United Nations, and
President of the Fifteenth General Assembly, epitomized
to me those qualities that my government had come to
expect from Irish representatives abroad. Also, Ireland,
like Canada, had played its full part in the United Nations
peace-keeping operation in the Congo. At my press conference in Dublin I noted: "There is between our two
countries that friendship which is so necessary for international goodwill and peace."

Before visiting Dublin, we had journeyed to Belfast,
where we were the guests of Viscount Brookeborough,
the Prime Minister of Northern Ireland. This was a visit
that provided a most amusing experience. The day before
our departure from Ottawa, I was chatting with my confidential messenger, Gilbert Champagne. Champagne had
served Prime Ministers Borden, Meighen, King, Bennett,
and St. Laurent in this same capacity. I asked him if he
wouldn't like to accompany us to Ireland. He was as-
tounded; he had never before been invited to travel anywhere. Of course he agreed. In order to make our hosts in
Belfast aware of this addition to my party, a telegram was

sent by External Affairs to this effect: "PRIME MINISTER WILL BE BRINGING CHAMPAGNE." I gather that this caused some annoyance among the officials responsible for our welcome in Belfast. Their reaction was that I was bringing my own because I feared the champagne in Ulster inferior. It was a case of "B.Y.O.L."; it appeared to them that I was initiating the practice internationally of bringing your own liquor. But they rose to the occasion. When our airplane landed, a panel truck equipped with wine racks wheeled onto the tarmac to accommodate our Champagne. Brookeborough was most amused. He personally directed that a special table be set in an alcove for Gilbert at the state luncheon in my honour, and that several bottles of champagne be within his reach.

During the Prime Ministers' Conference in London in 1957, Lady Churchill invited Olive and me to luncheon. During the course of my conversation with Sir Winston, he offered to share one of his dearest possessions, some Napoleon brandy. He said: "Will you have shome?" I replied: "I'm a teetotaller." He couldn't understand what that meant. He checked his ear-piece and had me repeat it. I explained that I did not drink hard liquor. He asked: "Are you a prohibitionist?" I said: "No, I have never been a prohibitionist." He considered this for a moment and then remarked: "Ah, I see, you only hurt yourself."

When I attended the Prime Ministers' meeting in London in 1957, there were but nine members of the Commonwealth. Malaya joined our number in 1957; Nigeria in 1960; Cyprus, Sierra Leone, and Tanganyika in 1961. The floodgates were opening: there are now over thirty Commonwealth members. In size and diversity the Commonwealth was becoming much like the United Nations or its agencies. But there were, and are, important differences. From a Canadian point of view, the Commonwealth was a much clearer window on the world than the United Nations. If our common institutional heritage was diminished in practice, British parliamentary democracy and the Rule of Law assumed an ideological force that made the Commonwealth an important bulwark against the spread of international communism. Further, while each member was free to criticize any other, we did not attempt to establish common policies. Each member of the Commonwealth was responsible for its own policies, whether domestic or foreign. To consent to any other practice would be a complete reverse of responsible government and a repudiation of the Balfour Report. The day when Commonwealth Prime Ministers' Conferences decide issues by vote will be the day that marks the end of the Commonwealth. The real issue, however, was whether the Commonwealth could serve as a bridge of understanding in preventing serious antagonisms from developing between the rich nations and the poor. In large measure, this was dependent upon the ability of the older members within the Commonwealth to assist the new ones in Asia and Africa through such arrangements as the Colombo Plan. I was so impressed with this scheme that, beginning in 1959, I increased Canada's annual contribution from $35 million to $50 million.

On the tenth anniversary of the Colombo Plan on 14 January 1960, I issued the following statement:

On this occasion which marks the Tenth Anniversary of the concept of the Colombo Plan, I share with all Canadians and the peoples of the other Colombo Plan countries a feeling of justifiable pride in the great accomplishments which the Plan has made possible. The Colombo Plan arose out of, and in turn has contributed to, the realization that the economic progress of all parts of the world is an essential element of any satisfying and enduring peace. I refer not only to the large hydroelectric projects, the irrigation schemes, the fisheries plants and the cement plants and the many other major undertakings which have been carried out under the Colombo Plan, but, as well, to the spirit of international cooperation and goodwill which is such an essential and inherent part of the Colombo Plan concept. Undoubtedly these many large projects for years to come will serve as worthy monuments to the skills, both human and mechanical, which went into their construction. Even more, they will stand as a lasting symbol to the spirit of international cooperation which has moved the peoples of a score of very different countries to pool their ideas and resources in what was, in 1950, and still remains, a unique and exciting experiment devoted to the welfare of humanity. The implementation of the Colombo Plan is an outstanding example of what individual nations can achieve when they unite in meeting their obligations to one another.

Canadians, together with the peoples of other Commonwealth nations, are especially proud of the role of the Commonwealth in starting and sustaining this great plan. That the original idea was so quickly and effectively extended to other nations is an indication of the important and useful part which the Commonwealth can play in international affairs.

Our association with these other nations in Asia has been one of mutual cooperation from which all have been able to benefit to a significant degree. Canadians have contributed money, materials and personal skills and, in return, have gained enormously from the experience of working closely with the many people with whom they are associated in this venture.

For the future, the Colombo Plan idea holds great promise of advancement toward the fuller and better life which is the goal of the people of the many different nations which have had the good fortune to be joined together in it.

The success of the Colombo Plan as a form of co-operative action to provide assistance for economic development in Asia commended it as a model for a Commonwealth program for Africa. I considered that Canada, by virtue of its position in the Commonwealth, its reputation in the United Nations and in other councils of the world, its relatively advanced economy, and its bilingual culture, was perhaps in a better position than any other member of the Commonwealth to take a lead in proposing a constructive program for Africa. It was apparent that the new nations of Africa feared the resurgence of colonialism. A Canadian initiative might overcome these fears. Moreover, we had already begun to move in this direction with the Commonwealth Scholarship Scheme and with the preliminary Canadian program for technical assistance to Commonwealth countries in Africa (two of the accomplishments of the 1958 Commonwealth Trade and Economic Conference). In consequence, I took an initiative on this question at the Commonwealth Prime Ministers' Conference in May 1960. It was agreed that consideration be given to co-operative action among the members of the Commonwealth in assisting the economic development of the Commonwealth countries in Africa, which had recently attained or were approaching independence. On 22 September 1960, the Commonwealth Finance Ministers met to create a Special Commonwealth African Assistance Plan (SCAAP). Canada's contribution was to be $10.5 million over its first three years.

Nearer home, I was particularly interested in the then emerging Federation of the West Indies. I have a fondness for those island states that were formerly part of the British West Indies. Each year, Olive and I have tried to vacation in one of the Commonwealth countries in the Caribbean, or in Bermuda or the Bahamas. I have already mentioned that in the autumn of 1958 I was able to announce the intention of my government to ask Parliament to appropriate $10 million over a period of five years to provide capital and technical assistance to the West Indies Federation. I had been much impressed with the federation idea in several conversations with my close friend, Sir Grantley Adams, Prime Minister of Barbados, whom I admired greatly. His dream was of a great federation of British islands from Jamaica to Trinidad and Tobago. When the federation idea began to collapse because of the rivalry for predominance between Trinidad and Jamaica (which resulted in a rather foolish commitment during a by-election contest by Premier Manley of Jamaica to a local referendum on the question), Sir Grantley came to me for help. He proposed that I tour all the islands concerned to speak in favour of the federation idea. I very much regret that I did not make the time to do so. My schedule was so pressing it did not seem possible for me to get away from Ottawa for the time required. Had I been able to go, I might have been able to bolster the sagging federation idea.

The two new boys at the Prime Ministers' Conference in 1957 were Kwame Nkrumah and myself. Of course, all the Canadian arrangements for the conference had been made in advance of the 1957 election. In consequence, Canadian officials had arranged matters in expectation that the government of Mr. St. Laurent would be returned. Mr. Pearson was to be the Dominion Day speaker to the London Canadian Club. I took his place. This occasion provided me the opportunity to review Canada's long association with the Commonwealth idea. It is of interest that the original concept belonged not to South Africa's Jan Christiaan Smuts but to Canada's John Alexander Macdonald. It had been Macdonald who had fought for a recognition of the existing political plurality of the Empire, and Macdonald who achieved that recognition with the creation of the office of Canadian High Commissioner in London in 1880. It was Macdonald who saw the future evolution of the Canadian, Australian, and New Zealand colonies to a Commonwealth association of autonomous nations. As a point of interest, Sir John Macdonald was the first Canadian to be made a member of Her Majesty's Imperial Privy Council; I will be the last.

My successor as Prime Minister in effect abolished this distinction for Canadians, but not before accepting it for himself. One of the first things I did when I arrived in London as a young lieutenant in 1916 was visit St. Paul's Cathedral, there to view among the busts of some of the great heroes and creative geniuses of British civilization that of Sir John Macdonald, the only Canadian ever so honoured.

As a point of minor interest, Nkrumah was also to become an Imperial Privy Councillor. Indeed, his name remained on the Privy Council List until his death, even though Ghana became a republic, far removed in its practices from the rest of the Commonwealth, with Nkrumah as its President and Saviour. I came to know Nkrumah reasonably well. He had a pathological fear of assassination, which caused him to react nervously at the sound of any sharp noise. I visited him once at the Ghanaian High Commission in London. When I arrived, I was physically jostled by his aides and it took me a moment to realize that in fact I was being frisked for weapons lest I be the assassin he feared. During the course of our conversation that evening, he inquired if I had ever consulted necromancers. I had not, but I told him about Mackenzie King's propensity in that regard. Nkrumah, like King, I discovered, was a believer in mediums and extra-terrestrial communication, and the like. He told me of a prophecy made of him by a renowned female psychic: that he would become his country's first Prime Minister; that he would become his country's first President; and that he would marry an heiress. At the time of our conversation, he had achieved all these. I said to him, "Isn't that amazing; is she ever wrong?" He replied, "I hope so, she also predicted that I would be the victim of a *coup d'état*." This, too, was to be fulfilled. But in each case, it was in consequence of his own actions. The supernatural was only a part of his vision of himself.

In this chapter, and earlier, I have outlined a variety of reasons, both international and domestic, why my government was prepared to give the Commonwealth that attention it had not received from Canada since 1921 (the years 1930–35 excepted). My 1957 proposal to divert fifteen per cent of Canada's imports from the United States to Britain, while intended to help solve Canada's adverse balance of trade with the United States, served to focus the attention of the entire Commonwealth and the world at large on Commonwealth questions. It was also a direct challenge to British industry and initiative. In 1956 Britain's exports to Canada totalled $485 million. I proposed to see this total increased some one hundred and thirty per cent, to about $1,110 million. I further said: "We are prepared to explore with you every avenue to make this possible." It was up to Britain to meet the requirements of the Canadian market. I have never understood how some critics were able to portray this proposal as a piece of selfishness on the part of my government. Although we had a vested interest in diversifying our trade so as to lessen our dependence on the United States, the opportunity to reverse recent Commonwealth trading patterns was there if Britain wanted to take it.

Initially, Prime Minister Harold Macmillan was my most important supporter. At the 1957 Prime Ministers' Conference, I outlined my reasons for calling a Commonwealth trade conference. Had Prime Minister Macmillan not supported me in this, I doubt that the conference would ever have taken place. Thus, the Commonwealth Trade and Economic Conference in Montreal in September 1958 was held because of my initiative and British backing.

Traditionally, Commonwealth trade had been encouraged by tariff preferences. As we approached the 1958 Commonwealth Economic Conference, many observers, recalling the Imperial Conference of 1932 in Ottawa (which was convened on the initiative of Prime Minister the Right Honourable R. B. Bennett), expected tariffs to be the focus of the conference. Investigation and study of this question suggested that these expectations were mistaken. The type of tariff action undertaken in Ottawa in 1932 reflected the fact that the world was experiencing an unprecedented depression, and that the United States, in a mood of extreme isolationism, had raised its own tariff barriers to an unprecedented height. The circumstances in 1958 bore no resemblance to those of 1932. My government had tested the waters of tariff preferences at the meeting of Commonwealth Finance Ministers at Mont Tremblant, Quebec, in September 1957, when we made this offer:

The Canadian government is not now proposing a new system of tariff preferences, or of restrictions against trade with non-Commonwealth countries. On the other hand, if fellow-members of the Commonwealth could reciprocate, and if it seemed that Commonwealth trade could be promoted on a mutually advantageous basis, we would be glad to engage in discussions relating to tariff adjustments.

The only response we received was from Britain, that we might unilaterally restore in favour of Britain a number of tariff preferences that had been reduced during the General Agreement on Tariffs and Trade negotiations.

Our conclusions, which served as part of the instructions to the Canadian delegation to the Montreal conference, were threefold. First, there was no disposition whatever amongst Commonwealth governments to form a separate or regional bloc for trade, for development, or for any other purpose. No Commonwealth country wished to take steps to cut off or estrange itself from the United States; the United States not only provided the greatest single market and richest source of capital in the world, but was also the heir to the world responsibility which Britain had carried for two hundred years. This became particularly evident at the conference in the discussion of tariff preferences and quota discrimination. Most of the external economic problems affecting Commonwealth countries were of a world-wide nature. In short, the Commonwealth countries were looking towards economic expansion not at the expense of other countries, but together with them. We wanted to achieve "an expanding Commonwealth in an expanding world economy".

Second, we had concluded that the chief trade interest of the forthcoming conference was likely to relate to commodity arrangements and agricultural protection. All the Commonwealth countries, other than Britain, were heavily dependent on the production and export of primary products, including farm products; indeed, some were almost completely dependent on these exports. Thus we had a common interest in exploring solutions to prevent international agricultural dumping and to promote international commodity price stabilization.

Third, we anticipated that the main emphasis of the conference would be on economic development, particularly in under-developed countries, and in the financial measures needed to sustain world-wide expansion of both development and trade. When Prime Minister Harold Macmillan visited Ottawa towards the end of June 1958, he was particularly interested in the proposal for a Commonwealth Bank. He recognized that it could be argued that a Commonwealth Bank was unlikely to mobilize additional savings, either within the Commonwealth or from other sources, and that in practice the existence of such a Commonwealth institution might lead to a reduction in lending to Commonwealth countries by the International Bank, but he did not regard these possible objections as insuperable. In particular, he was not convinced that a Commonwealth Bank would fail to secure for investment purposes additional savings within the Commonwealth. The Indian Maharajahs and the merchants in Hong Kong had savings which were not now making any contribution towards the economic development of Commonwealth countries. To mobilize these savings, he considered that it might also be necessary to mobilize a Commonwealth mystique. I was attracted by this idea, and quite disappointed when Mr. Macmillan subsequently informed me that his government had reluctantly come to the conclusion that it would not be wise to proceed with it.

The Commonwealth Economic Conference met at the Queen Elizabeth Hotel in Montreal from 15 September to 26 September 1958. I had written to Prime Minister Macmillan on 18 July 1958 urging him to give "some further thought to the question of ending discrimination in your import restrictions and those of other members of the sterling area." I suggested that dropping discrimination would expose his government to fewer risks than the formal establishment of the convertibility of sterling, and "would really be in your own interests as much as ours, since your over-all balance of payments position should be better if you buy in the cheapest markets. The same should be true of other Commonwealth countries in the sterling area." From my point of view, the Commonwealth Trade and Economic Conference became a success the moment the British agreed to sweep away the greater part of their trade discrimination against dollar countries. This made the system of preferences within the Commonwealth, so far as they applied to Canada, a reality, with important implications for Canada's long-term trade with Britain, the West Indies, and the colonies. I was able to report to the Canadian people on 29 November 1961, on CBC television's "The Nation's Business":

Last year our total trade with Commonwealth countries, including of course the United Kingdom, amounted to $2,124 million—that is, 20% of our total world trade. That our Commonwealth trade has been progressing upwards is shown by the fact that there has been an increase of over $350 million since we took office. In the same four years our exports to Commonwealth countries have increased by $195 million, that is, 18%.

This is a remarkable achievement during a period of increasing trade competition and hemispheric recession.

It is part of the very significant overall increases in our total exports since 1956 during which time our sales abroad have increased by 12%. Our trade is still increasing. In the first eight months of the current year, another new high has been reached—$3,716 million worth of export business, an increase of 4.8% in eight months.

Our imports from Commonwealth countries and the United Kingdom have increased to greater proportion than from the United States.

I might note before leaving this subject that the Conference emphasized the need that a European Common Market and European free-trade area should be outward-looking, in the interests of an expanding world trade and world economy.

Much has been made of my government's supposedly uncooperative attitude to Britain's attempts to negotiate an entry into the European Economic Community. This was a matter that received great attention in the Liberal press and a highly theatrical opposition from the Liberal Party in the House of Commons. The economic policies of my government with regard to Canada's external trade never once threatened us with the internal disruptions that were so evident from the first days of Mr. Pearson's government. (One of the ironies óf recent Canadian history is that Walter Gordon, a man whom I had met only for a few minutes when he delivered to me his Royal

Commission Report, has stated that he decided to do everything in his power to make Mr. Pearson Prime Minister because he hated me and feared that my policies would wreck Canada!) To set the record straight, from the beginning in 1957, my government's policy towards all the European regional trade plans was, while recognizing their broad political and strategic implications, to safeguard our own trade and economic interests. It was always a question of finding a balance: we were in favour of a stronger Europe but not if in consequence Canada were to be locked into a continental economic union with the United States, or if the Commonwealth were to be destroyed. We were concerned about some of the proposed rates for the Common Market tariff on key Canadian exports, and the serious danger of highly restrictive arrangements for agriculture. It is to be remembered that the initial response of the United Kingdom to the formation of the EEC was to seek to embrace the Six in a broad European free-trade area. We went along with this on the clear understanding that our agricultural interests in the United Kingdom market would be fully safeguarded. When these negotiations broke down, Britain, together with other European non-EEC countries, formed the European Free Trade Association. Their main purpose was to strengthen their bargaining power in future negotiations with the Six for wider European arrangements.

The European Economic Community, as things turned out, enjoyed a much greater success than Britain had anticipated. On the other hand, Britain continued to be in a difficult economic position and continued to experience a serious balance-of-payments problem. The resurgence in the British economy that Prime Minister Macmillan had predicted in conversation with me in June of 1958 did not take place. Consequently, domestic pressures forced the Macmillan government to renew negotiations with the EEC. I received notice of the British intention to do so in September 1960.

To me, this was a matter of considerable concern to Canada until President de Gaulle finally closed the Common Market door on Britain in January 1963. On 12 October 1961, I provided President Kekkonen of Finland, who was visiting Ottawa, with a brief explanation of our position. I noted that it was a principle of the Commonwealth association that individual Commonwealth countries should retain their freedom of action but that each should avoid damaging the interests of the others so far as possible. Britain, in this sense, had a right to become a member of the EEC. At the same time, it had to be realized that Canada had been extending tariff preferences to Britain since 1897, and that since 1932 our trade relations had been on a contractual basis. More recently, the Montreal Trade and Economic Conference in 1958 had placed a new emphasis on the expansion of Commonwealth trade. As things had turned out, the resultant advantages to Canada coincided with Britain's increasing interest in entering the EEC. With the exception of Canada, the economies of the Commonwealth countries were in large measure complementary to Britain's. I maintained that it was imperative that Commonwealth agriculture be protected in any British arrangement with the EEC. The problem was not purely economic, however. Since important political problems were raised by the proposed British move, we could not be sanguine when we contemplated the effect of British entry on the Commonwealth relationship and, in particular, on Britain's role in the Commonwealth. If Britain turned inward to Europe without protecting the interests of the Commonwealth, the Commonwealth might cease to exist. My government could not be certain that the French would continue to refuse derogations from the Rome Treaty. If they did, British membership in the EEC would be forestalled. If they softened, the future was uncertain.

In terms of specific Canadian interests, if I may again quote from my television broadcast on 29 November 1961:

If we had not taken a stand on behalf of Canada we would have been criticized for failing to do so. Our exports to the United Kingdom, amounting to $915 million in 1960, are about 17% of our total exports, of which a large proportion enter free or with preferences. 76% of our United Kingdom exports would be affected by Common Market tariffs.

Trade affects every segment of Canada's economy. About one in every four Canadian workers derives his livelihood from external trade.

I have here a complete analysis of the effect on certain Canadian exports if the United Kingdom had agreed to adopt the Common Market external tariffs under the Treaty, without having provisions made to maintain a high degree of Commonwealth preferences.

Let me give you a few examples taken quite at random.

Durum wheat is now free to enter the British market, but would eventually face a tariff of 20%.

Other wheat and flour exports (amounting this year to $133 million) are now free, but would eventually face the same high tariff.

It is a long list taking only the items which now enter free but which would be subject to substantial tariff barriers—frozen and canned salmon, butter, cheese, plywood and other lumber products, steel bars, aluminum, magnesium, plastics, drugs and chemicals, cotton fabrics, newsprint and book and other papers, marine engines, machinery, aircraft engines and parts, and so on.

In direct contrast to the casual, and even negligent, approach of the [St. Laurent] government of which Mr. Pearson, Mr. Pickersgill and others were members, we have gone all out for trade expansion. It is a matter of record that their days [in office] were more notable for the loss of overseas markets than for any visible concern for new markets.

At the Commonwealth Prime Ministers' meeting in London in 1962, and as I have already written in Chapter Four, I told my Commonwealth colleagues that I did not think Britain would be successful in her attempt to enter the European Common Market. I had known for a long time that General de Gaulle had had grave misgivings about Britain's intentions in Europe. My contention was that as long as he remained President of France, there was no possibility of British success. The Right Honourable Edward Heath, Britain's chief negotiator with the EEC, was flushed with anticipated success, confident that Britain would be admitted to the Common Market within a few weeks. Prime Minister Menzies asked how I could have ever come to such an absurd conclusion. I could only repeat what I knew to be true. I felt obliged, however, to re-emphasize the Canadian position that the decision on whether Britain should seek entry was for Britain alone to take after the present consultations and such further consultations with the Commonwealth as would be desirable. I might add that in his message to me, dated 29 January 1963, telling me of the French veto of his government's application, Prime Minister Macmillan ended with an expression of appreciation for "the understanding attitude" of the Canadian government "throughout these difficult negotiations".

Shortly after de Gaulle's decision was made public, the French Ambassador to Canada told one of my officials that a major consideration in the General's decision had been the Nassau Agreement of December 1962 between Prime Minister Macmillan and President Kennedy; that it had proved to de Gaulle that Britain was, in fact, turning its back on Europe in favour of the United States' conception of an Atlantic Community dominated from Washington. President Kennedy apparently, and no doubt inadvertently, had given President de Gaulle a final proof when he secured Britain's agreement to end its Sky Bolt missile program and become part of a new American-controlled defence strategy. A United States-dominated Britain had no place in the kind of Europe that de Gaulle envisaged.

Had I remained Prime Minister following the election of 1963, Canada would have launched a major initiative on Commonwealth and international economic questions. The plans were ready but could not be presented until events had run their course; until a clear decision against Britain's bid to join the EEC was finally made, there was no point in tendering any new proposals for the Commonwealth. What I had in mind was a series of positive actions that would permit Britain to achieve a major part of her own economic objectives without disturbing the existing pattern of Commonwealth relationships. I felt that success in the implementation of this program would mitigate substantially the adverse economic effect of the EEC, reduce trade discrimination, provide a framework for the rational allocation of investment capital, and encourage balanced and sustainable economic growth on a broad basis. It would not destroy the fabric of the preferential system, but on the contrary would permit its adaptation to changing circumstances in return for full and adequate payment by the countries that would benefit, notably the United States, the EEC, and other principal trading countries. It was a program designed also to provide considerable room for the expanding trade of the developing members of the Commonwealth and to make a significant contribution to economic progress in those areas. This Canadian alternative for the Commonwealth was a practical program that would have provided a new focus for closer Commonwealth consultation and co-operation, consistent with the realities and needs of trading in a changing world.

An evening that will live forever in my memory was that of Tuesday, 4 November 1958, when I spoke in London's famous Albert Hall. Over five thousand people turned out that evening to the Anglo-Canadian rally sponsored by the Commonwealth and Empire Industries Association. My theme was one of the themes of Canada's foreign policy throughout the period of my government: the necessity of expanding trade and economic co-operation among the nations of the free world as a means of meeting the Communist world-trade threat. I dwelt on the importance of the Commonwealth in meeting this challenge, on its uniqueness, embracing as it did peoples of all continents; on the need of the Commonwealth to be more than simply a remnant of Empire but rather a new and vital force in world affairs. I talked about my dreams for the future and my vision of the Commonwealth's "new appointment with opportunity and destiny". "Living in the second Elizabethan age, this is no time for little faith. You see the picture, the opportunity and the challenge. Let us rekindle once more the greatness of our past, strengthen and maintain the traditions and principles of the present. Let us build together a future of peace and prosperity. Let us lift our horizon and above all banish those fears and those doubts." I quoted Alfred Lord Tennyson to convey the essence of my message: "Pray God our greatness may not fail through craven fear of being great."

I remember that I was ill that evening. I had come down with a high fever in the afternoon. Those who have experienced such things know their enervating physical effects. At the reception preceding the meeting, I was forced to find a chair and simply sit there, hoping that no one would think me rude. When we proceeded to the platform, I feared that I would not be able to speak; indeed, I wondered if I would be able to walk from my chair to the rostrum. I was introduced by the Right Hon-

ourable The Lord Balfour of Inchrye, P.C., M.C. With un-
steady step, I took my place before that great audience. I
somewhere found the strength I needed, and no one
knew the extreme of my physical discomfort. Prime Minister Macmillan spoke in response to my remarks. His
words were beyond anything I could have asked for. He
said of me: "He has faith in his fellow-countrymen, in
himself, and in the tasks which Canada has to undertake
and the contribution that she has to make to the whole
world. He has faith in the continuing and indeed ever-increasing moral and political value of that unique combination of nations which we call the Commonwealth." I
suspect that it was this faith, and this alone, that gave me
the necessary strength to address my audience that evening. What began as a probable disaster ended in triumph. In its report of my speech on 5 November, the London *Times* noted: "More than 5,000 . . . were there to
enjoy and be inspired by the experience when he spoke
on the theme of the new and living Commonwealth. . . .
The whole audience, including the Prime Minister, Mr.
Macmillan, stood and applauded Mr. Diefenbaker at the
end of his speech."

I had faith in the Commonwealth; I still have. It required faith to meet the Commonwealth's most pressing
problem: our Association of Nations had to be made
"colour blind". We in Canada have a long history of opposition to racialism. The actions of Upper and Lower
Canada in the early 1790s to rid Canadian society of the
damnable abomination of slavery stood some forty years
in advance of the British. Only Denmark, in the whole of
the Western world, took measures to abolish this curse
earlier than the Canadian colonies. Pioneer Canada thus
struck important first blows against the enslaving of human beings. Unfortunately, slavery is but the extreme
course of denying human beings their God-given rights. I
have spent my lifetime in opposing discrimination on the

basis of race, colour, and creed.

The issue of racial equality within the Commonwealth came to a head at the Prime Ministers' Conferences of 1960 and 1961. Before 1960, all the member nations of the Commonwealth, except the United Kingdom and Australia, had made it clear in the United Nations General Assembly that they strongly disapproved of the Union of South Africa's apartheid policies. There had been, however, no serious move to force a show-down with South Africa over its fitness for membership in the Commonwealth. South Africa, with that strange stubbornness born of a messianic interpretation of her history, now placed herself in the dock and demanded final judgment.

I informed the House of Commons on 29 January 1960 that I would not bring before the forthcoming Prime Ministers' Conference, or indeed support, action that would exclude South Africa from the councils of the Commonwealth. The killing by South African police of sixty-seven black Africans at Sharpeville caused me profound concern, but as I stated in the House on 25 March 1960: "The important consideration is not whether any action or statement by Canada would relieve Canadian feelings but what practical effect such action or such a statement would have in South Africa itself." The problem, as I said on 27 April 1960, was: "What shall we do in order to bring about before it is too late a realization [in the Union of South Africa] that discrimination wherever practiced is a forerunner, first of tyranny, and then of ultimate change by force . . . ?" I was asked at my press conference when I arrived at London airport for the Prime Ministers' Conference on Friday, 29 April 1960, if there was any difference of opinion on the question of apartheid in the Canadian House of Commons. I explained that there was unanimous disapproval of racialism and discrimination in race, and dismay at the results of the policies of the Union of South Africa. The Leader of the Opposition, the Honourable L. B. Pearson, the Secretary of State for External Affairs, and I nevertheless took the stand that as long as channels of communication between South Africa and the other governments of the Commonwealth were maintained, there would be hope that even yet an improved situation might be achieved.

When the Commonwealth Prime Ministers met on 3 May, strong feelings against apartheid were immediately voiced. The wise and statesmanlike Prime Minister of Malaya, Tunku Abdul Rahman, made a convincing case that the Commonwealth had to preserve its standards of conduct and its moral principles of equality of men irrespective of colour, and of justice and fair play. The policies of the Government of South Africa, he said, seemed to many people to be at variance with these principles; and while he had no intention of interfering in the domestic affairs of another country, recent events in South Africa had exceeded the limits of purely domestic concern. I agreed with Mr. Macmillan when he replied that in his view it would be preferable for the subject to be discussed informally in small groups rather than in plenary sessions where advisers were present and a record kept. Moreover, it was a settled convention of Prime Ministers' Conferences that the domestic affairs of any member or any question in dispute between two members would not be discussed in open sessions. Mr. E. H. Louw, South Africa's Minister of External Affairs, agreed to private discussions on the subject.

I had two private conversations with Mr. Louw, and informed him that Canadians had no sympathy for policies of racial discrimination. I said to him: "I'm not here to argue the question of every man a vote, not at all, but what I do ask is this: in your country's interest and in the interests of its survival, will you at least take a step forward and give to the black and the coloured peoples of the Union the same representation [three Members] that they had in the House of Representatives under Field Marshal Jan Christiaan Smuts? The restoration of those three constituencies would be a start, a symbol." And his answer was: "No, not even one Member." His answer was unacceptable and indicated a stubborn, a truculent, refusal to appreciate the fact, as I told him, that sooner or later a blood-bath would take place. I said, "You can't carry on like this. Your nation's stand will turn the whole continent of Africa, with the exception of the Portuguese colonies and Rhodesia, against you. Your policies are not only wrong, but dangerous." He would not be moved. The newer Commonwealth Prime Ministers had even less success than I had with Mr. Louw. At least he listened to me. They were unable even to present their views because of his obstinate refusal to do anything except expound his own point of view. General annoyance came to a head when he held a press conference giving his side of the apartheid question while it was still supposed to be under private discussion among Prime Ministers. The Tunku retorted with a heated press statement of his own. However, discussions of the subject continued during private consultations between various Prime Ministers over the weekend of 7 and 8 May, and during a restricted meeting of heads of delegations.

Then Mr. Louw unexpectedly brought before the Conference the question of a proposed South African referendum on whether to change her constitution from a monarchy to a republic. What he sought was assurance that South Africa would be welcomed back into the Commonwealth should she change her constitution. For my part, I stated that a decision by the present meeting that South Africa should remain in the Commonwealth, if the result of the referendum were in favour of a republic, would anticipate the referendum and amount to interference in an issue of domestic policy, or could be so interpreted in South Africa. It had been established that the question of republican or monarchical status was a matter for each country to decide for itself. I regarded it as a dangerous development if any decision of the meeting appeared to be interfering in the process of constitutional development of any member country. I was therefore opposed to giving an assurance of the kind requested by Mr. Louw. After considerable discussion the conference affirmed the view that the choice between a monarchy and a republic was entirely the responsibility of the country concerned. However, in the event of South Africa's deciding to become a republic, and if the desire was subsequently expressed to remain a member of the Commonwealth, we agreed that the South African government should then ask for the consent of the other Commonwealth governments either at a meeting of Commonwealth Prime Ministers or, if this were not practicable, by correspondence.

On 16 May 1960, I reported to the House of Commons:

Many observers have pointed out that the proceedings of the meetings did not result in any perceptible change in the attitude of the South African government. It was not to be expected, however, that magic improvements could take place in a situation of such tension and complexity. . . .

Despite the profound differences which prevailed and persisted throughout, it was possible for a communiqué to be issued. This was difficult with two inherently conflicting elements to be reconciled. First, it had become essential that a way be found for Commonwealth governments to make clear their intentions on this central question of racial relations.

Second, it was desirable that this should be done without violation of the traditional practice of these meetings that the internal affairs of member countries are not the subject of formal discussion. I believe now, more certainly than I did when I spoke here on 27 April, that any departure from this last principle would mean an end to the Commonwealth as we know it. . . .

The communiqué, with respect to this question, reads as follows: "Whilst reaffirming the traditional practice that Commonwealth conferences do not discuss the internal affairs of member countries, Ministers availed themselves of Mr. Louw's presence in London to have informal discussions with him about the racial situation in South Africa. During the informal discussions, Mr. Louw gave information and answered questions on the Union's policies, and the other Ministers conveyed to him their views on the South African problem. The Ministers emphasized that the Commonwealth itself is a multi-racial association and expressed the need to ensure good relations between all member states and peoples of the Commonwealth."

On 19 May 1960, in an address on "The Nation's Business", I said:

Much has been said regarding the question of South Africa and the policy of apartheid which has been in effect since 1948. Through the years I have taken a strong stand against racial discrimination. Indeed, I said long ago that the Indian population of Canada ought to have a representative in Parliament and should have the vote. After the present Government assumed office the Indian population was given its first representative in Parliament when James Gladstone was appointed a member of the Senate of Canada. And at the present session the Government brought in legislation which will, for the first time, give all Indians the vote in Canada without in any way taking away any of their rights.

I abhor discrimination and always have. As I said in the House of Commons several weeks ago, no nation can win a race war. The equality of man, whatever his race and colour, is a principle that must be accepted. This is so because the brotherhood of man denies any other view, and because Communism is advanced whenever Christians allow themselves to practice discrimination.

On 3 August 1960, Prime Minister Verwoerd announced that the Union government had decided to hold a referendum on the republican issue on 5 October 1960, and that if the result was in favour of a republican form of government, it was the intention of the Union government to make the customary request to the Commonwealth Prime Ministers that South Africa be permitted to retain its membership in the Commonwealth. He expressed confidence that the Commonwealth would welcome the membership of the Republic of South Africa.

On 9 August 1960, I received a letter from Prime Minister Tunku Abdul Rahman of the Federation of Malaya concerning a decision by his government prohibiting the import of all South African goods. During the summer, Ghana and Nigeria adopted similar policies. These Commonwealth governments thus joined India, which had banned South African imports for several years. I replied on 8 September:

I appreciate the feelings which inspired your boycott action but I find it difficult to believe that such action is likely to induce the Union to move or, to speak very frankly, that it is a desirable precedent to set. As I announced in Parliament in April, Canada does not contemplate placing any restrictions on its trade with South Africa. There is no evidence that I have seen which would indicate that any of the governmental or trade union boycotts in various parts of the world have had the slightest effect on Union policies. South Africa, with its abundant natural resources and industrious people, seems unlikely to be moved by outside economic pressure. In fact, such "foreign interference" might well strengthen those tendencies which we are seeking to reverse and at the same time cause real economic hardship for African labourers. . . .

I abhor the denial of fundamental freedoms in South Africa,

but if every country in the world refused to trade with every other nation whose domestic policies were repugnant to it, the international economic scene would be very distorted indeed. Moreover, it would do a disservice to peaceful international relations by limiting the opportunities for the healthy interchange of goods, ideas and people, which is the best hope for breaking down barriers of ignorance and prejudice.

I have no particular suggestion of my own to make at present regarding alternative positive measures, but I shall continue to give earnest consideration to this question. I have an open mind on the usefulness of a conference being held in the future and would be glad to hear more about this idea should there be widespread support for it. . . .

In a conversation with His Excellency Willem Dirske-Van-Shalkwyk, the South African High Commissioner to Canada, on 15 August 1960, I informed him that South Africa's optimism about automatic re-admission to the Commonwealth should it choose a republican constitution in its referendum was misplaced. I questioned the reasoning behind his government's decision to have a referendum at this time, given conditions of such uncertainty throughout Africa. I told him that Mr. Louw would not listen to any arguments advanced, even from those who had been good friends to South Africa and desired above everything else to remain so. I added that I had done everything I could to deny the introduction of a motion of censure in our House of Commons, which I believed would have been passed unanimously had the question come to a vote. For Prime Minister Verwoerd to delude himself into believing that the application of South Africa to rejoin the Commonwealth as a republic would receive a unanimous vote was to have no regard whatever for the world situation and the position taken by several Commonwealth countries. Mr. Dirske-Van-Shalkwyk took the stand that reason demanded that South Africa be re-admitted. I replied that, as one with experience in the courts as counsel for the defence, whatever the demands of reason might dictate, no jury with four of the jurymen being either brothers or close relations of some of the Crown witnesses would ever bring in a verdict for the defence.

The South African plebiscite, held on 5 October, excluded all the non-whites (who constituted 80 per cent of the population) but included the electorate of South West Africa (thus defying a large body of world opinion which regarded this territory as an international mandate and not as an integral part of the Union). Subsequently, the government announced that on 31 May 1961 a republican constitution would be proclaimed which would be virtually identical with the existing one except for the exchange of President for the Crown.

I did not see how I could support South Africa's re-admission if the Union government continued to refuse to pay even lip service to the concept of racial equality. I was convinced that major concessions were unlikely, and judged also that public opinion in general in Canada was so aroused on this issue that unless the South Africans made some move, I could not, against my personal devotion to the equality of all human beings regardless of colour or race, adopt at the next Prime Ministers' meeting an attitude as favourable to South Africa as I had had at the last meeting. When the moderate wing of Dr. Verwoerd's party favoured a few parliamentary seats for the half-caste Cape Coloureds, the Union Prime Minister rejected even this, and stated that his party would have to "stand like walls of granite" on the race issue.

By early January 1961, I began to wonder if the onus could be placed on the Government of South Africa to make necessary concessions on the race question; if, as an alternative, it would be possible to put the Union government on probation by allowing it a conditional re-entry into the Commonwealth. I realized my past statements on South African racial policy, taken together with the passing of the Canadian Bill of Rights, had created a general expectation that I would either advocate or support a move to expel South Africa from the Commonwealth. But South Africa's outstanding record in two world wars and her historical connection with the Commonwealth made it impossible for me conscientiously to assume the responsibility to vote for her expulsion without a further opportunity being given her government to change its racial policies. South Africa, however, indicated she would not accept a qualified re-entry or a period of probation that would permit the main decision to be deferred. Moreover, I did not think from our soundings that all the other Prime Ministers would be prepared to assent to this proposal. Nor did there appear to be any means of leaving the subject without action because, in the absence of a decision, South Africa would cease to be a member of the Commonwealth at the end of May 1961. This would require interpretation by the various Prime Ministers: *ex post facto* decision-making was not a desirable course.

I have been charged with driving South Africa out of the Commonwealth. At the Prime Ministers' Conference on 13 March 1961, I again appealed to Dr. Verwoerd to take some measure which would indicate that he was prepared to move towards according some representation to those South Africans who were at present disenfranchised. He and Mr. Louw ridiculed the suggestion. In reply to his observation about the lack of representation of North American Indians in the Canadian Parliament, I patiently explained that although they had full voting rights, they constituted only some six to eight per cent of the Canadian electorate and were not sufficiently concentrated in any one area to form a majority; accordingly special measures had been taken to represent their interests in Parliament. When Prime Minister Verwoerd handed me a clipping from the morning press indicating that a black man had been denied admission to a leading hotel in Edmonton, I found my position rather difficult. I could not argue effectively that the question of civil rights was within the determination of the provinces. I had to admit there was discrimination in Canada. I pointed out that there was discrimination everywhere in the world; certainly we had it in Canada. But it was individual or group discrimination, not a state-declared policy, and that there was a vast difference between the two. Discrimination cannot be removed by statute. A government can declare against it, can prevent its active implementation, but unless there is a change of heart on the part of the persons concerned, it will remain at their level. I found it hard to understand why it was (and why it still is) that in the enlightened state of the Union of South Africa discrimination against the blacks and the coloured not only had been given official sanction, but had been upheld and dignified by scriptural quotation.

On 13 March, I told my fellow Prime Ministers there could be no gainsaying that the long history of close relations between Canada and South Africa had recently been clouded by the racial policy of the Union. This policy was repugnant to the Canadian people. So long as it was possible to regard this as a purely internal affair of South Africa, the Canadian government had not expressed any serious criticism; but now any racial question was bound to have international repercussions, and the attitude of Commonwealth countries to this question would be closely watched all over the world. The Canadian government believed that some public recognition of the multi-racial character of the Commonwealth was necessary if the association was to be preserved. All members of the Commonwealth should subscribe to the principle of non-discrimination between human beings on the grounds of race or colour. This was essential, and a declaration to this effect should be issued by the Conference.

In our discussions the next day, I agreed with Mr. Menzies about the dangers of attempting to interfere with the domestic policies of a member government. But South Africa's racial policies had such far-reaching effect that their impact was international rather than domestic. A declaration of Commonwealth principles was not a notice to South Africa to quit; it was rather a statement of abiding principles to which the Commonwealth adhered. It might be true that some of the member countries fell short of the ideals it expressed (Dr. Verwoerd had taken particular exception to the domestic policies of the Nkrumah government); but it was essential for the preservation of the Commonwealth itself and for its standing in the eyes of the world that they should declare and recognize their faith in the principle of non-discrimination on grounds of race or colour to which they had indeed already subscribed by adhering to the Charter of the United Nations; there was no principle other than non-discrimination which could unite the Commonwealth. Such a declaration should not be regarded as an attempt to sit in judgment on the South African government.

At our meeting on the afternoon of 14 March, I read out the last paragraph of the draft communiqué: "They considered that this policy [apartheid] was inconsistent with the basic ideals on which the unity and influence of the Commonwealth rest, and with the Charter of the United Nations. They affirm their belief that for all Commonwealth governments, it should be an objective of policy to build in their countries a structure of society which offers equality of opportunity for all, irrespective of race, colour or creed." I asked Dr. Verwoerd whether he would accept this in the communiqué. He refused. He offered a revised version which I considered unacceptable.

The impasse over the communiqué continued in our discussions the next afternoon. Finally Mr. Macmillan suggested that we adjourn for tea. When we returned after twenty minutes or so, Dr. Verwoerd announced: "In the circumstances I wish formally to withdraw my request for South Africa to remain a member of the Commonwealth after she becomes a republic on 31 May next."

I greatly regretted the South African decision. As I told the House of Commons on 17 March 1961: "We tried to do whatever was humanly possible to avoid a break without making a sacrifice of basic principles. South Africa sought consent on the ground that continued membership was a virtual formality." When she finally accepted that this was not the case, she withdrew of her own volition. As a footnote, I liked Prime Minister Verwoerd. When I saw him and Mrs. Verwoerd at Buckingham Palace the final evening of the Conference, there was no suggestion that anything had happened to either surprise or shock them.

In retrospect, I consider it fortunate that the South Africans withdrew their application. Had this issue remained before us, a vote would have taken place. Regardless of how the votes were cast, the Commonwealth would have been destroyed. I was not alone among the Prime Ministers in regarding as intolerable any association of nations which subjected its members to decisions by a majority vote. Had it come to a vote, South Africa's application would have been turned down. The majority of Prime Ministers were committed to this course. It is probable that the only votes in favour of South Africa would have come from the white members of the Commonwealth. A division on this issue along racial lines would have ended the Commonwealth. Had South Africa been re-admitted, without any amelioration of apartheid, where would Britain, Australia, New Zealand, and Canada be today? South Africa has become a pariah among nations, virtually a world outlaw. If the four founding nations of the Commonwealth had refused to stand for the abiding principle of liberty, a principle which all the nations of the Commonwealth were presumed to uphold, what could the future bring except continuing pressure from the African and Asian members to expel South Africa, and criticism of the older members for crass hypocrisy. The apartheid issue was not about to die. Our high principles, and with them the Commonwealth, might have disappeared for naught.

It did not take long for those who were initially outraged by reports that I was the only white Prime Minister to take a lead on the apartheid issue at the 1961 Commonwealth Conference to realize that any other course of action would have been fatal to the Commonwealth concept. When I talked with the Right Honourable Earl Attlee on 22 May 1961, he told me that our course had been the right one, and that in his opinion the day was not far off when the blacks in South Africa would form secret societies and massacre all the whites. The events of 1976 in South Africa indicate that at last "the winds of change", to use Harold Macmillan's phrase, are blowing. They confirm that there will be the blood-bath that I feared. Today South Africa has the support of no nation, while to her north there are millions of blacks not unwilling to go to war. The white population of South Africa are as specks of sand when compared with the continent's blacks.

On 25 February 1963, I was made a Freeman of the City of London. This was a great honour. The Freedom of the City of London is a gift, and the greatest civic distinction to which any man or woman can aspire. No one can demand it; no wealth can buy it; no power command it. The occasion gave me the opportunity to reflect upon the Commonwealth. I said in my address at the Guildhall:

Confederation for Canada was a typical accomplishment of the

British instinct for government meeting the needs of the democratic impatience of her peoples overseas. That process continues today to create new nations in many parts of the world.

The Commonwealth is the only proven pattern of mutual tolerance, understanding, and co-operation, whose principles show the pathway to a world at peace through goodwill among men.

The Commonwealth has not disintegrated as the sceptics have so often prophesied, but has flowered into the fullness of a free association of peoples such as the world has never seen.

Many trials and difficulties have had to be met. Others will arise.

Was it not Rossetti who asked, "Does the road wind uphill all the way?", and promptly answered: "Yes, to the very end."

These difficulties will be met and I foresee a continuing expansion of the Commonwealth in the years ahead. Its base has been so broadened since the last war that no democratic nation which would desire to join us should or would be denied admission. This is the dream and the reality of the new Commonwealth.

In these last few years thirteen new nations have attained independence and have chosen to remain in the Commonwealth.

Two have left, and one elected not to join. Yet the peoples of these nations know that the light is still burning in the window. It may be that in the fullness of time they will join us in our faith that within the Commonwealth is to be found a political, economic, and spiritual ideology that in its principles, in brotherhood, and in co-operation, meets the needs and aspiration of the human soul.

"And from this hour
The hearts of brothers govern in our loves
And sway our great design."

As we go forward together there is work to be done—internally, in the strengthening of the Commonwealth; externally, in bringing its influence to bear more and more on the problems of the world.

25 & 26. In October 1958 Prime Minister and Mrs. Diefenbaker left Ottawa on a six-week world tour that took them to fourteen countries. *(Left)* In Paris Mr. Diefenbaker had his first meeting with General Charles de Gaulle. *(Below)* A few days later he conferred with Chancellor Konrad Adenauer in Bonn.

27 & 28. Following meetings with President Ayub Khan of Pakistan, Mr. and Mrs. Diefenbaker visited the fabled Khyber Pass. Near the Pass the Prime Minister received this gift of goats and, following tradition, touched them, and returned them as presents to the donors. *(Below)* On his arrival in Delhi, Mr. Diefenbaker is greeted by Prime Minister Nehru.

29 & 30. *(Above)* Prime Minister and Mrs. Menzies welcome the Diefenbakers to Canberra. *(Left)* Mr. Diefenbaker greets Queen Elizabeth at Torbay, Newfoundland, at the beginning of her 1959 visit to Canada.

31. *(Above left)* The official opening of the St. Lawrence Seaway in June 1959, the realization of a dream of more than a century, was graced by the presence of Her Majesty Queen Elizabeth, Prince Philip, and President and Mrs. Eisenhower.

32. *(Left)* Prime Minister Harold Macmillan during his March 1959 visit to Ottawa.

33. *(Above)* A visit to Sir Winston and Lady Churchill in London, May 1960.

34, 35, 36, & 37. (Above left) A very proud moment — the opening of the South Saskatchewan River Dam project, 30 May 1959. (Below left) With the Prime minister's brother, Elmer Diefenbaker, Christmas 1960. (Above) In France, on the fortieth anniversary of the Armistice, 11 November 1958, at the Verdun Monument. (Left) Governor General Georges Vanier escorts President John F. Kennedy and the Prime Minister through the grounds at Rideau Hall, May 1961.

38 & 39. *(Above)* In January 1961 at a special convocation Mrs. Diefenbaker received a Doctor of Laws (honoris causa) degree from Brandon College. *(Below)* The thirteenth Prime Minister of Canada, the Right Honourable John G. Diefenbaker, M.P.

Conceived and born in London, an institution that has made a contribution to justice and freedom and to ever-rising economic standards among all its people, the Commonwealth has much unfinished business yet to do.

This is no hour for little aims and big fears. The Commonwealth needs to go forward in the things of the spirit in strength, for it has a mission for all mankind.

We must fully explore what can be done to expand trade within the Commonwealth as well as with all like-minded nations. We must expand the educational and cultural exchanges within the Commonwealth. We must produce greater designs for assistance to the under-developed countries within the Commonwealth.

We have our responsibilities as well outside our own fellowship.

In the last few years the united strength of the Commonwealth membership has espoused the great causes of the brotherhood of man, and the folly of the armaments race.

At the 1961 Conference of Prime Ministers we decided that racial discrimination as a policy was not compatible with the Commonwealth's abiding principles.

At the same Conference a joint and united stand was taken for peace and disarmament by advocating abolition of both nuclear and conventional weapons and the establishment of a world authority for inspection and control. This was a forward step, being the first time in peace that the members of the Commonwealth have acted as a collective influence on world affairs.

My Lord Mayor, as I have already said, this day brings back to us the glory of our milestones and our memories.

How can we hold such memories in our hearts and not be moved?

Before us lies the far-flung community that God has built by your hands and the hands of its member nations everywhere in the world.

Shall we not resolve to strive to expand the concepts, for the good of all peoples, without difference of kind or race or origin? To strive for their freedom, for their right to lift themselves up from day to day and behold the things they have hoped for?

And may we not lift up *our* eyes to the great tracts of life yet to be conquered in the cause of righteous peace, of those yearnings which lie in the hearts of peoples and outlast all wars and errors of men?

. . . My Lord Mayor, I thank you from the heart that I have been so honoured and am now a Freeman of the greatest city of the world.

I can offer in return for so great an honour and privilege only my humble and heartiest gratitude.

And as your newest Honorary Freeman, I pledge undying loyalty to one of your own company, our most Gracious Queen, whom we are proud to serve as The Queen of Canada.

CHAPTER EIGHT

※

I DON'T KNOW how many meetings I addressed or how many miles I travelled during the 1958 election campaign. I am told that I spoke to eighty-six major meetings and travelled seventeen thousand miles. Each meeting and mile became part of the next; something indefinable made me forget the long hours, the labour, the distance. Everywhere, people raised their eyes to see the vision of Canada's greatness, and realized something of their own greatness. Then, as today, they yearned for those things that the Liberal Party since the days of Laurier has never been able to offer. "Where is Canada going?" was their question. I offered an answer. Canadians responded with their hearts, their hopes, their imagination. The "New Frontier" was North America's last frontier. It offered us a future uniquely Canadian; it offered us the opportunity to be uniquely ourselves. The response was overwhelming when I appealed to my fellow Canadians to "join with me":

Canadians, realize your opportunities! This is only the beginning. The future programme for the next five to seven years under a Progressive Conservative Government is one that is calculated to give young Canadians, motivated by a desire to serve, a lift in their hearts, faith in Canada's future, faith in her destiny. We will extend aid to economically sound railway projects, such as the Pine Point Railroad to Great Slave Lake.

We will press for hydro-electric development of the Columbia River, which now awaits completion of an agreement with the United States.

We're going to call a national convention on conservation to map a national conservation policy to extend the principles of farm rehabilitation to all Canada, to maintain a continuing study of soils and land use. We have under consideration a possible second Trans Canada Highway route.

There is a new imagination now. The Arctic. We intend to carry out the legislative programme of Arctic research, to develop Arctic routes, to develop those vast hidden resources the last few years have revealed. Plans to improve the St. Lawrence and the Hudson Bay Route. Plans to increase self-government in the Yukon and Northwest Territories. We can see one or two provinces there.

"One Canada" was my message in 1957; "One Canada" was my message in 1958. This continues to be my message; perhaps more than ever before. In 1958, I asked for a mandate:

It is for those things that I ask a mandate. These are the reasons that I appeal to the Canadian people, a mandate for a clear majority.

We need a clear majority to carry out this long-range plan, this great design, this blueprint for the Canada which her resources make possible.

I want to see Canadians given a transcendent sense of national purpose, such as Macdonald gave in his day. To safeguard our independence, restore our unity, a policy that will scrupulously respect the rights of the provinces, and at the same time build for the achievement of that one Canada, is the major reason why 35 of our 112 members in the House of Commons are sufficiently young to belong to the Young Progressive Conservatives. They caught that vision. I am here for the purpose, as a Canadian to give you a picture of the kind of Canada the long range plans that we have in mind will bring about.

Any political party can make promises. Indeed, Mr. St. Laurent uttered these words during the 1957 campaign: "An election promise is a mere cream-puff of a thing, with more air than substance in it." The Liberals had stood on their record in 1957 and had been repudiated by the electorate. We had been given the opportunity to make our promises good. I was prepared to be judged by our record. I could stand before an audience (as I did at Saskatoon on 13 February 1958), point to my government's Agricultural Stabilization Act, and say: "If the farmers of Western Canada, and throughout Canada in general, will read that Bill, they will find that it is the greatest single advance on behalf of agriculture ever made in the history of this country." When I told Prairie audiences, "One of the major reasons for my being in public life is to do something for Canadian agriculture," they knew the Conservative Party was no cream-puff affair. We had proven true to the faith the electorate had placed in us.

It was the Liberals who suffered a credibility gap with the public. When Mr. Pearson promised a $400 million temporary tax cut, he looked ridiculous. He and his Liberal high command had been aware of the impending economic crisis before the 1957 election when common economic prudence would have dictated a balanced budget, an easing of tight money, and the preparation of public works so that government expenditures would offset any decline in the public sector. His sudden discovery in February 1958 of the needs of the Canadian taxpayer, farmer, and small businessman smacked of hypocrisy. The electorate apparently came to the same conclusion.

One area that concerned me in particular during the

1958 campaign, one that generally has been lost sight of in the commentaries on this event, was what we could do to assist small business. I presented our platform on this question (a platform that was soon to become reality) at Brantford, Ontario, on 17 February:

Across this nation, as in every nation, small business constitutes to a major degree the backbone of small communities, and even larger communities, throughout our nation. For many months now, representatives of retailers and wholesalers met with representatives of the government in an effort to deal with the question of small business. Small businessmen throughout this nation—and I have had letters from them in great numbers—realize the desire of this government to help small business. In return, they have been anxious to do anything that they can to assist in furthering our success in the achievement of their purpose. They have urged that there should be some focal point within the administrative machinery of government to which they can refer their problems.

Consequently, it is our intention to set up a Small Business Section within the administrative machinery of government, to which any small business organization, or small businessman, or anyone concerned with the general field of welfare of small business, can make representations and receive advice. A particular group of retailers and wholesalers has set up their own advisory committee in order that they will have a ready means of presenting to the government the concerted views of those they represent. And I say to small business in this connection—that it is our intention that any individual or organization shall have ready access to the government's Small Business Section, whose function it will be to maintain a continuous study of the problems of small business, to act as a liaison between the Cabinet and small business in presenting the problems and needs of the business community, and to advise on the measures necessary to meet these problems.

This office will also look into the establishment and setting up of a Small Business Loan Fund, and recommend the terms on which economic assistance shall be given to such Fund.

In Chapter Three, I dealt with my government's positive and comprehensive action on the Atlantic Provinces Adjustment Grants, which began 1 April 1958, and our legislation to help develop power resources in these provinces. The slow rate of economic growth in this area affected one and three-quarter million people, or ten per cent of Canada's population. In 1926, average income per capita in the three Maritime Provinces was 38 per cent below the average for the six other provinces; in 1939 it was 32 per cent; in 1946 it was 24 per cent; but in 1955, it was 37 per cent (including Newfoundland)—a disparity greater than in 1939. I found Premiers Stanfield, Flemming, and Matheson of Nova Scotia, New Brunswick, and Prince Edward Island quite responsive to my views concerning assistance to their provinces.

Premier Smallwood of Newfoundland had a disposition that was anything but in keeping with what one expects from a provincial leader. One could not help having trouble with him. He had a popular appeal and a considerable ability as a public speaker, but his actions showed that he did not understand that the essence of democracy is the right to disagree. One example that I will never forget occurred during one of our visits to St. John's. We landed at Argentia. Our route from the air base took us through a number of small villages. In one of them, there was a sign in front of a pub that read: "Welcome John". My information is that Smallwood's supporters were annoyed and began action to have that old soldier's liquor licence cancelled. Smallwood made one major slip during the 1958 campaign, however. I had a meeting in St. John's on 19 February. We arrived late because of fog over the Avalon Peninsula. Prior to my arrival, the Premier handed out a copy of a letter he had delivered to me. To his discomfiture, I used that letter in my address to indicate that despite his noisy declarations that the Diefenbaker government would be defeated, he really didn't believe a word of it. His letter asked me to take action in the new Parliament in support of amendments to our legislation on assistance to hydro-electric power development. I simply read that portion of his letter to my audience, and thanked him for his powers of prophecy which indicated that the election result had been predetermined.

Political prophecies, however, carry no guarantees. Sir John Macdonald once wrote (I have the original letter): "Any election is like a horse-race, in that you can tell more about it the next day." I made my election predictions on the basis of a combination of individual summaries from each of the constituencies and on my personal reaction following meetings in each province. I knew that things were going well, certainly as well as they had gone for Mr. St. Laurent in 1949, when he elected 190 Members. I simply could not believe that we would break the back of the Liberal Party in Quebec; not since Sir John Macdonald's greatest electoral triumph in 1882 had the Conservative Party made such an impact on Quebec. However, the Honourable Daniel Johnson, in a letter to my mother, wrote that everything was going well for me in Quebec and that Conservatives would win in at least thirty constituencies.

On election day, Olive and I were at home in Prince Albert. The first result from the East did not show great promise; in five elections, I never had any real political success in Newfoundland. In 1958, we retained our two seats, out of a possible seven. When I saw these results, I wondered if my hopes of victory would be fulfilled. With the assistance of Allister Grosart, I began to draft speeches to cover both eventualities. Then came the first counts from Nova Scotia: we were leading in all twelve ridings. I stopped thinking about one of the eventualities.

In P.E.I., we led in all four. We were faring well in New Brunswick. Before the polls closed in Prince Albert, I knew that Quebec had come our way with fifty Conservative victories. Ontario gave us sixty-seven; Manitoba, fourteen; Saskatchewan, sixteen; Alberta, seventeen; and British Columbia, eighteen. The Conservative Party in 1958 received the largest majority in the House of Commons ever recorded in the history of Canada: two hundred and eight seats.

In my message to the Canadian people that night, I spoke of the first inaugural speech of President Lincoln, who said we should rely on: "Intelligence, patriotism and Christianity and the firm reliance on Him, who has never yet forsaken this favoured land." I had asked my countrymen to "catch the vision"; they had, overwhelmingly. I had my mandate; the "tidal wave at the polls" merely confirmed Canada's "date with destiny". On 1 April, Olive and I returned to Ottawa. There was work to be done.

On a normal morning, as Prime Minister, I would get up at half past five or a quarter to six. On first rising, I would have half a grapefruit or an orange and coffee. Then I would dictate memoranda, letters, etc., for an hour or so before I set off on my morning walk. I did not have security guards to follow me wherever I went; I've never had them. I did take the obvious precaution of not always walking the same route, and thereby inviting trouble. Often I would walk along Sussex Drive as far as the Mint and back, or across to Rideau Hall Park, or up John Street, or into Eastview (now Vanier), or in the general direction of the Japanese Embassy in Rockcliffe. I would try for a mile and a half each day, at about 140 to 160 paces a minute. When I returned home, my wife would join me at breakfast. I arrived at the office, ready for the day ahead, by eight o'clock. How the present Prime Minister can take the days and weeks of holidays he does is beyond me. Although I never considered myself overworked, a 14-hour day was the norm.

On becoming Prime Minister, I cut out a lot of the frills that were part of Mr. St. Laurent's routine. For example, he attended dinners at various embassies and high commissions. During my period in office, however, the number of diplomatic missions in Ottawa increased to around sixty. If I were to visit each of them once a year for two and a half hours or three hours, that would be, say, one hundred and eighty hours; when I had them back, even six at a time, the total time spent in often aimless social activity amounted to thirty eight-hour days. I did away with this.

When I arrived at my office each morning, the first person I saw was my Executive Assistant. To begin with, I looked at the messages from foreign countries and from our various missions abroad, then at the background papers covering Cabinet business, reports from the United Nations, and my correspondence for the day, including letters from private individuals. There were many letters that did not require my personal attention. I would ask from time to time, however, to see random samples of these, just to make certain that they were being answered properly. Then, there were discussions of expected developments in the House, and meetings with various ministers who often wanted to speak to me before Cabinet if they had a particular problem. I tried at all times to make myself easily accessible. Incidentally, this applied to the man in the street as well as to those who were highly placed. There was never a time when I did not want to find out what people were thinking. I recall one occasion when a farmer from Alberta had an appointment with me. An important Canadian industrialist arrived and demanded to see me right away. Well, he had to wait his turn. He simply couldn't understand this, that a man of his importance should have to wait while this "rustic", as he described him, got in to see me first.

More often than not, I had lunch at my desk. Once or twice a week I would have lunch at the Cabinet table in the Parliamentary Restaurant. The Rideau Club I rarely visited. It is one of the most prestigious private clubs in Canada. I was the only Prime Minister who did not seek membership in it.

When the House was sitting, I tried to be at my Commons desk as often as possible, although I did not manage this to the extent that Prime Minister St. Laurent had. I felt it important that, as Prime Minister, I should participate in the debates under our parliamentary system, but this requires a lot of effort if one is not content to have others prepare final drafts of his material. When I participate in debate, I do not recite or read scripts, I enter into the current of discussion. To me, this is what Parliament is all about.

On the question of prime-ministerial decision-making, one group has said I delayed everything; another has claimed I decided things too quickly. I don't know how to reconcile these two points of view. When a matter was difficult and complex, when there was deep uncertainty, I took my time before deciding. Time is often the politician's best friend. Sir John Macdonald was called "Old Tomorrow". I read extensively, I read all the recommendations that came in, the suggestions of various departments, and then I would get the Clerk of the Privy Council to fill in the areas where I required more information, and on that basis I would make my decision. I might add parenthetically that the official upon whom I relied most, and who gave me a loyalty and an objectivity that causes me to give him a special reference, was the Clerk of the Privy Council, Mr. Robert B. Bryce. He was a man of great ability, indefatigable in research, with a wide knowledge of domestic and international affairs, and, above all, he was a man who at no time allowed political considerations to divert him from giving me his innermost thoughts. Obviously, the final responsibility for decision rested on the Prime Minister, and on no one else. To use the words of Harry Truman, over each Prime Minister's desk there is an imaginary plaque that reads, "The buck stops here." He takes the best advice he can get, but decisions on vital matters must be by his determination. When things turned out right, often a particular Cabinet Minister would do his best to take all the bows. But when things turned out wrong, the "old man" was always the goat.

In response to the criticism that my government could not act swiftly to meet the pressing needs of the nation, let me give one example to the contrary. When the non-operating unions of the two national railways called a strike for 3 December 1960, the government decided that the strike was not in the national interest. We had no desire to intervene directly, but circumstances left us no choice. Was the national economy to be plunged into chaos? The answer was no. When efforts at conciliation failed, a bill was introduced on 29 November 1960 to provide for the continuation of railway operations. The House voted on this legislation at 4.30 p.m. on 2 December; the Senate approved it at 6.00 p.m.; it was signed into law by the Governor General at 6.30 p.m. Here was decision, together with parliamentary debate and immediate action. To digress for a moment, never did we adopt the methods of labour settlement embraced by our successors. The "Pearson formula" for ending labour disputes affecting the national interest, for example the 1966 settlement with the Montreal longshoremen, set off in Canada a spiralling inflation from which we have yet to recover. This is a subject about which I will have more to say in my next volume. The average rate of inflation in Canada during my period in office was 1.2 per cent: "the lowest in the Western world", as President Kennedy, no friend of my government, once admitted.

In advancing my views on Parliament and politics, I am fully conscious that there is more than one side to every question. But memoirs are by definition a series of personal views. The experience of being Prime Minister affords one a unique perspective on events and institutions. Journalists may write their worm's-eye views. Prime Ministers deal with broader vistas. Each undoubtedly has its place in the history of a nation.

When we were in office, I decided there would never be any effective examination of government expenditures, proper or improper, as long as the government controlled the Public Accounts Committee through the nomination of its chairman. I decided this must end. In consequence, we established the practice which allowed a Liberal Member, Alan Macnaughton (now a Senator), to serve as Chairman. It was a system that worked well. In the whole period of my prime-ministership, we spent a total capital outlay of a mere $18,000 on the Prime Minister's residence. I had to pay $5,000 a year rental, as had Mr. St. Laurent and as would Mr. Pearson—a situation that no longer applies. This rental, I might add, was not tax-deductible. As Prime Minister, I had an annual car allowance of $2,000 (as had all ministers) but had personally to pay half the cost of the chauffeur's salary. Today, the Prime Minister drives a bullet-proof car that cost the taxpayers $75,000. Unfortunately, the philosophy today is spend, spend, tax, tax; that it is the public's money is of no account. A Prime Minister does much to set the mood of government. I insisted that expenditures should not be made unless essential to the needs of the people.

In caucus, I would place before our Members those matters that were to come up in the House. Often, I would advance arguments in favour of propositions that I did not in fact have in mind at all, in order to have them challenged. I wanted the caucus to be alive to the issues; to challenge and to weigh. Nothing was more helpful when I advanced a proposition and asked, "Would this be the proper course?" than to find that there were Members who would say, "No," and who were prepared and able to argue the reasons for their opinion. Often these presentations were very full, very thorough, and very convincing. There must be give and take in caucus, otherwise private Members do not believe that they are taking their proper part in the process of government. I believe that one of our major difficulties after the 1958 election was that we had too large a majority. Perhaps we would have been much better off had we only elected the one hundred and ninety won by Mr. St. Laurent in 1949.

Contrary to the practice of recent years, the ministers in my government attended the House of Commons. The idea that ministers ought not to attend because they are so overworked, which with one or two exceptions is not true in the first place, indicates a general contempt for the House of Commons. Further, one of my admonitions to Cabinet was that when a member of the Opposition advanced something worthwhile, I wanted to know about it forthwith. There was never any hesitation on my part to improve a piece of legislation. Prime Ministers Mackenzie King and St. Laurent were occasionally amenable to this approach, and to a lesser degree, so indeed was Pearson; but there is none of that today.

In the 1958 election, the Liberal Party was reduced to forty-nine Members. Social Credit was wiped out completely. The CCF retained only eight of its twenty-five Members. I think now that it was a mistake on my part to agree that the CCF should be treated as a separate party in the House, with its leader, in consequence, being given the right to speak on every issue. Parliament is stronger when there is a two-party House of Commons. As I wrote in Volume I, the bifurcation or trifurcation of recognized Opposition parties simply does not permit the House of Commons to operate as effectively as it should. It is a denial of the basic principle of Parliament in the British tradition that there is a Government and an Opposition. The eight CCF Members should have been recognized only as independent Members, not as a party. Given so large a majority, however, I feared that if I took this stand, it would be interpreted as autocratic. It might have been the course of political wisdom to have left the Opposition to guard against the abuse of political power by the government instead of assuming this responsibility myself. I sought to establish a new style, or, rather, to re-establish an old style, in the operation of the House of Commons. I acted to return government from the corporate level of the St. Laurent operation back to the democratic level.

Parliament is the most maligned of our institutions. In every generation it has been the object of criticism, but in the last few years all our institutions, the monarchy and Parliament included, are under attack. Some are critical because of a desire to improve; others desire to annihilate our traditional institutions and symbols. Parliament, of course, has been a favourite subject of satirists and columnists for three hundred years. Among questions most commonly asked of it are: "Why doesn't Parliament get down to work?"; "Why does it talk so much?"; "Why is there an Opposition?"; "Why shouldn't Members go to Parliament and all unite?"

Parliament can deal only with legislative matters that the Cabinet decides to bring before it, except for the very limited right of the private Member to introduce bills other than money bills. The Cabinet places before Parliament its measures, and in discussion changes and improvements can be effected. Sir Ivor Jennings, a recognized authority on Parliament, wrote, and rightly: "The function of Parliament is not to govern but to criticize, to modify Government policy and to educate public opinion." To those who say that Parliament should be turning out legislation in quantity, my answer is that its mission is freedom, and the assurance that all the people shall receive justice. Parliament is not a slot machine into which a slug is dropped to produce ready-made legislation.

Parliament is a place honoured by tradition and hallowed by the greatness of its history. By tradition, nobody is allowed within its confines. The gallery is presumed to be empty, even though a portion of the gallery has been set aside for the press. Visitors to the gallery are expected to observe the proprieties; it is not a place for private conversations. At any time a Member may rise in his place and say, "Mr. Speaker, I spy strangers." The galleries are then emptied of all observers. This course was followed once or twice during the Second World War.

The Members of the Government and the Opposition sit eighteen feet apart. That is a distance at which only the points of opposing swords can touch. The Queen and the Governor General are not allowed into the Commons Chamber. In the days of Pym and Elliott and Hampton and Charles I there was a practical reason. Today it is tradition. Freedom of speech is the essence of Parliament, but the exercise of that freedom is circumscribed by a code of decent behaviour and respect for the rights of others.

Parliament's paramount responsibility is to preserve freedom. Parliament is the place in which abuses and grievances are aired and where the rights of the private citizen are preserved. Its authority is legislative, and with it is exercised executive and administrative control. Its major responsibility is to require that expenditures of the people's monies shall be kept under control and that taxation shall not be levied without its consent.

There is a widespread failure in this country to comprehend the institution of Parliament. The very continuity and stability of the system of British parliamentary democracy and the absence of any recent social or constitutional upheavals may have induced a measure of contempt bred of familiarity. As Walter Bagehot once observed: "The characteristic danger of great nations, like the Roman or the English, which have a long history of continuous creation, is that they may at last fail from not comprehending the great institutions which they have created." I do not argue that Parliament is perfect or that there must not be change to meet changing conditions.

I regret that I did not bring about a physical change in the House of Commons. I shared with Winston Churchill the opinion that there will never be any incentive to a full attendance in the House as long as there is a seat for every Member. There will never exist that cut and thrust of debate, without which good legislation is not possible, so long as there are desks. The House of Commons Chamber if cut down to three-quarters, if not half, its present size and the desks removed would be vastly improved. Then, no one could come in to read his speech, unless a Minister presenting a carefully detailed departmental report. In consequence of this physical change, the House would have rationalized its own procedure automatically, for no one could speak in debate unless he had some knowledge of his subject. The rule prohibiting the reading of speeches would be easily enforced. Parliament should be a place where there is discussion, debate, disagreement or agreement; a place where consensus is reached following argument and the presentation of varying views.

As to whether Parliament should be televised, I think it would be another effective means of ensuring attendance by Members. At the same time, this would provide an expanded source of information for the people as a whole. Today, because there is no television in the Commons Chamber, Ministers of the Crown often say the very antithesis of what they have expressed in the House during the abbreviated session before the television cameras outside the Commons' doors. There are, of course, Members and Ministers who realize that they would be shorn of some of their mystic power if exposed to the people through television. Expediency and hypocrisy are very quickly revealed by television. The performance of a Prime Minister, who makes only a handful of speeches in the House, and reads them at that, and who regards the House as an inconvenience and its Members as "nobodies", might appear as a revelation to Canadians if they were able to see it. There are, however, practical difficulties in televising Parliament: who is going to determine what shall be broadcast; who is going to allocate time between Government and Opposition Members? These, however, are problems that will only be solved in practice; the televising of Parliament should begin immediately.

Some have suggested that Parliament would be improved if we had a permanent Speaker of the House of Commons, as in Westminster. To begin with, this would be most difficult in a bilingual country. Others contend that the Speaker should not have to be elected as a Member of Parliament; that when he is chosen, he should be given a special, non-representative constituency in Ottawa (Parliament Hill has been suggested) set up for this purpose. I, for one, could not support it, among other reasons because Mr. Speaker is first among equals in the House of Commons. He can be this only when elected. How could he be the first commoner if he is not a commoner? Believing as I do in a non-partisan Speaker, however, and recognizing the difficulties in asking a person actively engaged in politics to totally dissociate himself from the partisan consideration of the party to which he belongs, I see merit in having an unwritten rule that once a Member is chosen as Speaker, he should not be opposed in his constituency by the party representing Her

Majesty's Loyal Opposition. If I may take the case of the Honourable Lucien Lamoureux, former Liberal Member for Stormont–Dundas, who was elected Speaker in 1966. His partisanship ended when he was chosen as Speaker. He endeavoured throughout his period in the Chair not only to act fairly but at the same time always to seem to act fairly. In the general election of 1968, he became an Independent. It was not a Conservative who ran against him but an NDP candidate. In the 1972 election, he was opposed by both Conservative and NDP candidates. In my opinion, this was not as it should have been.

While I am on the general subject, I might mention the question of dress in Parliament. The dignity of Parliament is an important consideration. Parliament is the repository of Canada's freedom. I can just imagine what the House of Commons would look like if Members developed a propensity for coming into the House in shorts, sandals, and open shirts. The Honourable Member for Mount Royal, now the Right Honourable Prime Minister, had to be taught a lesson in this regard during the 1966 Session. Surely proper dress is to be expected. I do not advocate a return to the days when everyone wore silk hats and morning coats. When I was first elected to the House, there were still one or two who wore their hats in the House, and a Member could do it today if he chose. This hasn't been done, however, since the "people's Member" from Toronto, Tommy Church, left our company.

One of my regrets is that we did not abolish closure in the House of Commons when I was Prime Minister. In the debate on the Address in Reply to the Speech from the Throne on 16 October 1957, I said:

... There is need for careful examination, full consideration and debate that is not muzzled in anticipation by the application of closure.

I mention this as one of the most serious examples of the curtailment of the ancient rights of Parliament. . . . the essence of Parliamentary government is full discussion. You say, what are we going to do about that? Well closure had its place, if properly used, in order to prevent an unjustifiable action on the part of the opposition as against the government of the day after a debate lasting for a very considerable period of time. We found out, however, that closure, necessary as it has been proven to be in times past, not only in our own Parliament but in other Parliaments within the Commonwealth, under our rules constitutes an open invitation to the curtailment of fair and reasonable debate, indeed to the imprisonment of Parliament by the government.

During the election campaign I said, and I am unchanged in this viewpoint, that having regard to its potential danger, as was evidenced so clearly so short a time ago, we intend at the first opportunity to move the necessary motion in order to remove closure from the rules of the House of Commons, to the end that Parliament will be restored to something of its ancient glory.

On 9 December 1957, a motion for the repeal of Standing Order 33 of the House of Commons was introduced in my name, as Prime Minister. Standing Order 33 read as follows:

Immediately before the Order of the Day for resuming an adjourned debate is called, or if the House be in Committee of the Whole, or of Supply, or of Ways and Means, any Minister of the Crown, standing in his place, who shall have given notice at a previous sitting of his intention to do so, may move that the debate shall not be further adjourned, or that the further consideration of any resolution or resolutions, clause or clauses, section or sections, preamble or preambles, title or titles, shall be the first business of the committee, and shall not further be postponed; and in either case such questions shall be decided without debate or amendment; and if the same shall be resolved in the affirmative, no Member shall thereafter speak more than once, or longer than twenty minutes in any such adjournment debate; or, if in Committee, on any such resolution, clause, section, preamble or title; and if such adjourned debate or postponed consideration shall not have been resumed or concluded before one o'clock in the morning, no member shall rise to speak after that hour, but all such questions as must be decided in order to conclude such adjourned debate or postponed consideration, shall be decided forthwith.

The constitutional argument for the abolition of closure turns on the distinction between responsible and irresponsible obstruction by the Opposition in the House. Irresponsible obstruction is a deliberate attempt to frustrate the will of the majority. Sir Wilfrid Laurier believed that this form of irresponsibility would be severely punished by a free electorate. Obstruction is adopted by a responsible Opposition only when it is convinced that its views correspond more closely to the basic interests of the people than do those of the government. By obstruction, which might better be termed "extended debate", the Opposition can attempt to force an issue to be submitted to the electorate. Presumably, it would not risk such a course unless it had good reason to believe its stand would be endorsed by the people. Without this ultimate weapon of extended debate, a parliamentary minority would be virtually powerless should a dominant majority fail to understand that democracy is as much a matter of gaining the consent of minorities as it is of giving effect to the will of the majority.

To give an example: when Sir Wilfrid Laurier introduced the Canada–United States Reciprocity Bill in the House of Commons in 1911, the House sat for weeks on end. The Opposition carried on the fight for more than four months. Laurier refused to resort to closure. Finally, the life of Parliament expired. The government was forced to go to the country and was defeated. Sir Wilfrid Laurier took the stand that as a great issue was before the people, the Opposition was exercising its parliamentary rights and discharging its duty. He, knowing Parliament, did not deride the Opposition as obstructionists. He was a great parliamentarian, as was the Right Honourable Ernest Lapointe, who held the same views.

In 1957, I was prepared to take it as proven that the then existing rule of closure was dangerous and contrary to the spirit of parliamentary government. For this reason, it merited abolition. With Laurier, I believed that for very practical reasons the abolition of closure was unlikely to tempt minorities to frustrate capriciously the will of the majority. I considered that abolition would increase the awareness of all parties and all Members of their individual and collective reponsibility for the effective working of the parliamentary system. Aware of man's inherent limitations, and aware that the majority is not always right in the short run, and is sometimes prone to trample on the rights of minorities, I believed in the necessity of setting up rules to check the abuse of power or the concentration of too great powers in the hands of any group, and not excepting a majority ruling in the name of the people. Thus I served a notice of intention to proceed with the abolition of closure at the next session of Parliament.

The election intervened, and in the new Parliament there always seemed so many more urgent items demanding our attention. It is a fact that I felt there was no urgency; I believed that never again would any government in Canada impose closure after what had happened in the Pipeline Debate. However obstreperous the Opposition became, I was never once tempted to invoke closure. On 25 March 1962, I wrote to Oakley Dalgleish, editor of the *Globe and Mail*: "Tomorrow I am bringing in the motion dealing with the subject of closure. That was one of the promises I made and have not yet carried out which is most often referred to. I know there are varying views on the subject. A re-reading of the debate in May of 1956 on the pipeline bill is convincing evidence that never again will any government dare to bring in closure. That being so, the argument that the power is needed in the rules becomes academic." That I was wrong need hardly be said. We, on the Conservative side of the House, had learned the lesson of the 1956 Pipeline Debate. I was convinced that the Liberals had learned as well. We were to discover in 1965, however, that the Liberals had learned nothing from their experience.

On the question of Senate reform, I told the House on 27 June 1955:

While it is interesting to speculate as to whether or not the Senate could be abolished by an amendment passed by the House of Commons and the Senate—and I believe it could without any resort to Westminster, provided there was in fact a majority in the Senate desirous of achieving the execution of that body—it is my personal belief that it would be the derogation of one of the major constitutional foundations upon which Confederation was built. Therefore, I do not go with those who believe we should end the Senate, but I do believe that the responsibility facing people today, and in particular facing this Parliament, is that it should do its part—if I may use a phrase of Dr. R. A. MacKay—not to end but to mend the Senate.

I added that whether the British North America Act was regarded as a legislative act or as a "moral" compact among the provinces of Canada, "it was an agreement, and the Senate was a necessary and requisite part of that agreement." In my opinion, it followed, therefore, that general agreement of the provinces, the public, and both Houses of Parliament was an essential prerequisite of reform dealing with constitutional amendment, though not of reform requiring only changes in the rules and, more particularly, changes in the attitude of the government towards the Senate. I considered that effective reform must include both constitutional amendment and changes in legislative practice. I have not had reason since to substantially alter my views.

The constitutional functions of the Senate, as intended by the Fathers of Confederation, were to provide regional representation of the rights and interests of the provinces, to revise or suspend unwise or hasty decisions of the elected representatives of the people, and to "trim and polish" the bills coming to it from the House of Commons. Sir John Macdonald described its legislative functions as follows:

There would be no use of an upper house if it did not exercise, when it thought proper, the right of opposing or amending or postponing the legislation of the lower house. It would be of no value whatever were it a mere chamber for registering the decrees of the lower house. It must be an independent house, having a free action of its own, for it is only valuable as being a regulating body, calmly considering the legislation initiated by the popular branch, and preventing any hasty or ill-considered legislation which may come from that body, but it will never set itself in opposition against the deliberate and understood wishes of the people.

At best, these expectations were never fully realized, and in recent years they had become little more than a memory.

In the 1920s, Mackenzie King made effective use of Senate reform as a rallying cry for the radical element in the Liberal Party. King and the Liberal Party thought of reform not as a means of increasing the usefulness and independence of the Senate, but of bringing the Senate, in his words, "into line with the Liberal government and the House of Commons". King preferred the method of "reform from within", which he sought by requiring every new Senator to pledge that he would "be prepared, once a measure passes the Commons, to give it his support". Senators would be appointed, he stated, "with that understanding, and as providence takes away a few older members, you will have a Senate pledged to bring about the reforms for which the administration stands." Although I was always curious to know the exact number of Liberal Senators who had taken the pledge, Mr. King would not reveal the figure. In fact, his only intent was to render the Senate subservient to the executive. Mackenzie King actually stated, in reply to a question from Agnes Macphail, "Well, I am reforming the Senate. As the Tory Senators die I am appointing good Liberals in their places." When he had achieved a Liberal majority in the Senate, he could quite honestly say that he had "reformed" the Senate. Some years before he accepted a Senate appointment for himself, Grattan O'Leary observed: "A Senatorship isn't a job, it's a title. Also it's a blessing, a stroke of good fate, something like drawing a royal straight flush in the biggest pot of the evening, or winning the Calcutta sweep. That's why we think it is wrong to think of a Senatorship as a job, and wrong to think of the Senate as a place where people are supposed to work. Pensions aren't given for work."

I was present in December 1950 when the Holland government in New Zealand, fulfilling an election promise to reform their upper chamber, created a suicide squad of new appointees to the New Zealand Legislative Council, each one pledged to its abolition. I talked to two or three of those so appointed. After the fact, they recognized the "exceptional" importance of the upper chamber to the legislative process. Given the opportunity, they would have changed their votes. Although not suspicious by nature, I had some doubt about their motives. The title "Legislative Councillor" or "Senator" has about it a pleasing ring to the ears of those who hold it.

When we came into office in June of 1957, there were only five Conservative Senators out of a total of one hundred and two designated seats. "Providence" had served the Liberals well. If Senate reform required the consent of the Senate, as it did, I could not consider the matter worth serious attention. There is no way under our constitution to create sufficient numbers of new Senators to vote it out of existence. In today's world, the Senate is simply an anachronism. Theoretically it is still possible the Senate could save the nation in a very serious situation against headstrong action on the part of the House of Commons; but I can hardly regard that as anything more than a pious expression of hope. The bicameral system in Canada would be justified if the Senate performed those functions that Sir John Macdonald envisaged, something between the United States Senate and the British House of Lords. The first bicameral system was created for the Canadas with the passing of the Constitutional Act in 1791 (which was in fact the Quebec Act amended); the famous debates over this Act between Pitt the Younger, Fox, and Burke are as lively today as they were when spoken. I believe it was Fox who expressed the view that if the British had set up a House of Lords in the thirteen colonies there never would have been an American Revolution. This may have been wisdom two hundred years ago. It does not apply today.

My experiences with the partisan employment of the Senate by the Liberal Party led me to conclude that it was in danger of becoming no more than a political pawn. In 1961, the Honourable L. B. Pearson used the overwhelming Liberal majority in the Senate to amend measures passed by the House of Commons to alter the Customs Act in the interests of infant Canadian industries. I noted at the time, "This government will not accept the amendment—this bill will provide many thousands of jobs but is to be prevented by the overwhelming majority of Liberals in the Senate. . . . " This was a question of principle: I regarded the action of the Senate as unconstitutional, a reversion to oligarchic government, threatening the effectiveness of the House of Commons. The action of the Senate Banking Committee to embarrass my government at the climax of the Coyne episode will be discussed in the next chapter.

If the Senate could not be improved, if it could be neither ended nor mended, I was determined not to make it any worse. I tried my best to appoint good men to the Senate, men who had achieved something in their own lives, men who had devoted long service to the public weal, men whose reputations were not tainted by unsavoury dealings. I took great care in each appointment; if there was even a hint of scandal, no appointment was made until the matter was disproved to my satisfaction. Occasionally, I took the wrong advice and did not appoint someone who truly deserved it. I also used the Senate to provide minorities with parliamentary representation which they might never achieve otherwise. For example, I mentioned in Volume I the appointment of a native Indian Senator, Chief James Gladstone. I also drew up a list of distinguished black Canadians for possible Senate appointment, as I considered it unlikely that a black M.P. would be elected in the foreseeable future. However, when I met Lincoln Alexander, my present desk mate in the House of Commons, I changed my view. Initially, I considered appointing him an ambassador; but before an opening occurred, the 1963 election took place. In 1965, I urged him to run as a candidate in Hamilton West. I wanted him to run because he was a good man for the riding, not because he was black. Although he was defeated in 1965, he made an exceptionally good showing. In the 1968 election, the voters in his constituency recognized his sterling qualities and elected him to the House of Commons. He has justified their confidence and become a first-rate parliamentarian.

One final note to conclude this discussion of Parliament: during my period in office, we endeavoured to bring about the "patriation" of the Canadian constitution. There are those who argue that the British North America Act and its amendments are a foreign piece of legislation. Nothing of the kind! All the terms of the B.N.A. Act were determined in Canada by Canadians at one or other of the two conferences held in Charlottetown and Quebec. This was a statute of the British Parliament in 1867 because it involved a union of the British North American colonies. Its subsequent amendments were all made in Canada by Canadians, then perfunctorily passed by the Parliament at Westminster; British statesmen would be pleased if they could rid themselves of this obsolete responsibility. The inability of Canadians to solve their domestic constitutional problems is hardly the responsibility of Britain. We have had the right to patriate the British North America Act(s) since the passing of the Statute of Westminster in 1931. Any action to do so, however, has hinged on the unanimous agreement of the Dominion and provincial governments to an amending formula. To this date, no such agreement has been possible. To bring the B.N.A. Act home without the agreement of the provinces to an amending formula could have been done at any time, but would have amounted only to a gross public deception. To date, the provinces, and Quebec in particular, apparently feel that their legislative powers are better protected by a Canadian constitution that continues as a British statute. Thus, the constitution of this great nation has never been nationally enshrined.

We almost achieved the necessary agreement to bring home our constitution while I was Prime Minister. On 1 December 1961, Canada's Minister of Justice, the Honourable E. D. Fulton, announced that he had transmitted to the Attorneys General of each of the provinces the official text of the formula which had been worked out over the previous fifteen months by the Conference of the Attorneys General of the Dominion and the Provinces to ensure that all future amendments to the constitution would be made in Canada. That text had been approved by representatives from each provincial delegation and the federal delegation as being a satisfactory draft of the formula arrived at by the conference. If only we had pressed on instead of delaying to permit the further consideration of one or two minor matters, I believe the final step would have been taken. Parliament would have adopted the necessary address to Her Majesty praying that she cause the proposed formula to be laid before the United Kingdom Parliament for enactment as an amendment to the British North America Act. This would have been the last amendment to the B.N.A. Act to be made in Westminster, as by it all further power of amendment would have been transferred to Canada. But we decided there was no rush; we believed that the plan would be accepted and acted upon. The result was that the provinces of Saskatchewan and Quebec found some new grounds for objection. We were so close to success. But we failed. That this was an area where no one has ever succeeded did not lessen my sense of loss and regret.

As I have written in my first volume, it was my abiding purpose to see every Canadian not only secure in his liberty, but secure in the knowledge of his fundamental rights and freedoms. It distressed me that those who were neither British nor French in origin were not treated with the regard which non-discrimination demands. I was even more distressed that many contended they would never become Canadians.

In 1912, I took part in the Boys' Parliament of Saskatchewan, held in the Third Avenue Methodist Church in Saskatoon. In the course of debate, I moved a resolution calling for the designation of an unhyphenated Canadian

citizenship. Thirty-four years later, I participated in ceremonies in the same church following the passage of the
Canadian Citizenship Act. In my days as a young lawyer
I began the drafting of a Canadian Bill of Rights. The 1938
election manifesto of the Conservative Party in Saskatchewan, authored by me and issued under my leadership,
began with the following statement: "The Conservative
party pledges itself to maintain the rights of freedom of
speech, freedom of assembly, freedom of religion, and
freedom of the press, reaffirms its implicit belief in democracy and democratic institutions, and its absolute
opposition to the principles of both Fascism and
Communism." From the time I was unanimously elected
leader of the Saskatchewan Conservative Party on 29 October 1936 until its realization on 10 August 1960, I consistently advocated a Canadian Bill of Rights.

I was concerned in 1936 about the continuing extension
of the powers of the Crown at the expense of the individual. My concern was greatly intensified by experiences
during and after the Second World War. On 2 May 1946, I
moved an amendment to the Citizenship Bill in an attempt to have a Bill of Rights included in its provisions. I
wanted to see Canadians assured by statute of freedom of
religion, freedom of speech, and the right to peaceable assembly; that *habeas corpus* should not be suspended except by Parliament; and that no one should be required to
give evidence before any tribunal or commission at any
time if denied counsel or other constitutional safeguards.
My amendment was opposed by the King government.

In January 1947, I placed on the Order Paper a Private
Member's resolution calling for a Bill of Rights. In May of
that year, I explained to the House:

A Bill of Rights must deny the right of government to interfere
with my right to speak within the law; my right to serve my
Maker as my conscience demands; my right to be free from the

threat of a police state, whether consciously or unconsciously administered; my right to live my own life within the limits of the law, without regard to race or colour or creed; my right to belong to an unpopular minority anywhere in this country; my right to have recourse to the courts to guard me against the intrusions or the invasions of the state.

I spoke on this again on 12 April 1948.

On 10 June 1948, I spoke to the nation over CBC radio from Winnipeg. The title of my speech, "A Bill of Rights for Canada". I quote at length from it because it was a fairly complete expression of my philosophy. Speaking of the Mackenzie King government, I said:

This government has flouted the constitution. It has denied equality under law by Orders-in-Council providing that any Canadian may be discriminated against at the will or whim of a Minister. The constitutional liberties of an individual guaranteed by *habeas corpus*, which, since 1670, has provided that no person shall be imprisoned without trial, was departed from two years ago. . . .

. . . [In] a recent case in the Exchequer Court, when the Judge, having come to the conclusion that the rights of an individual had been infringed upon by a Minister of the Crown, had to come to the conclusion that he could do nothing to protect the citizen's rights. Is there any wonder that he used these words, "There are, in my judgment, far too many encroachments from Ministers, Deputy Ministers, and functionaries in the judicial as well as the legislative field."

I am against discrimination on the basis of colour or race. This government dared to provide, under Order-in-Council, for deportation of native-born Canadians whose only offence was their colour. . . .

The time has come to assure that this government shall be shorn of its arrogant disregard of the rights of the people. It does not rule by Divine right as did the Stuart Kings, even though the Prime Minister . . . would indicate that criticism by an opposition is a wrongful act. . . .

Parliament placed the freedoms of the Canadian people in the custody of the Canadian government for the period of the war. I am convinced that the Ministers of this government have found it easier to carry on by short cut methods outside of parliament and are endeavouring to make permanent the precedent of war in peace time. This must be stopped. . . .

A Bill of Rights for Canada is the only way in which to stop the march on the part of the government towards arbitrary power, and to curb the arrogance of men "clad in a little brief authority". . . .

. . . Some say that it is unnecessary and our unwritten constitutional rights protect us. They have not in the past. They can not unless you and I have a right to the protection of law in the courts of the land. There are others who claim that the Parliament of Canada cannot pass laws to preserve the constitutional freedom of Canadians. If that be true, then Canadian citizenship is a provincial variable. There will be nine kinds of Canadians in Canada whose freedoms will be based on the home address of each of us. If that contention be true, Canadian unity is a meaningless term. . . .

I stand for freedom that will secure for the individual his inherent constitutional rights; Freedom maintained by the equality of every person in this country before the law. Freedom is the most sacred thing of the human personality. Freedom is founded on the sacredness and dignity of the human being. I believe in freedom which will secure for you and me equality of opportunity, that will assure the business man of a fair return, the farmer of fair prices, the man who works of fair wages. I believe that you and I must be assured of that freedom from fear that comes from fluctuations incident to the operation of economic laws. I believe that by legislation freedom shall be secured that will provide for you, and for me, a minimum standard of security and health. I believe in the maintenance too of the political freedoms, of the constitutional freedoms which can not be preserved if economic freedom is denied. Our political freedom is an abiding and a living thing.

It is part of our heritage. Without a Bill of Rights, having regard to the experience of recent history, that heritage of which we are trustees, will not be passed along to those who come after us. There are some who contend that freedom cannot be assured by a written document. In part that is true, for when the spirit of freedom dies in the hearts of people, statutes cannot preserve it. But the ideal of freedom is kept before the people in a declaration of their rights, and when coupled with a declaration that these rights may be fought for in the courts of the land, the danger to freedom by a powerful state is diminished, if not completely denied.

On 26 October 1949, I again placed a Private Member's resolution on the Order Paper, in which, among other things, after asking for a Declaration of Human Rights, I requested that: "As a preliminary step the Minister of Justice do submit for the opinion of the Supreme Court of Canada, the question as to the degree to which Fundamental Freedoms of religion, speech and of the press, of the Constitutional Rights of the individual, are matters of Provincial or Federal Jurisdiction." Every year thereafter in Opposition, I placed a Private Member's resolution on the Order Paper calling for a Canadian Bill of Rights.

The protection of minorities is fundamental to democracy. My advocacy of a Bill of Rights was to assure Canadians, whatever their racial origins or surnames, the right to full citizenship and an end to discrimination. This was basic to my philosophy of "One Canada, One Nation". It was to give Canadians a new sense of national greatness and the opportunity to pridefully declare it that the 1961 decennial census for the first and last time asked the question: "Are you a Canadian?" Hundreds of thousands of Canadians answered: "Yes," with pride. This change was disapproved by the Liberal Party and by some members of the Ottawa bureaucratic establishment and was discontinued after I left office.

One of the first items of Cabinet business following the

general election of 31 March 1958 was Bill of Rights legislation. The question before us was whether to submit a
draft Bill of Rights to the Supreme Court for its opinion
or to bring it straight before Parliament. We decided that
the proper first step was to present the bill to Parliament
for its consideration. The Supreme Court would have
their say in due course, although little did I anticipate
that it would take a full decade before they had anything
significant to say with regard to it.

On 5 September 1958, I moved for leave to introduce
Bill No. C-60, for the Recognition and Protection of Human Rights and Fundamental Freedoms. The Cabinet's
plan was to introduce the Bill of Rights at the end of the
first session of the new Parliament in 1958; to give it first
reading; to withdraw it; and to re-introduce it at the earliest possible date. The interim would provide Members
and Senators and interested individuals and organizations with the opportunity to study the proposed bill, so
that they might give us their observations and criticisms.

The drafting of the bill was difficult, and I want to pay
tribute here to those Liberal and ccf Members whose
amendments in Committee contributed to improving the
wording of this most important Act. I wanted to keep the
Canadian Bill of Rights strictly within the constitutional
powers of the federal Parliament and to avoid any en-
croachment upon the provinces. There are grey areas in
the division of constitutional authority in Canada. The
aim and purpose of the Bill of Rights was to give Parliament the opportunity to remove any dangers to the fundamental freedoms of our country, so far as they related
to Parliament's legislative competence. It was also our
objective to clothe the bill in simple language. Human
Rights and Fundamental Freedoms do not require grandi-
loquent words to contribute to their greatness and importance.

Further, we decided to enact the Bill of Rights as a simple statute rather than as a constitutional amendment. I considered that it would be impossible to pass an amendment to the British North America Act which would be binding both on the provinces and on the Dominion. My experience with the provincial goverments indicated that they were too jealous of their jurisdiction over property and civil rights to support any amendment applicable to themselves. I have little hope that their attitude will be altered in the years ahead. To have made provincial agreement a condition for enacting a Canadian Bill of Rights would have meant a complete failure to achieve this important objective. As I said on introducing this legislation in the House:

... I realize there are many who feel that there should be a constitutional amendment binding on the federal Parliament and the provincial legislatures.

All I have to say in that regard is this, Mr. Speaker. Let us clear our own doorstep first. . . .

The cynics will say it does not go far enough. It is a first step. As the Chinese say, every journey by mankind, even a journey over a thousand years, begins with just one step taken by some individual who sees the possibilities for the future and tries to make it possible to equalize the opportunities for those of his own generation. The bill will not do everything, but I do think fair-minded Canadians will agree that it is a major step forward.

. . . Realize this: that henceforth, except within the limitations that security demands, Canadians will know their rights are not to be loosely disregarded, and Parliament will have before it at all times the warning which is emphasized in this Bill of Rights, namely that fundamental rights and freedoms within the federal jurisdiction shall not be made light of by this or future Parliaments.

Under my philosophy, the Bill of Rights was based

upon the belief that certain rights and liberties of the citizen are so fundamental to our way of life that no law and no force should be allowed to encroach on them. There were critics who contended that a statute containing the Bill of Rights could be repealed by any subsequent Parliament. The experience of the *Habeas Corpus* Act, passed at Westminster in the reign of Charles II, indicated that no Parliament would dare to repeal a freedom statute. No government would so foolishly court the wrath of public opinion. Such action could not be kept secret because, under our legislation, any government desiring to circumvent the provisions of the Bill of Rights would have to pass legislation through three readings in the House of Commons and three readings in the Senate justifying its decision to pass a law "notwithstanding the Bill of Rights". Sixteen years have now passed and we have yet to see a piece of legislation passed by Parliament "notwithstanding the Bill of Rights".

On Dominion Day, 1960, I moved the second reading of the Bill of Rights (now C-79) in the Commons. In doing so, I could not help reflecting on the genius of the Fathers of Confederation, and on the contribution they made in their day and generation to the setting up of a national political organization which, despite the many vicissitudes of national and international events, has proven to be one of the most forward-looking constitutional accomplishments among the nations of the democratic world. I noted that during the intervening years we had been able to add steps which more and more had expanded the democratic rights of Canadians as a whole. I was justifiably proud that during the session then in progress we had passed legislation to provide for the first citizens of Canada, the Indian and Eskimo people, the full right of franchise, thus removing any suggestion that they or any other Canadians were in a position of second-class citizenship.

The Bill of Rights can be summed up in a few words. In Part I, clause 1, the following fundamental freedoms are provided:

a) the right of the individual to life, liberty, security of the person and enjoyment of property

Not the ownership of property, notice, which is a matter within provincial jurisdiction.

and the right not to be deprived thereof except by due process of law;
b) the right of the individual to equality before the law and the protection of the law;

I consider this worth emphasizing because above everything else in the world today there is no element more dangerous to freedom everywhere and to the nations which espouse freedom than the practice of discrimination. Clause 1 continues:

c) freedom of religion;
d) freedom of speech;
e) freedom of assembly and association; and
f) freedom of the press.

The courts had held that freedom of the press was within the exclusive jurisdiction of the Parliament of Canada, but this was the first time in Canadian history that freedom of the press was given recognition under law.

To ensure that the courts would have to determine the ineffectiveness and inapplicability of any law, or section thereof, that violated this declaration by Parliament, it was provided in clause 2 that:

Every law of Canada shall, unless it is expressly declared by an Act of the Parliament of Canada that it shall operate notwithstanding the Canadian Bill of Rights, be so construed and applied as not to abrogate, abridge or infringe or to authorize the abrogation, abridgement or infringement of any of the rights or freedoms herein recognized and declared, and in particular, no law of Canada shall be construed or applied so as to

a) authorize or effect the arbitrary detention, imprisonment or exile of any person;

b) impose or authorize the imposition of cruel and unusual treatment or punishment;

c) deprive a person who has been arrested or detained

i) of the right to be informed promptly of the reason for his arrest or detention,

ii) of the right to retain and instruct counsel without delay, or

iii) of the remedy by way of *habeas corpus* for the determination of the validity of his detention and for his release if the detention is not lawful;

d) authorize a court, tribunal, commission, board or other authority to compel a person to give evidence if he is denied counsel, protection against self crimination or other constitutional safeguards;

e) deprive a person of the right to a fair hearing in accordance with the principles of fundamental justice for the determination of his rights and obligations;

f) deprive a person charged with a criminal offence of the right to be presumed innocent until proved guilty according to law in a fair and public hearing by an independent and impartial tribunal, or of the right to reasonable bail without just cause; or

g) deprive a person of the right to the assistance of an interpreter in any proceedings in which he is involved or in which he is a party or a witness, before a court, commission, board or other tribunal, if he does not understand or speak the language in which such proceedings are conducted.

I should like to underline the provision "of the remedy by way of *habeas corpus* for the determination of the validity of his detention and for his release if the detention is not lawful." *Habeas corpus* has not been denied in Britain in the last century except by Parliament, and only then when the security of the state demanded it. In time of war, freedoms may have to be placed in pawn as security for victory. Here in Canada, *habeas corpus* was denied in September 1945 by Order-in-Council, following the arrest of certain individuals following the revelations of Igor Gouzenko. This must have been passed without much consideration because when I asked about it in the House in December 1945, the Minister of Justice, the Honourable Louis St. Laurent, said there was no such Order-in-Council. Then, in May 1946, the Minister of Justice explained that he was not overly concerned about the matter. I found it difficult to understand how a distinguished barrister could have said this about an Order-in-Council that swept aside a basic foundation of individual freedom. That Order-in-Council stated that anyone detained would be considered as being lawfully detained; in other words, no one, however unlawfully detained, could successfully apply to the Court for a writ of *habeas corpus*. This grave danger to freedom can no longer happen under the Canadian Bill of Rights.

There is further provision in the Bill of Rights that no one shall be denied the right to a fair hearing in accordance with the principles of fundamental justice; and that no court, tribunal, commission, board, or other authority shall compel a person to give evidence if he is denied counsel, protection against self-crimination, or other constitutional safeguard. This provision put an end to a practice that had placed individual rights at the mercy of some Commission or another under legislation like the Excise or Exchange Acts. A further example of the sort of practice made unconstitutional by the Bill of Rights was Orders-in-Council which legalized taxation before Parliament legislated it. Some bureaucrats were outspoken in their condemnation of the Bill of Rights, realizing as they did that the days of the bureaucratic tyranny in Canada were over. The critics of the Bill referred to the fact that no penalties are provided therein. Penalties cannot be enforced on Parliament. However, Parliament can no longer pass a statute or a section thereof that contravenes any of the provisions of the Bill of Rights. From the time it became law, any statute or portion thereof passed by Parliament since 1867 having the effect of contravening any of the freedoms therein set out would be null and void.

It is often asked why I did not have legislation brought before Parliament to repeal the War Measures Act. The reason was simple: Canada was living in dangerous times internationally, and hanging over the world was the fear of an atomic holocaust. I explained this in the House of Commons on 3 August 1960 when I said: "The War Measures Act, either in its present form or better still in amended form, must remain in effect under the trying and dangerous times in which we live." We did not intend, however, to provide that the Government of Canada again be endowed with absolute power beyond the authority of Parliament. We decided that Parliament should have the right to review the circumstances under which the War Measures Act is invoked. In effect, this amendment preserves the rights of Parliament, and prevents the government, with its majority, from continuing to use the War Measures Act after the initial period of its invocation unless Parliament so approves, as it did, and mistakenly, in October 1970. I expected that action by Parliament to bring to annulity the War Measures Act would take place only in the most extreme of situations since it would cause the defeat of the government and produce a difficult situation in war or threatened insurrection. The important thing was that in principle it preserved the rights of Parliament and was a defence against the government's using the War Measures Act under circumstances where it really was not justified.

Thus, Part II, section 6, of the Canadian Bill of Rights read:

6. Section 6 of the War Measures Act is repealed and the following substituted therefor:

"6. (1) Sections 3, 4 and 5 shall come into force only upon the issue of a proclamation of the Governor in Council declaring that war, invasion or insurrection, real or apprehended, exists.

2) A proclamation declaring that war, invasion or insurrection, real or apprehended, exists shall be laid before Parliament forthwith after its issue, or, if Parliament is then not sitting, within the first fifteen days next thereafter that Parliament is sitting.

3) Where a proclamation has been laid before Parliament pursuant to subsection (2), a notice of motion in either House signed by ten members thereof and made in accordance with the rules of that House within ten days of the day the proclamation was laid before Parliament, praying that the proclamation be revoked, shall be debated in that House at the first convenient opportunity within the four sitting days next after the day the motion in that House was made.

4) If both Houses of Parliament resolve that the proclamation be revoked, it shall cease to have effect, and sections 3, 4 and 5 shall cease to be in force until those sections are again brought into force by a further proclamation but without prejudice to the previous operation of those sections or anything duly done or suffered thereunder or any offence committed or any penalty or forfeiture or punishment incurred.

5) Any act or thing done or authorized or any order or regulation made under the authority of this Act, shall be deemed not to be an abrogation, abridgement or infringement of any right or freedom recognized by the Canadian Bill of Rights."

It was not until ten years after the Parliament of Canada had enacted the Bill of Rights providing that human

rights and fundamental freedoms shall exist without discrimination by reason of race, national origin, colour, religion, or sex, that a case bearing upon this great principle
reached the Supreme Court of Canada. A charge of
drunkenness in a public place had been laid against Joseph Drybones, a Dogrib Indian of Yellowknife, Northwest Territories, under the Indian Act, which provided
more severe penalties than those specified in liquor laws
under which non-Indians would be charged. Drybones
was acquitted on the ground that conviction would im-
pair his rights under the Bill of Rights. The Supreme
Court upheld his acquittal.

Naturally, I was greatly pleased. The courts, while
never denying the constitutional significance of the Bill of
Rights, had shied away from it in their judgments, sometimes indulging in juridical acrobatics to avoid having to
deal with it. Critics condemned it as a pious and ineffec-
tual declaration. The Drybones judgment ended this. The
Bill of Rights stands today as the protector of the liberties
of every Canadian, however humble, despite recent judgments of the Courts, which indicate a desire to chisel
away at some of the freedoms Parliament intended to
protect.

This is not to say that the Canadian Bill of Rights remained for ten years without effect. Those law professors
and politicians who condemned it had closed their eyes
to what was happening. All the laws of this Dominion
were made to conform to it. It became the standard and
the pattern for those Canadian provinces that wished to
enact their own provincial Bills of Rights. No less important were the individual acts of fine citizenship which the
Canadian Bill of Rights inspired. For example, I was most
impressed when my long-time friend and colleague, the
Honourable David Walker, in consequence of his commitment to the concept of non-discrimination, initiated,
as President of the prestigious Lawyers' Club in Toronto,

the sweeping aside of any barriers preventing Jewish membership. When I spoke on the Bill of Rights on Dominion Day, 1960, I included the following declaration:

I am a Canadian, a free Canadian, free to speak without fear, free to worship God in my own way, free to stand for what I think right, free to oppose what I believe wrong, free to choose those who shall govern my country. This heritage of freedom I pledge to uphold for myself and all mankind.

CHAPTER NINE

✴

THE SPEECH FROM THE THRONE, opening the first session of Canada's twenty-fourth Parliament on 12 May 1958, announced the government's intention to proceed with our mandate. On the economic front there were additional public works programs, the further extension of unemployment insurance, projects for slum clearance and urban re-development under the National Housing Act, for rivers and public buildings, the expansion of airports and airways, the Pine Point Railway, Roads to Resources, Arctic research, the South Saskatchewan Dam, new harbour facilities at Fort William and Port Arthur, and new agricultural and small-business legislation. In his budget speech on 17 June 1958, the Minister of Finance, the Honourable Donald Fleming, announced:

With a budgetary deficit of $640 million, and a total cash requirement of about $1,400 million, it is not in my judgment necessary for economic reasons to propose any further major tax reductions. The stimulating effect of the policies that we have already and promptly put into effect should, in the absence of any further adverse external events, sustain economic activity and provide the economic climate for an early resumption of economic expansion. . . . It seems to me that we have, for the time being at least, a fairly sensible balance of fiscal policy, investment policy and income maintenance policies. . . . The principal tax changes affecting the present fiscal year were introduced and approved by Parliament last December. Those changes amounted to tax reductions of $178 million in a full year. The further changes now submitted add up to $26 million in a full year, and it can therefore be fairly said that our total tax reductions in our first year in office exceed $200 million.

He had forecast a large borrowing program for the current year to meet new cash requirements amounting to $1,423 million, and to pay off maturing securities of $1,950 million, making a total of $3.4 billion.

Shortly after his budget speech, Mr. Fleming informed me that our approach would have to be changed in view of the fact that between 1 January 1959 and 1 September 1966, approximately $10 billion of government securities would fall due for payment. These were the fifth, sixth, seventh, eighth, and ninth Victory Loans, all bearing interest at three per cent. He said that the immense volume of these bonds overhung the market and made it very difficult to launch any new long-term issues with any prospect of success. The market trend in recent years had been towards shorter loans, and to complicate the situation further, a major break had occurred in the United States bond market just before his budget was brought down. This break had spread to Canada, and while there was nothing he could have done to prevent it, the budget had contributed to it. Thus, a number of bond-holders had been caught with unmarked supplies of government issues, particularly the guaranteed CNR issue of 1 January 1958, and confidence in the market had been shaken. He considered that, for the time being, we could not proceed with our projected borrowing program, and that to meet immediate cash needs, it was necessary to borrow $400 million from the Bank of Canada.

This was rather disturbing news. We had been given a

mandate for a vast development program. Now we could not proceed. We had to wait until we had paid for the Second World War! There was a possible solution, he told me. He recommended that in order to restore confidence in the market and give future borrowings a better chance of success, a Conversion Loan be issued for the $6.4 billion in bonds of the fifth and ninth Victory Loans. Holders of Victory Bonds would be offered four varieties of bonds in exchange: twenty-five-year bonds at an interest rate of four and a half per cent, fourteen-year bonds at four and a quarter per cent, seven-year bonds at three and three-quarter per cent, three-and-one-quarter-year bonds at three per cent. In addition, there would be cash adjustment payments bearing from a maximum of $25 per $1,000 of bonds to $15 per $1,000 of bonds, depending on the issue the holder selected. Other Victory Bond holders could opt for any of these four issues. This proposal, if agreed to, would lift from the market the burden of the substantial amount of early maturities. For years ahead, debt management would be simpler. Above all, this would restore confidence and give us the opportunity to carry on with our national development plans.

On the other hand, the proposal was not without risk. A mammoth effort would be required in view of the fact that the season of the year (5 August to 15 September) was not what we would have chosen had there been any alternative. I agreed when the Minister of Finance suggested that a number of leading investment men in the country be called to Ottawa and informed in confidence of the proposals and asked to comment on them. Initially fourteen had been invited. A further twenty-three were then invited. I thought it ironic that a number of these gentlemen began by criticizing us for spending too much money. When the details of the Conversion Loan were explained to them—something that was going to cost us in excess of $50 million a year in additional debt charges—and the sound of cash registers in their respective brokerage houses began to ring in their ears, they became quite enthusiastic. They weren't taking any chances; we were. All were soon at work to further the role of their own organizations in the campaign. On the plus side of the campaign ledger was the fact that over $3 billion in Victory Bonds was held by the Bank of Canada, other government agencies, and the chartered banks; we could be reasonably certain that they would convert their holdings, and that a strong response from them would encourage others to do the same. I was concerned that the Opposition would attack the price we were paying to achieve a manageable situation and some flexibility in government finances. Nevertheless, I have always regarded the remarkable success of the Canada Conversion Loan–1958 as one of the government's outstanding successes.

I launched the campaign with an appeal over national television and radio on 14 July 1958. I said, in part:

... This, the largest financial project in our history, offers an opportunity to all holders of Victory Bonds which were purchased as an act of patriotic faith during the war years, to reinvest them for the greater development of a greater Canada.

These monies that were advanced during the days of war, and which contributed to the victory, we now ask to be made available to speed the pace of peaceful progress and the programme of national development. Now that the Speech from the Throne has been concluded, and as soon as the Budget resolutions are considered, we shall be placing further details of that national development policy before Parliament.

The action we are taking will make it possible for our nation to embark on a new era of peacetime prosperity far and beyond anything we have ever known. I sincerely believe that great objectives can and will be attained by the faith and enterprise of all our people. To that end, your Government believes that the steps we are taking are necessary in order to create the climate in which this can come to full fruition. . . .

In saying that a major result of this new loan is to make other necessary funds available for immediate participation by the federal government in the development of resources, I need hardly remind you that such participation is not, by any means, an end in itself. Its chief objective is, of course, to provide essentials such as access roads, railroads, and energy sources, and the business climate which will attract private investment to newly developing and lesser developed regions in our country, in amounts many times in excess of the government investment. It is confidently expected that the debt refinancing which we announced today will clear the decks for greatly increased private investment in our future, just as surely as it will do so for government investment.

This, of course, is in keeping with our whole philosophy of the role of the government in the progress of the nation—which is to stimulate the enterprise of private capital by a national policy of development of those resources which would not otherwise be brought into production or be long delayed. . . .

In the *Bank of Canada Report* for 1958, the Governor of the Bank, James Coyne, commented favourably on the Conversion Loan. There were, however, disturbing aspects in his *Report* which tended to confirm my view that he had been principally responsible for the budget introduced by the Honourable Walter Harris in the spring of 1957, which in some measure contributed to the Liberal Party's defeat a few months later. It was apparent that he rejected the proposition that the prime task of economic policy was to ensure, not assume, the appropriate level of aggregate demand necessary to maintain reasonably full employment. Our economic projections indicated that unemployment would remain a serious problem until at least 1961. Coyne was content to assume that the level of demand would be adequate for sustained growth if our economic policy embraced the goal of "sound money". He apparently belonged to the economic school which had considered that the only way out of the Great Depression was to have more depression, and that the only way to cure unemployment was to create more unemployment. My government, as we again made most clear in the House on 19 January 1959, gave unemployment priority over inflation. And, if I may repeat the point, we managed, despite this priority, to hold inflation to 1.2 per cent.

I recognized from the beginning that Coyne was inflexible in his ideas to the point of being unbalanced on the question of "sound money" policy. Early in our government we came up against his assumption that he, not the elected representatives of the people, would determine economic policy. We, however, had democratic responsibilities. The people of Canada had not given their mandate simply to balance the federal budget. The following letter from Donald Fleming to Coyne in November 1957 catches the essence of the early stages of this problem:

I acknowledge receipt of your letter of the 19th instant. I thank you for your very full statement on your views concerning the "minimum liquid asset ratio of 15%" which has been maintained by the Canadian chartered banks. The essence of your views appears to be contained in the following statement on the third page of your letter:

"Although we made it clear that in our judgment the operation of this working stand should be continued for the indefinite future, the banks could if they chose vary the agreement or abolish it. However, I should think it likely that they would wish to discuss the matter with the Bank of Canada before coming to such a decision. If the banks were to suggest dissolving their agreement or changing it in a way that did not appear sound to the Bank of Canada then I would feel it to be our duty to urge the chartered banks to continue to adhere to what the Bank of Canada regarded as a sound practice."

Having regard to relations between the Bank of Canada and the chartered banks it does not appear to me that this position leaves the banks with very much freedom to depart from the 15% ratio. We have already reviewed on several occasions the views of the Government on this subject, and I do not know whether there is any use in asking you to reconsider the subject. I should, however, again stress the view I expressed that to attempt to make the 15% liquid asset virtually permanent would be to usurp the legislative function of Parliament.

On 5 November 1959, I received a letter from Neil McKinnon, President of the Canadian Bank of Commerce, suggesting a study of Canada's monetary system. The following excerpt catches the government's essential problem with James Coyne:

A part of this study should automatically involve the organization of the Bank of Canada, the powers vested in the Governor, the relations of the Bank of Canada to the Government and the relations of the Bank of Canada to the chartered banks. As you know in the past it has always seemed to me and has come to be expected by the banks that the Bank of Canada to a very large extent harmonized its policies to Government objectives and then gave leadership to the chartered banks so that there would be in turn a harmony of policies in that field, too. This was all informal but none the less effective and it is only in the past few years that it has not seemed to work.

I cannot accept that the root of this problem lay with the government. Mr. Fleming, who was an inherently cautious and responsible person, was not likely to advocate undermining the economy by printing money at a foolish level. But he did have some degree of flexibility in his approach to this matter. As he said in the House on 18 May 1959:

If the banks find they have not an ample amount of money to meet the extraordinary demands for credit that are made upon them today as a result of the upsurge in the Canadian economy, then certainly it is not the intention of the Canadian government to inflict on the people of Canada a repetition of the tight money policy of our Liberal predecessors.

By Act of Parliament passed in 1934, and subsequently confirmed on the several occasions when the Act was before Parliament for amendment, the Bank of Canada was given the duty "to regulate credit and currency in the best interests of the economic life of the nation, to control and protect the external value of the national monetary unit, and to mitigate by its influence fluctuations in the general level of production, trade, prices and employment, so far as may be possible within the scope of monetary action." To this end, the Bank of Canada had the sole right of issuing paper currency; it had the power to buy and sell broad classes of securities, to make short-term loans to the chartered banks, and otherwise to establish and give effect to the appropriate monetary policy from time to time. Under this Act the government of the day had no authority whatsoever over the manner in which the Bank of Canada should act in these matters. That said, it was obvious that fiscal and monetary policy could not be at war with each other. To deal with the serious problems of economic recession and unemployment, it was not only necessary to pursue a bold and effective fiscal policy, it was also essential that monetary policy be directed to the same goal of facilitating economic expansion and new job opportunities.

Coyne seemed to develop an obsession with his own infallibility. We took the stand that the government must make policy, not the administrators, whether the Governor of the Bank of Canada or anyone else. They were there to give their advice, but it was for the government to decide whether to act upon it. To have followed any other course would have been to create an aristocracy of higher-echelon civil servants, which would have been intolerable. Coyne was not alone. His attitude became public because he rushed into the public arena making speeches to promote his point of view. It was apparent that his actions were designed as a political campaign against my government. He was an unregenerate Grit, and Liberal Party strategists used him for their own ends. But when the Liberals came into power in 1963, they took action to change the Bank Act to make certain there would never be a repetition of Coyne's arrogant conduct.

On 18 January 1960, Coyne addressed the Canadian Club of Winnipeg. His address was entitled "Living Within Our Means". He said, among other things: "We must realize, however, that it would have meant that we would have built fewer houses and perhaps lower cost houses. . . . This would have meant a smaller consequential expenditure on streets, sewers, etc. by municipalities. We would have also built fewer miles of new high-cost highways and would have tried to finance more of various expenditures by governments and government enterprises out of revenue instead of out of borrowing. We would have had somewhat less in the way of resource development. . . . " Or, as he said, to the forty-seventh annual convention of the Retail Merchants' Association in Saskatoon on 22 March 1960: "What is required is rather a reduction in total spending and reorientation of part of our total spending towards the purchase of efficiently produced goods and services of domestic origin in place of imports together with whatever increase can be achieved in the efficient production of goods and services for export." He felt that "we have . . . been living beyond our means on a grand scale." To state the obvious, his view of Canada and of Canada's potential was not our view of Canada and of Canada's potential. He had not the slightest compunction about publicly advising us on fiscal policy, while privately refusing any advice from Mr. Fleming on monetary policy. He had created a state of affairs that could not be tolerated.

Indeed, even the Leader of the Opposition, the Honourable L. B. Pearson, recognized the impossibility of the situation when he stated on 26 June 1961: "Parliament intended the Bank to be independent of control in that sense and to act independently of government control within its own sphere but not, of course, to act in a fashion that would frustrate the policies of the government." This was exactly our point of view when we asked Parliament on 23 June 1961 to change the Bank of Canada Act so that the office of the Governor of the Bank of Canada might be deemed to have become vacant. We had asked him to resign, and he had refused. He made the correspondence public and demanded a public hearing before a parliamentary committee. Mr. Fleming refused. My own view was that we should have agreed. However, once Mr. Fleming had taken his position there could be no change; certainly I was not going to countermand him on this issue. Had we set up the committee of the House of Commons, we could have destroyed Coyne for all time. The Senate Banking and Commerce Committee gave Coyne his final forum. Loaded with Liberal partisans, it gave the worst possible interpretation to the actions of my government. Grattan O'Leary observed the proceedings. He sent me this note on 14 July 1961:

I sat in on one of the Senate Committee hearings the other night and what I saw and heard left me discouraged and dismayed: the mental confusion, the intellectual dishonesty, the cheap melodrama, the "ham" acting, the incompetence of some "cross-examiners"—all so disgusted me I could barely restrain myself from standing to protest.

Almost as bad was the reporting of the press: the pitiful stuff about "drama", the reporters who pride themselves on being "hard-boiled" turned into sob sisters, into unsophisticated dupes incapable of seeing through what was palpably phony.

One of the results of our huge majority was that, generally speaking, the press became the Opposition; no matter what we did, however beneficial, the powerful press condemned us. The pundits, at least as they described themselves, regarded their words as possessing all the authority of having been uttered *ex cathedra*. There was never any policy declared by me on behalf of the Conservative Party which was not first thoroughly canvassed, considered, and examined. That was something I had learned from my practice at the bar. To read the press for the period of my government, however, is often to read the opposite of what actually took place. Occasionally, however, I had the last laugh. During the period of Coyne's contest with my government, I was in Winnipeg to unveil the Shevchenko Monument on the grounds of the Legislature. Someone had placed a sign of large dimension in praise of Coyne under the drape at the statue's base. The word got around. There was a covey of expectant photographers gathered, cameras ready, waiting for me to unveil the monument with this sign about Coyne. Their expressions when the drape was pulled away made me wish that I had brought a camera. One of the Winnipeg policemen, checking beforehand to make certain that the unveiling would go off without a hitch, had found the sign and removed it.

Coyne finally resigned to a flurry of journalistic trumpets on 13 July 1961, his war against poverty won (at his request, the Board of Directors of the Bank had increased his pension to $25,000 a year on 15 February 1960, whereas Mr. St. Laurent's pension as former Prime Minister was a meagre $3,000). The Cabinet appointed Louis Rasminsky to succeed him. Rasminsky believed in the need for a careful and consistent meshing together of all the various aspects of financial policy and general economic policy in the effort to attain the broad economic objectives of high-level employment, price stability, and sustained economic growth. He saw monetary policy, fiscal policy, and debt-management policy as interdependent and to some extent interchangeable, necessitating a high degree of co-ordination to ensure that the blend or "mix" of these policies be purposefully directed towards attaining the over-all economic objectives of the community. As he wrote to Mr. Fleming before his appointment:

I shall wish to play my full part in achieving the close working relationship with the Minister of Finance which is indispensable if the Bank is to discharge its responsibilities in a satisfactory way. I would hope to have frequent contacts with the Minister of Finance of the same character as I have had over the past years in my capacity of Executive Director of the International Monetary Fund and International Bank. In addition, in order to ensure beyond doubt that continuing high importance is attached to maintaining lines of communication, and even though such precaution may now seem unnecessary, consideration should be given to setting up a routine procedure for regular meetings at fairly frequent intervals between the Minister of Finance and the Governor.

It is significant that James Coyne's resignation coincided with the end of the recession in Canada. We had not been content, however, to wait on either event to carry out our mandate. Our national agricultural policy was announced in the House of Commons on 30 August 1958. It promised a vigorous program to increase sales of wheat and other products, a comprehensive Crop Insurance program, a 4-H Bank program, farm credit expansion, an Agricultural Prices Stabilization Act, and an Agricultural Rehabilitation and Development Act. Our objective was to increase farm cash income in a manner equitable to all farmers and acceptable to the majority of Canadians. As an alternative to the two-price system for wheat, we put through Parliament a vote of $142 million for acreage payments to Western farmers in August 1960. When there were charges of political interference in the operation of the Prairie Farm Rehabilitation Act and the Prairie Farm Assistance Act, I instructed the Minister of Agriculture, Alvin Hamilton, on 29 December 1960 to remove the causes of complaint of the officials in both these operations. When drought struck Western Canada in 1961, my government agreed to pay half the cost of shipments of fodder to Manitoba, Saskatchewan, and Alberta to assist the farmers in wintering their livestock.

I personally favoured acreage payments over deficiency payments. In a speech to the Manitoba Conservative Association in Winnipeg on 17 November 1961, I said:

I love to see the interest of the Liberal party in the Western farmer. My memory goes back a few years. We said they were losing markets. They said no.

We said there should be widespread price supports. They said no.

We said there should be cash advances on grain. They said it couldn't be done.

We said they should bring in crop insurance. They said it couldn't be done.

We said there should be widespread extension of farm credit. Mr. Martin, agricultural expert of the Liberal party today, said no.

We said there should be acreage payments in order to help the small farmer. We brought them in; the Martins, the Pearsons and also the Argues said "Peanuts". [Argue, then CCF leader in the House, received his reward. Now a Liberal Senator, he has proved that the "paths of glory" lead but to the gravy.]

We have acted. I mentioned the sales to China. . . . The CCF said it couldn't be done. Then they said there hadn't been a sale. Now they say, "We certainly did a great job in prodding the government." . . .

Prairie Farm Assistance Payments for this crop year are estimated at $60 million . . . we expect to have $25 million in the hands of the prairie farmers before Christmas. . . .

The ARDA program was made necessary by the sweeping technological changes which had taken place in agriculture. A large percentage of farmers were handicapped in providing a satisfactory level of living for their families by a lack of productive resources resulting from unproductive land, uneconomic units, and poor farming methods. These "small" farms also suffered from underemployment of available family labour. My colleagues and I recognized what past governments failed to recognize or come to grips with. The small-farm problem was becoming increasingly acute in consequence of our higher national standard of living and the higher operating costs on small-farm units. In a period of twenty years, the number of independent farmers had decreased by 34 per cent, and the total labour force on the farm was down by about 45 per cent. Given the extensive acreage of submarginal lands which could be put to more intensive uses, consideration was given by the government to creating the ways and means whereby these lands could be purchased, taken on lease, or exchanged. We thought it important that, in the reallocation of lands, primary emphasis be placed on the establishment of economic family farm units. What we sought was a program, in co-operation with the provinces, which would provide an improved level of living for farmers on small farms through (1) better land use; (2) consolidation of small farms into more productive economic units; (3) better agricultural technical training; (4) facilitating off-farm employment for members of farm families; (5) extension of Unemployment Insurance benefits to certain classes of farm workers; and (6) expansion of the vocational, technical, and training agreement in order to assist the provinces to cope with that portion of the farm population which wished to enter other occupational fields.

Soon after he became Minister of Agriculture on 11 October 1960, the Honourable Alvin Hamilton sent me a memorandum on national agricultural policy. His conclusion:

It can be seen that to push our National Agricultural Program to a conclusion we must take the final step of an Agricultural Rehabilitation and Development Act (ARDA). I expect I will need about $15 million a year after it gets rolling. At first, this will run about $6 million a year in the West and $9 million a year in the East if I can persuade the provinces to accept the ideas advanced. Eventually the costs will decline in the West and rise in the East where there is so much to be done.

Thus we brought into being a threefold program embracing alternate land use, rural development, and water conservation to make the best use of our nation's arable land. As indicated above, this would require considerable expenditures (every program did), but without our action the problems would remain. The 1956 census listed one hundred and twenty thousand farmers in Canada with incomes of less than twelve hundred dollars a year. This was *not* a situation that should or could be tolerated. ARDA was an integral part, an essential conclusion, of a campaign that George Perley and I had begun in Opposition many years before to give agriculture its rightful place in our national economy. When the House of Commons divided on this Act after third reading on 31 May 1961, the vote was "Yeas", one hundred and eighty-two;

"Nays", nil. In my response on 10 March 1959 to the Western Farm Delegation which had journeyed to Ottawa to make various representations to my government, I said:

I say this, it will be my undeviating purpose and those associated with me to do what we can to assure that degree of prosperity for agriculture, without which the Canadian economy cannot be maintained. . . . believing as I do that agriculture must remain dynamic and not static, my purpose, Ladies and Gentlemen, so long as I occupy this position, will be to continue to press, to assure those steps be taken that ultimately will bring about a comprehensive policy for agriculture and give to the farmer of Canada that hope which too often has been lost to him.

I was amused when Mr. Wesson, the Chairman of the Farm Delegation, suggested that I would not be able to appreciate their problems. In support of his own credentials, he pointed out that he had first come to Saskatchewan in 1906. In reply, I reminded him that he had stopped at our homestead shack for breakfast en route to his home in Maidstone. He had forgotten. It was an incident that cleared away further questions about my understanding of farm problems.

My government also decided to establish, for the first time, an independent, federal Department of Forestry. We were fortunate in having as the Department's first Minister the Honourable Hugh John Flemming, former Premier of New Brunswick. He and his family had been in the lumber business for many years. His portfolio, therefore, was in keeping with his wide knowledge of the industry.

Premier Flemming had been defeated in the provincial election of 1960. His government had brought in a universal health insurance scheme requiring direct contributions from its recipients. He felt that if social security costs were paid for directly by the people, there might be a general realization that while politicians may promise what they will, the people cannot escape the cost. The idea seems to be widespread that governments can simply create the money for expenditures, not only for social security, but in all fields; that somewhere there is a bottomless bank which governments operate to provide the funds necessary to fulfil those political promises so conducive to winning elections. The provincial Liberals promised that, if elected, they would bring in similar legislation for which no one would have to pay (directly). They campaigned successfully by exploiting the popular notion that if one did not pay directly for government services, these services would somehow be free.

Mr. Flemming thus became available to join the federal Cabinet as Minister of Forestry. Over three hundred and fifty thousand Canadians earned their living in forestry and in the pulp-and-paper industry. Most of the publicly owned forests were administered under the constitutional jurisdiction of the provinces. Although we had no desire to encroach upon provincial rights and responsibilities in this field, we considered that the federal government had an important duty to acquire new knowledge needed by provincial forest administrators, if the forest industry were to do its full part in expanding the national economy. The more important functions of the Department were outlined by the new Minister of Forestry on 24 January 1961:

a) The conduct of comprehensive programs of research relating to forestry and the utilization of forest products.
b) Economic studies of the forest resources and the forest industries, and co-operation with the Department of Trade and Commerce in matters relating to improvement of trade in forest products.
c) To keep the public informed regarding forestry and the for-

est industries, and to promote public interest in the proper management, protection and use of the forest resources.

d) Provision of appropriate assistance to the provinces or to co-operate with any persons under agreements authorized by the Governor in Council in order to expedite progress in specific forestry programs.

e) Provision of forest surveys, technical advice and assistance to other agencies of the Dominion Government who are responsible for the administration of forest lands.

f) Co-operation with international organizations concerned with forestry and in which Canada maintains membership.

Our national development policies were aimed at extending, rationalizing, and expanding our three economic frontiers of farming, forest, and mining. In relation to the latter, I was determined that any new exploitation of Canada's North be in the interests of all Canadians. Canada's North comprises seven-tenths of our entire land area—more than 2½ million square miles. This includes the Yukon and Northwest Territories, and a very sizeable part of every province in Canada except the three Maritime Provinces. Lying mostly beyond the fringes of existing settlement, we saw in these lands the promise of even greater prosperity to the people of Canada than that which resulted from the development of the West. Our essential task was twofold: to provide, first, the basic services necessary to development; and second, to ensure the general economic climate in which private enterprise could feel confident that its efforts would be fairly rewarded if it put money and effort into northern development.

Nothing in the Liberal legacy was comparable to their regulations on northern development. Under their regulations, almost 100 per cent of our oil-reserve lands would go to the discovering company. Canadian industry was not encouraged. All that the Canadian people would get would be the usual royalty of 12½ per cent. Under regulations brought in by my government, the Crown reserved over 50 per cent of our oil-reserve lands, and we guaranteed Canadian financial participation. Our preliminary studies indicated that we had from 300 million to 1500 million of potential oil and gas acreage. The vastness of what the St. Laurent government, through lack of interest, was willing to give away is indicated by the fact that in ten years Alberta received over $1 billion in revenues from oil and gas. It was estimated that Canada had from three to fifteen times this potential in the Yukon and Northwest Territories. In 1956-57, total expenditures by the federal government on northern development amounted to only $11.9 million, whereas for 1958-59 the Department of Northern Affairs and National Resources spent approximately $33.0 million. Of this increase of $21.1 million, capital expenditures alone (i.e., expenditures on development roads, bridges, buildings, and other works in the Yukon and Northwest Territories) accounted for $14.4 million. These figures on capital expenditures do not include the Roads to Resources program in the provinces, which in 1958-59 alone amounted to some $3 million.

When it is considered that we were embarking on a development that required the expenditure of vast sums of money, public and private, to discover and exploit northern oil and gas pools, it is well to remember the rather adverse general economic conditions that had first to be overcome. We were inviting hundreds of millions of dollars in Canadian-controlled investment into northern development. It is to be noted that following a ten-year period of rapid and virtually uninterrupted expansion beginning with the Leduc discovery in February 1947, the Canadian petroleum industry suffered a severe setback in the latter half of 1957 and early 1958. In 1947, Canadian production averaged 19,000 barrels per day, accounting for only eight per cent of our domestic consumption. In 1957, output had risen 26-fold to nearly 500,000 barrels a day, the equivalent of two-thirds of our total domestic requirements, which had tripled in the interim. This development had required a capital investment of $4.5 billion, of which $3 billion was spent on exploration and development directly, and $1.5 billion on facilities such as refineries and pipelines. Then, in mid-1957, the consistently upward trend in Canadian oil output was sharply reversed. There was a cutback in demand in established markets for Canadian oil: in the United States Pacific Northwest, in British Columbia, in the Prairies, and in Ontario. Only in the United States Great Lakes area was refinery demand sustained. The demand for Canadian oil in the late 1950s was the exact reverse of the demand in the mid-1970s: the success of the Canadian oil industry was heavily dependent upon United States markets when my government came into power. And on at least two occasions we were forced to make vigorous protests to the United States government against their discriminatory oil-import quota restrictions.

We were not dismayed by these difficulties. We rose to meet them. Oil and gas permits to private industry increased from fewer than one hundred to a thousand a year. We expected that private industry, in the period from 1960 to 1967, would spend a minimum of $255.6 million in oil and gas exploration. But most important, we enacted new northern oil and gas regulations that guaranteed independence, not continentalism, to the Canadian people.

On 11 February 1957, I said in the House of Commons:

We do not want a day-to-day course wherein there are great developments in Canada depending on the world situation, but a plan...whereby Canada in the days ahead will remain an independent Canada and will not inexorably drift into economic continentalism; one whereby Canada will maintain her economic independence and her sovereignty; a policy that will provide national development for a greater Canada in which growth and prosperity will not be purchased at the expense of our economic independence and our effective national sovereignty.

Our major thrust northward began in 1958, when we announced our national development program. This had three main objectives:
1) To ascertain what resources we had, where and how much, under a continuing inventory;
2) To develop the energy resources of the nation;
3) To inaugurate a conservation approach so that the best use would be made of resources.

To carry out these objectives, various projects were launched amongst which were:
– Roads to Resources in the Territories;
– Roads to Resources to northern areas in the provinces;
– The Pine Point Railway;
– The Frobisher Bay development.

Furthermore, in 1958 Canada made a major proposal at the International Law of the Sea Conference in Geneva. The Canadian resolution to give sovereign rights to the bottom of the sea to the littoral state was accepted. Since then, the required twenty-two nations have ratified the Convention and Canada now has the sole right to develop the sea-bed contiguous to the Canadian mainland. Our development program included:
– Polar Continental Shelf Explorations, which began in 1959;
– A ten-year program of a magnetic survey of the Cordillera and the Canadian Shield;
– Completion of the gravity-meter survey of the same area;

- The doubling of the Hydrographic Survey capability;
- The establishment of an Oceanography Institute; and
- The modernization of oil, gas, and mining regulations.

In this latter connection, my government moved immediately in 1957 to cancel the regulations in effect under the St. Laurent government. Under the Territorial Lands Act, we brought in new Oil and Gas Regulations which became effective 13 April 1960. Section 32 stated that no oil and gas leases were to be granted:

a) to a person unless the Minister is satisfied
  i) that he is a Canadian citizen, or
  ii) that he is a bona fide resident of Canada and that he will be the beneficial owner of the interest to be granted by the lease;
b) to a company incorporated outside of Canada; or
c) to a company, unless the Minister is satisfied
  i) that the shares of the corporation are listed on a recognized Canadian stock exchange, or
  ii) that at least fifty per cent. of the issued shares of the corporation is beneficially owned by persons who are Canadian citizens or are bona fide residents of Canada.

We were looking to the future. But, as I have noted above, the immediate results were gratifying. The *Edmonton Journal* reflected this in its comments on 4 December 1961: "One of the brightest aspects of the economic scene in Canada, as 1961 enters its last month, is the success of the national oil policy."

I do not claim that unemployment was not a serious problem throughout much of my time as Prime Minister. As an economic indicator, however, I would suggest that there was more than one way of viewing the figures relevant. Total employment in February 1956 was 5,249,000; total employment in February 1962 was 5,840,000. This represented an increase of 591,000 jobs. Thus, when I said, "More Canadians are working than ever before," this was obviously correct. The economy was expanding. The fact was that the nature of the Canadian economy was changing; an imbalance had developed between the labour demands of goods-producing and service industries. The labour force had increased by 834,000 in the period between February 1956 and February 1962. Unemployment in the same period also increased, but at a rate lower than that in the United States. However, if one examined the statistics on the men and women unemployed in February 1962, they revealed that the vast majority were men and that unemployment was heaviest among unskilled workers and among those with relatively low levels of education.

Increased unemployment insurance was not an answer, although we increased the benefit period from sixteen to fifty-two weeks and extended eligibility. Nor did I regard the vast program of public works projects undertaken by my government as more than a stopgap. It is true that public works projects provide jobs not only for those who participate in their actual construction, but also for the trades that feed the necessary requirements of a public works program. Dollar for dollar, however, I must conclude, on the basis of my own experience, that there is not the value in public works so often ascribed to it. Further, I do not think that any country has been able to alleviate unemployment to any great extent by public works. Too often these result in projects that are ever after a drain on the public purse. Only when public works stimulate economic growth and revenue-producing capacities are they truly worthwhile.

Much more effective was the legislation we introduced in 1960 which empowered the federal government to enter into agreements with the provinces to provide financial assistance for the costs incurred in providing technical or vocational training programs. The Honourable Michael Starr, as Minister of Labour, deserves much credit here.

This was an approach that offered some prospect of solution in the long term. Under this legislation, the federal government, for the first time, shared in the costs of providing technical or vocational training in science or technology. Not only did we share the cost of teachers, instructors, supervisors, or administrators to carry out the training program but, most important, to meet the need for additional training facilities across Canada we agreed to provide contributions of up to seventy-five per cent of the cost of new facilities and equipment. These included technical and vocational schools, technical institutes, and trade schools. In consequence, some four hundred schools were either built, enlarged, restored, or rehabilitated; and hundreds of thousands of Canadians, youths and adults, received a technological training that would not otherwise have been available.

I took a very strong personal interest in this program. While education is, of course, a provincial, and not at all a federal, responsibility, I firmly believe that if we are to provide a proper and relevant education for Canadians, then the only way in which we can possibly attain our objectives is by federal aid and assistance. There is no reason why even the total cost of education at the secondary level should continue to fall on the shoulders of the homeowner.

It is interesting to note that we were several paces ahead of industry in recognizing the need for technological education. Every sophisticated industrial structure in the world had established a level intermediate between the trades and the professions. Canadian industry, perhaps reflecting its own stage of development, was slow to avail itself of the pool of talent that we helped so substantially to create. When the Pearson government arbitrarily closed our program down, the provinces determined to carry on without federal aid in maintaining what we had created. I was doubly shocked by this Liberal action when I thought back on the difficult negotiations we had with each of the provinces before we could bring our scheme into effect. This, however, became the common practice for our Liberal successors. The National Productivity Council, which might have greatly eased our industrial and technological transition, was terminated by the Pearson government before it had a chance to show more than its promise. This too was the fate of the Atlantic Development Board. Even Winter Works was abandoned. It was as if the Liberals were bent on destroying every visible evidence of my government's existence.

To return to the subject of education, my reading does not convince me that the Fathers of Confederation ever intended the provinces to exercise exclusive jurisdiction beyond the secondary level. The universities now find themselves in a desperate financial position. It was bad enough when I was Prime Minister: we increased our grants to almost double what they had been under the Liberals. Five years from now, I cannot imagine how the nation's universities will survive unless there are vast increases in federal support.

The only opposition we encountered over federal grants to universities came from the Province of Quebec. During the tenure of Premier Duplessis, federal grants were refused: $24 million had been built up in trust for Quebec's universities when we came into office. According to Mr. Duplessis, to accept this would amount to a gross interference by the federal government with provincial rights in education. I don't know whether we would have ever been able to come to agreement with him. He never gave any indication that he would change his position. When he died in September 1959, Colonel Paul Sauvé became Premier. He was a tribune of the people, a man of great ability, able to see Canada as a whole. He had none of the myopia or pretence that has afflicted certain Liberal Quebec leaders. As a matter of fact, had Sauvé lived, he might have become Prime Minister of Canada. Had he lived, we would have retained our majority in the 1962 election. He was a good friend and a fine colleague. We settled the educational issue with despatch. On 24 December 1959, I made public the following letter to Premier Sauvé announcing its solution:

If the Legislature of Quebec chooses to adopt the new plan and the Federal legislation is amended by Parliament in the manner proposed by the Government then for the next two fiscal years, commencing April 1st, 1960, and ending March 31st, 1962, the following terms will be in effect:

a) If the Legislature of Quebec should choose to raise the Provincial Corporation tax to 10 percent or more of corporation profits, corporations liable thereto will be allowed an abatement of 10 percent, instead of the present 9 percent, against the Federal tax on corporation profits;

b) The grant of $1.50 per capita of population which the Federal Government has with the sanction of Parliament been providing for universities would cease so far as the universities of the Province of Quebec are concerned;

c) The difference between the yield from the 1 percent additional tax abatement and the $1.50 per capita of population of your Province will be adjusted so that the fiscal position of the Federal Government remains unchanged. In other words, if the 1 percent tax abatement exceeds the equivalent of $1.50 per capita of population, as it will, the Federal Government will deduct this excess from the equalization payment now being paid to Quebec out of the Federal treasury in pursuance of the provisions of the Federal–Provincial Tax-Sharing Arrangements Act. By way of illustration, if the new formula were applied to 1959 data the Federal treasury would lose and the Provincial treasury would gain about

$9,250,000 from the change in corporation tax rates. On the other hand, the university grants on the basis of $1.50 per capita if applied to Quebec would amount to about $7,500,000; and the difference of $1,750,000 would be deducted from the equalization payment to Quebec, which in 1959 will be approximately $67,000,000.

When the Liberal Party came into power in Quebec following Colonel Sauvé's untimely death, the question of federal grants to universities was reopened by Premier Jean Lesage. It was not the principle that concerned him; it was how to get more money under the "Diefenbaker–Sauvé" formula.

In the broader field of public education, one of the important achievements of my government was to begin the reconstruction of Louisbourg on Nova Scotia's Cape Breton Island. We considered that a historic reconstruction offered a most dramatic means of teaching our nation's history to its citizens and to our visitors; that the more vividly history was illustrated by this means, the more indelibly would the facts and forces of history be impressed on the public mind. Prior to its second capture from the French by the British forces in 1758, Louisbourg was a complex and important community. As a seat of French colonial government, it had palaces and courtyards; as North America's strongest and most costly fortress, its cannons and vast fortifications and barracks were constant reminders of war and violence; it had wharves and merchantmen, fish flakes and coal yards, churches, a hospital, shops, taverns, dwellings, all thronging with people. Lest the lesson of history be lost, we judged that a restoration should try to achieve not only an accurate historical impression of a cross-section of life in Louisbourg at its height, but also an impression of the doom which befell it on capture and demolition. The lands contained in the 1745 and 1758 captures encompassed an area of about twenty-five square miles. The projected costs were substantial, and ran, depending upon the extent of the restoration, anywhere from $6,641,000 over a ten-year period to $18,664,000 over a fifteen-year period. This restoration also provided a source of new jobs in a hard-pressed area of Cape Breton.

There were critics who claimed that my "Vision" for Canada was no more than empty rhetoric, that there was no national plan. It is a fact that those who will not see cannot be made to see. When we embarked upon our great Roads to Resources program, we did not lose sight of the Maritime Provinces. If they had no new land resources to discover, they did have a physical beauty and attractiveness that could be exploited for tourist dollars. We therefore applied our road-building program to that end. The tourist value of the Louisbourg restoration was another aspect of this. As part of our national agricultural policy, we spent in excess of seven million dollars under the Maritime Marshland Rehabilitation Act. Had we remained the government, the economic position of Prince Edward Island would have been greatly enhanced. On 27 February 1962 the Cabinet agreed with the recommendation of the Honourable David Walker, Minister of Public Works, a man who at all times had a national perspective, that approval in principle be given to proceed with the Northumberland Strait Causeway project, as an alternative to the existing ferry system linking New Brunswick and Prince Edward Island. We wanted first to investigate the possibility of a combined causeway–tunnel crossing to handle road traffic. Thereafter, a further report would be submitted to the Cabinet as to the most economic basis for constructing a crossing. Under the Pearson government all this went the historical route of the ship–railway project of an earlier era to link the Bay of Fundy with the Northumberland Strait. The approaches to the Causeway, constructed before we left

office, stand today as a sad reminder of what might have
been.

Nationally, we completed the Trans-Canada Highway.
We extended the legislation covering its construction to
provide an additional fifty million dollars so that we
might be linked together by a national highway 4,877
miles long. We brought Quebec into this vital project for
the first time when the Honourable David Walker signed
an agreement with the province in October 1960. To complete this highway over the north shore of Lake Superior
was a considerable feat; to extend it through the Rogers
Pass route in British Columbia was a very difficult and
costly construction task indeed. Canadians now travel
from coast to coast in numbers that no one in 1956 would
have believed possible.

It is paradoxical but true that whatever assistance we
gave to the provinces redounded to the political credit of
the provinces. They forgot altogether the assistance that
had come from my government. I know of no exception.
This was true in Newfoundland. This was true in British
Columbia. This was true even in Manitoba. I take nothing
away from the achievements of Duff Roblin. In 1957, he
worked very hard on behalf of Conservative candidates.
He stood with me as Leader of the Opposition in the
meetings that were held in Manitoba. He might not have
become Premier had we not won the 1957 election. We
elected seven federal Members from Manitoba. We
formed a government which gave incentive and enthusiasm to our supporters throughout Canada. The hopeless-
ness and the defeatism of Conservatives everywhere was
supplanted by the hope that what had been done nationally could be done provincially. In the 1958 election, we
swept Manitoba's fourteen seats. Immediately thereafter
Roblin was able to elect a minority government. The following year he went to the people and achieved a majority. It was my government that asked Parliament to ap-

prove funds to provide a Floodway to protect the city of Winnipeg and surrounding communities from the ravages of floods when the Red and Assiniboine rivers overflowed their banks, as they intermittently did. (My maternal forebears had experienced this when they arrived at the Selkirk Settlement in 1813.) The proposition that this was a matter of national concern was strongly pressed by the Honourable Gordon Churchill. We had a full study made. We agreed to contribute thirty million dollars to the province for the Floodway. I have yet to hear a word of thanks or appreciation to the federal government for what we did. When I announced on 17 November 1961 that we would pay sixty per cent of the costs of this project, Premier Roblin took the credit; Gordon Churchill deserved it.

In Newfoundland, whenever anything was done—for example, the thirteen-million-dollar harbour improvement at St. John's—Smallwood would say, "Look me over. See what I've done," with that modesty that has characterized him at all times. On the other side of the country, in British Columbia, the Honourable W. A. C. Bennett, the Premier, a remarkable man, never gave us credit for completing the Trans-Canada at tremendous cost through the Rogers Pass. Indeed, knowing that we were going to have an official opening, he had his own opening for the province of British Columbia a couple of weeks in advance. I did not regard this as abnormal. This is politics.

When my government set up a Royal Commission on Health Services in June 1961, under the chairmanship of Emmett Hall, the Chief Justice of Saskatchewan, to make "a comprehensive and independent study of existing facilities and future need for health services for the people of Canada", the Douglas government in Saskatchewan moved on the medicare question. Some have contended that the Medicare legislation of the province of Saskatchewan was a political move on the part of that government to anticipate the findings of the Hall Report.

The outstanding example of pure politics that comes to mind, however, belongs to my successor as Prime Minister, the Right Honourable Lester Pearson. When the Pine Point Railway was officially opened (a project the Liberals had ridiculed when we decided to proceed with its financing), I did not even receive an invitation. Without our decision to subsidize the construction of this rail line from Roma, Alberta, to the shores of Great Slave Lake, one of the world's great base-metal formations would never have been mined. The entire operation has been a tremendous success.

The simple fact is that we did business on a national scale. As Prime Minister, I had to look at the problems of the entire nation; I tried to see the balance between immediate needs and long-term goals, between the economic needs and the social needs of all Canadians. I did not regard Canada as a series of Balkanized republics. My goal was to break down the barriers of region and race, not in the interests of cultural homogenization—anything but that—but to create a strong, independent, and viable nation.

One very important item of national business that many have forgotten with the passage of time might serve to illustrate further this question of necessary overview. In the years 1957 to 1963 we lived in anticipation of nuclear war, and had to think in relevant terms. The Free World was living on a razor edge, and we had to make plans accordingly. For example, there were various functions of government that would have been particularly essential in the early intense period of nuclear war: general direction of the defence forces; conduct of foreign relations concerning the war; general direction of civil defence activities; preservation of law and order; provision and allocation of housing accommodation; provision and distribution of food, fuel, power, and other essential supplies; provision and control of essential medical and public health services; maintenance and control of transport and communication facilities; basic management of public finances and whatever emergency financial measures were necessary to maintain the population and a workable economic system; direction and control of the production and distribution of various essential materials and services, including control of prices; and re-employment of manpower in accordance with emergency priorities. If the war ended shortly after this early shock period, there would then have been a period of rehabilitation and reconstruction, during which the functions of government would become more varied and complex as the immediate tasks gave way to those of longer term. If the war continued, the problems of government would be very difficult, particularly because of the need to allocate surviving resources between competing civilian and military demands.

We had to be equipped to adapt to the variety of contingencies that might arise in a major war. It was probable that attack would come with little or no warning. Our communication and transportation facilities were highly vulnerable. Normal peacetime arrangements for government in Canada would be of little use in the event of a major war. In consequence, we set about the development of a flexible federal system of emergency government, with central, regional, and some zonal elements. We worked out appropriate liaison in co-operation with provincial and municipal authorities. Much was made of our decision to create an emergency government centre outside Ottawa—probably one of the worst-kept secrets ever—and it was jocularly referred to in the press as the "Diefenbunker". But I can tell you frankly that with the awesome responsibilities in prospect, it was anything but a joke. The Emergency Measures Organization people insisted that a bomb shelter be constructed at 24 Sussex Drive, the Prime Minister's residence. And at a cost of less than four hundred and fifty dollars a small shelter was built between the rocks so that Olive and I would have some protection during a nuclear attack. Fortunately, nuclear war did not come. And if our senses are somewhat dulled to any current threat, the organization that my government created over twenty-five years ago is there if catastrophe strikes, ready to serve Canadians in any emergency, whether military or civil.

It is the clear responsibility of a government to take those measures demanded by considerations of national security. In my opinion, it was also the responsibility of government to provide an appropriate climate and opportunity for national economic development. This is the expression of a belief in the role of public or government enterprise as a necessary catalyst for the fullest functioning of our system of private enterprise. This belief envisages a policy of practical partnership between public and private enterprise. This philosophy was particularly applicable to northern development in Canada. In general, our policies were successful.

By early 1962, our economy had recovered from the recession. I wrote to the Honourable George Drew, Canada's High Commissioner in London, on 3 March that year: "The economic situation in Canada has vastly improved in the last few months. Economic indicators in almost all sectors are favourable to a tremendous expansion and even the Liberal leaders who have been voicing doom and gloom are being forced to admit that such is the case. . . ."

CHAPTER TEN

❋

WHEN I BECAME THE LEADER, the Conservative Party was regarded as a vanishing breed nationally. My endeavour was to broaden the base of Canadian citizenship. Ethnically, every Canadian would see the end of exclusion from the enjoyment of the full benefits and responsibilities of Canadian citizenship. This concept included French Canada. I believed in the constitution, and in the rights of French-speaking Canadians as constitutionally guaranteed. I publicly and privately accepted the position taken by Sir John Macdonald in the House of Commons on 17 February 1890: "I have no accord with the desire expressed in some quarters that by any mode whatever there should be an attempt made to oppress the one language at the expense of the other; I believe that it would be impossible if it were tried, and it would be foolish and wicked if it were possible." During my period of office I tried to do those things that ought to have been done under the constitution. Provision was made for effective bilingualism in the House of Commons through the introduction of simultaneous translation. In consequence, for the first time in our history, French-speaking Members could take their full part in debate. In the past, important debates had been in English; even a major speech in the French language had served too often to empty the House. The result was that until 1958, those Members from Quebec not fluent in English were excluded from democracy's most important process. This was recognized in Quebec at the time, and the response of French Canada to simultaneous translation in the House of Commons was overwhelmingly enthusiastic. For years, there had been far too few appointments in the higher ranks of the Civil Service for French Canadians. I remedied this through a program of actively recruiting the French-speaking talent which good government in Canada required. There was, understandably, desire and demand that government documents, cheques and the like be printed in both languages. The Liberal governments of King and St. Laurent had rejected the idea because the cost was too high. But, when in July 1962 all family allowance, old age security, and other card cheques, which accounted for almost ninety per cent of all Receiver General cheques, were issued in bilingual form, this was dismissed by partisan Liberals as of no consequence. Our critics asked: "Is that all? What else are you going to do?" I replied: "I'm going to continue to live up to the constitution."

In answer to a hostile press in Quebec which had never taken serious issue with the King and St. Laurent governments for *not* making the advances that were made by my government, the Honourable Noël Dorion said in Quebec City on 9 December 1960:

How can we say that the Prime Minister of Canada could think of bringing together in a sort of melting pot Canadians of French expression, origin and culture, and those of English expression, origin and culture along with all other Canadians? The present Prime Minister of Canada has not tried as others to flatter us at election time and to compliment grudgingly the ethnic group to which we belong. His thoughts and feelings he has expressed by his actions. He who has introduced simultaneous translation in the House of Commons, who has recommended one of ours, General Vanier, to occupy the most important position in the country, that of Governor General of Canada, cannot be the assimilator that some accuse him of being.

There were even those who took exception to our policies to make the nation's capital, Ottawa (not Ottawa–Hull or any other strange convolution), attractive to all Canadians. The Honourable David Walker deserves credit as Minister of Public Works for organizing the National Capital Commission, acquiring some thirty thousand acres of land for the Ottawa Green Belt, extending and developing vast new areas in Gatineau Park, closing down the old Union Station opposite the Château Laurier and building the new Hurdman's Station. He also brought an end to twenty-five years of disagreement between the governments of Canada, Quebec, Ontario, Hull, and Ottawa in an agreement to build the Macdonald–Cartier Bridge across the Ottawa River.

We were concerned also to preserve Ottawa's past, and we instituted policies to restore its historic architecture. Early in 1957, after I became Leader of the Opposition, I took strong objection to the destruction of the historic building on the west side of Parliament Hill which started as a barn and was later occupied by the Supreme Court of Canada. There some of Canada's most historic cases were tried. Several Prime Ministers of Canada had argued cases in that building. It had been the centre of Canada's freedom and should have been preserved, but during the 1957 election campaign it was demolished to provide a parking lot. To add a touch of drama for the many visitors to our capital, we initiated the Changing of the Guard ceremonies on Parliament Hill. When a subsequent administration decided that this ceremony was too "British" to be Canadian and attempted to do away with it, public outcry was so loud that they had to reinstate it. We also instituted, beginning on 1 July 1958, an annual Dominion Day national birthday celebration on Parliament Hill. It was to have the effect of bringing together Canadians of all racial origins through performances representative of the artistry of our many lands of origin. Canadians everywhere were joined together as national television and radio carried this celebration of Canada's greatness into their homes. The Trudeau government in 1976 cancelled the Parliament Hill celebration altogether.

I must point out that one of the early decisions of my government in 1957 was to re-establish the use of the word "Dominion" in Canada. This had fallen into gradual disfavour during the St. Laurent period, although this was as nothing when compared to its sacrifice since 1963. Liberals have tried to attach to "Dominion" the unsavoury connotation of colonial subservience. On the contrary, it stands as a proud word: "And they shall have dominion from sea unto sea" was the Scriptural inspiration of one of the Fathers of Confederation in suggesting an acceptable alternative to Sir John Macdonald's stated desire to call our confederation "The Kingdom of Canada". That the word "Dominion" was subsequently used throughout the Empire and Commonwealth to describe those colonies which had followed Canada's example in attaining full self-government is a tribute to our own nation. To suggest otherwise is to deliberately falsify the record. We are the Dominion of Canada.

And it was to prepare for the celebration of our country's One Hundredth Birthday that my government set in motion the plans necessary to co-ordinate activities at every level across this country to make possible the grand and appropriate Centennial Celebrations of 1967. It was Senator Marc Drouin and the Honourable Pierre Sévigny who first put forward the idea for Expo 67 in Montreal. Marc Drouin was a man of ability who had an understanding of Canada as a whole, and I appointed him to the Senate, where he served as Government Leader. His premature death was a great loss to Canada. I believe it was Colonel Sévigny who first asked me to do what I could to bring about Canada's selection as the site for the international exposition in 1967. The following day, Senator Drouin came to me with a more detailed proposal. Shortly thereafter, the Young Men's Board of Trade of Montreal made representations following a discussion with Senator Drouin. Out of all this came my decision to bring this matter before Cabinet. My colleagues agreed that we should do everything we could to bring the world exposition to Montreal in 1967. We vigorously pursued this objective internationally to compensate for the lateness of our application, and we succeeded.

There were other areas of our national policy that I considered of fundamental importance if Canada was to remain strong and free. Thus, the 1958 Speech from the Throne stated my government's intention: "To ensure that the Canadian Broadcasting Corporation and the privately-owned broadcasting stations work effectively together to constitute a national system to provide satisfactory television and radio services to all Canadians within reach." The real problem in national broadcasting policy was the conflict between the east–west flow of Canadian programs and the south–north flow of American programs. I did not agree with those who believed that the real conflict lay between the public and the private broadcasting systems. Canada's policy in national broadcasting was first developed by Prime Minister Bennett, who set up the Canadian Radio Broadcasting Commission, later to become the Canadian Broadcasting Corporation. Three royal commissions and thirteen parliamentary committees in the years intervening between his government and mine had not seen fit to challenge this policy in any substantial way.

From the point of view of quick profits, private broadcasters, with what amounted to a Liberal Party licence to print money, aided and abetted by a form of intellectual and artistic "dumping" from the United States, filled prime time with American-produced programs. Without a national broadcasting policy, Canadians were likely to be swamped by United States cultural and political values. Since our magazines were weak and our films already almost exclusively American, radio and television were the last bulwarks for a national policy in the field of communications. Indeed, there was a powerful argument that only in the realm of ideas could we find the ultimate safeguard against the erosion of our national consciousness and of our national economy. In my view, the CBC was as much to blame as the private stations. It may be the essential truth that the CBC had become so indoctrinated with the Liberal viewpoint that it indiscriminately embraced North American continentalism and could not differentiate, its academic and intellectual pretences to the contrary, between American national opinion and true internationalism. It was therefore important that national broadcasting policy be regulated by a body responsive to Parliament and to the needs of the Canadian nation.

The new Broadcasting Act was introduced in 1958. In general, this legislation followed the recommendations of the Fowler Royal Commission on Broadcasting, appointed under the St. Laurent administration. There were, however, a few substantial differences. Our Act was divided into two parts. Part one was concerned with the Board of Broadcast Governors, a new body created for the purpose of regulating broadcasting in Canada in all its phases, including the power to grant licences to new stations. Both of these powers had previously been exercised by the CBC. The Fowler Commission had recommended the creation of an independent body, solely responsible for regulation. The government agreed with this, but failed to see any justification that the CBC retain a licensing function. When the new Act came into force, the Board was established with Dr. Andrew Stewart as Chairman, Mr. Roger Duhamel as Vice-Chairman, and Mr. Carlyle Allison, nationally known newspaperman from Winnipeg, as the third permanent member. In addition to these three permanent members, there were twelve part-time members representing the nation as a whole. With the Board truly representative of all areas and sectors of the nation, we hoped that this body would become the means to the kind of national broadcasting system the nation deserved. Its function was not to adjudicate between the CBC and the private stations, but to ensure close and efficient co-operation between them. Otherwise, the stated objective of a single national system would be unobtainable.

The other substantial change made by this Act was to create a new corporation, maintaining the original name, the Canadian Broadcasting Corporation. This corporation was empowered to carry on the business of broadcasting over the national system but was in all respects to be subject to the regulations enacted by the Board of Broadcast Governors. Mr. Alphonse Ouimet was appointed President and General Manager. Mr. E. L. Bushnell, a man of wide experience and the former Assistant General Manager of the CBC, was made Vice-President and Assistant General Manager.

In a related area of national importance, I have already noted that Canadian magazines were far from strong. As we viewed the state of the periodical press in Canada, we were concerned. The publishers of Canadian national periodicals made repeated representations to my government to the effect that the growing competition of foreign periodicals threatened their future existence. This competition included the "overflow" into Canada of periodicals published in the United States, publication of "Canadian editions" of United States magazines, and printing in the United States of special "runs" of United States magazines to be sold in Canada for which Canadian advertising was specifically solicited. These representations obviously had some basis in view of the rapidly diminishing number of periodicals published in Canada. Canadian publishers urged that, if the present trends were permitted to continue, Canadian periodicals of popular interest would soon number no more than two or three.

The St. Laurent administration had attempted to provide some relief by means of the so-called "magazine tax" which imposed a levy of twenty per cent on the advertising revenue of special Canadian editions of foreign magazines. We asked Parliament to repeal this legislation in 1958. When recommending its repeal, the Minister of Finance, the Honourable Donald Fleming, in his budget speech of 17 June 1958, said:

The government has a sympathetic interest in the problems confronting Canadian magazines. We believe that Canadian magazines are contributing to the quality of our national life. But this interest does not blind us to the inequities introduced by this tax. When we were on the opposite side of the House we warned repeatedly that this tax would prove to be both unjust and ineffective. Experience has confirmed our views. . . .

I do not under-estimate the difficulties which Canadian magazines are facing. Likewise, I do not under-estimate the difficulties of government action in this field. If government is to give any special support it should be in a manner that infringes neither the freedom of the press nor the reading preferences of the public. A number of proposals have been put forward, but none has proved to be both practical and acceptable. While we are prepared to study any serious proposal to encourage a truly Canadian periodic press, it must conform with the principles I have stated.

My colleagues and I concluded that a Royal Commission should be appointed to investigate the entire question. In addition to the commercial and financial issues, the Commission could investigate and report on all phases of the problem, including its cultural ones. *The Report of the Royal Commission on National Development in the Arts, Letters and Sciences* had described Canada's periodical press as "our closest approximation to a national literature". For this reason, it was my hope that the Chairman of that earlier Commission would undertake the responsibilities of this new one. Accordingly, on 30 June 1960 I wrote to the Right Honourable Vincent Massey, who had retired as Governor General: "Because of your great interest in this subject, the experience you have gained and the thought you have given to the problems related to the development of a Canadian national entity, my colleagues and I believe that, if a Royal Commission is to be established, there is no Canadian better qualified than yourself to serve as its chairman and to guide its work. By doing so, you would make yet another notable contribution to the interests and progress of Canada." Mr. Massey regretted that he could not undertake this task. In consequence, I approached Mr. Grattan O'Leary, editor of the *Ottawa Journal*, who accepted this responsibility. Claude Beaubien, a public relations and advertising expert from Montreal, and George Johnston, an experienced and able public relations expert from Toronto, were his fellow Commissioners. They began their work on 16 September 1960, and on 15 June 1961 their *Report* was tabled in the House of Commons. Its principal recommendations were:

1) That periodicals containing advertising that is primarily directed to the Canadian market be no longer permitted to enter Canada from abroad.

2) That the deduction from income by a taxpayer of expenditures incurred for advertising directed to the Canadian market in a foreign periodical wherever printed be disallowed.

On 7 June 1961, I received a memorandum entitled "Royal Commission on Publications: Fiscal Proposals" from Mr. Fleming. He indicated that, if the two major recommendations were implemented, the Canadian editions of *Time* and *Reader's Digest* (in both languages) would cease publication and added that this appeared to be the intention of the Royal Commission.

The representatives of the Canadian Periodical Press Association strongly supported the two main recommendations of the Royal Commission *Report*, although they did not reject the possibility of modification. Thus, they referred to the claims that there ought to be a modification in the severity of the main tax proposal in order to avoid actually driving out of business an established operation in Canada, i.e., *Reader's Digest*. But they strongly supported the principle on which these and other recommendations were based: that a nation's advertising expenditures should support its own media of communications and not those of other countries. They argued that this applied to television and to other media in addition to magazines, but recognized that it would be difficult to apply it to these other media at least without full hearings such as had been provided by the Commission. They emphasized that the main tariff recommendation was designed to prevent the importation, not only of *Time* when printed in the United States, but also of many other United States periodicals, both consumer magazines and trade papers, carrying advertising directed to Canadian readers.

Strong representations were made to my government by the representatives of *Reader's Digest* and *Time*. It is important to record that they did not forecast the immediate cessation of their Canadian editions if the *Report* were implemented. Instead they felt the outcome would be that they would be forced, after an experimental period of some months or years, to discontinue these editions; meanwhile they would attempt, by various adjustments, to continue publication. The representative of *Time* explained that his firm was proceeding with arrangements to print their Canadian edition in Canada instead of in the United States, and to establish a staff of about a dozen persons in Montreal to edit its "Canadian" section. He anticipated that the presses and the staff would be installed by the end of 1961. At that time, they would cease to be affected by the main tariff recommendation and would instead be affected by the main tax recommendation of the *Report*. The basic question was whether some modification or modifications should be introduced into the main tax proposal to take account of the situations of *Reader's Digest* and *Time*, and permit them to continue.

On 22 January 1962, I informed the House that since the tabling of the *Report*:

... there has been time for a mature and searching appraisal by the government, and by the public, of the conclusions and recommendations of the commission and the information and argument on which they are based.

The commission, in vigorous and persuasive language, calls our attention to the unique role that Canadian magazines play, or ought to play, in our national life. The report states:

"So far as the printed word is concerned, it is largely left to our periodical press, to our magazines big and little, to make a conscious appeal to the nation; to try to interpret Canada to all Canadians, to bring a sense of oneness to our scattered communities. It is but necessary to note the veritable deluge of United States publications submerging Canadian print on our newsstands to understand the magnitude and, in the past, the impossibility, of their task.

"So pervasive, indeed, is this penetration, so obviously fraught with social and economic consequences, no examination of any aspect of Canadian communications can fail to take it into account. Here, inescapably, is the stuff of national concern."

I fully recognized that the issues at stake went to the very fabric of our culture. In relation to the *Report's* two main recommendations, I said:

It is the intention of the government to implement the first of these recommendations; that is to say, the government proposes, in due course, to prevent the importation of periodicals containing advertising that is primarily directed to the Canadian market. This will not in any way interfere with the continued importation into Canada of the many magazines that are printed and published abroad and that carry advertising that is primarily directed to their own home markets. It will, however, prevent publishers of magazines in other countries from preparing, as a by-product, and sending into Canada, adaptations of their magazines in which they carry advertising directed to the Canadian market.

As for the second major recommendation of the report, it is the intention of the government to implement it but with an important modification. If this recommendation were implemented without a change the result would be not merely to prevent the future establishment in Canada of foreign-owned, foreign-edited periodicals, but to put an extremely heavy, they claim, burden on those which have already been established here. The latter, in that they import most, if not all, of their reading matter as a by-product of their parent magazines abroad, have an unfair competitive advantage over their Canadian competitors; and this advantage must be offset. On the other hand, they have established themselves in this country in good faith, they employ Canadian labour, and they attempt to supply Canadian readers with a specially adapted product.

Accordingly, in applying the recommendation that advertising placed in non-Canadian magazines be no longer deductible as an ordinary business expense for tax purposes, the government will introduce an important, although partial, exception. As a general rule, the recommendation will be applied, and this tax change is expected to make it unprofitable to initiate the publication of any new by-product magazines in this country. However, there will be an amelioration in the case of non-Canadian magazines that are already, as of today, published and printed in Canada, and that are or will shortly be carrying on editing operations in this country. When Canadian advertisers place advertisements in these latter magazines, their advertising outlays will continue to be deductible expenditures to the extent of 50 per cent. In other words, half the burden proposed by the royal commission will be removed from those non-Canadian periodicals that have established their operations within this country.

Believing that the solution as above set out was eminently practical, the Cabinet decided to proceed accordingly. The events that prevented the bringing down of a budget following the 1962 election left this question unresolved.

Today, of course, the Canadian edition of *Time* magazine no longer exists. Having driven it from our shores, the Trudeau government has created a virtual monopoly situation for a national newsmagazine of questionable political judgment. The ambitions of various provincial governments to control cable television and the federal government's apparent fascination with "pay television" threaten the very existence of our national broadcasting system. I will have more to say about these matters later.

It might be appropriate, before I conclude this volume, to mention here my thinking with regard to the Glassco Commission, although an account of its findings and the policies of my government to implement its recommendations properly belong in my next volume. To give maxi-

mum effect to the decisions of Parliament, all Cabinets require the services of the best possible Civil Service. It is
not always possible for necessary changes in the structure and operation of the Civil Service to be effected from
within. This is particularly so when new emphasis is
brought to bear and new programs are instituted in the
majority of government departments within a relatively
short period of time. When operations become needlessly
complex and cumbersome, co-ordination breaks down
and effective political control becomes difficult. We had
embarked on so many new programs and had established
so many new priorities that this state of affairs was probably inevitable. It was a situation the Cabinet sought to
rectify. On 7 September 1960, Mr. Grant Glassco of Toronto accepted my invitation to direct what was to be the
Canadian equivalent of the Hoover Commission in the
United States. We decided that it was in the national interest to set up a Royal Commission to make a comprehensive and detailed inquiry into the best means of promoting efficiency, economy, and improved service in the
operation of the departments and agencies of the federal
government. This report was to be completed within two
years. Mr. Glassco was a distinguished chartered accountant and corporate director. I considered that because of his wide experience in business, he might be
able to do for Canada what former United States President Hoover had done for the Truman administration in
the United States; or what the Bridges secret committee
had done in its investigation of British government. At
Mr. Glassco's recommendation, R. Watson Sellar, former
Auditor General in the federal government, was appointed to the commission. The third member appointed
was F. Eugene Thérien, Q.C., president of La Caisse Nationale d'Économie.

The Glassco Royal Commission was instructed to report upon measures that might be taken in the organiza-

tion of the federal bureaucracy for the purpose of:

1) Eliminating duplication and overlapping of services;
2) Eliminating unnecessary or uneconomic operations;
3) Achieving efficiency or economy through further decentralization of operations and administration;
4) Achieving improved management of departments and agencies or portions thereof, with consideration to organization, methods of work, defined authorities and responsibilities, and provision for training;
5) Making more efficient use of budgeting, accounting, and other financial measures as means of achieving more efficient and economical management of departments and agencies;
6) Improving efficiency and economy by alterations in the relations between government departments and agencies, on the one hand, and the Treasury Board and other central control or service agencies of the government on the other; and
7) Achieving efficiency or economy through reallocation or regrouping of units of the public service.

While leaving the detail for later, I wish to note that our implementation of the many particulars of the Glassco *Report* saved Canadians millions of dollars without in any way diminishing the quality of the public service.

When I spoke to my fellow Canadians on CBC television's "The Nation's Business" on 21 June 1961, I said:

If I were to take special pride in any one aspect of the accomplishments of these four years it would be the advances we have achieved for the average Canadian in the broad field of social justice.

This includes many aspects of our life from the protection and preservation for all time of the individual rights and personal freedoms in the Bill of Rights to the many measures taken to ease the burdens of those of our fellows who, for reasons beyond their own control, are least able to bear them. We have given Canadians equality under the law, whatever their race or creed; we have outlawed discrimination based on surname, racial origin or colour.

As to specific social security matters, I added:

... We have almost doubled the total amounts paid each year by the federal government in Old Age Pensions, Blind and Disability Allowances, Unemployment Insurance and Assistance, Hospital Insurance and Hospital Construction Grants, Health Grants and Veterans Pensions and Allowances....

Although, in the end, it is by individual effort that freedom lives and expands, my government was not forgetful of the poor and the under-privileged, and endeavoured as well to bring new hope to the inmates of penal institutions to enable them to take their place in society. The Minister of Justice, the Honourable Mr. Fulton, introduced and initiated important and long-overdue reforms in the general field of justice. We established the National Parole Board in 1959, consisting of five members, one of them a woman. This was part of a new policy designed to make increased use of parole as a release method while at the same time giving full consideration to the protection of the public. During the first two years of its operation, the Board granted 4,497 paroles, experiencing only a 6.7 per cent failure rate in relation to the number of paroles granted, a failure rate that was one of the lowest in the world. The Board also initiated changes whereby an inmate could qualify for remission of his sentence by reason of good conduct and industry. It was hoped that earned remission would operate as an incentive to an inmate to apply himself towards his own self-improvement. The Board expanded the use of the pre-release system. Further, we took measures to transform Canada's penal system into a modern and effective correctional program.

New penal institutions of various types were opened; two of the existing eight maximum-security institutions were transformed to medium security; and the programs of treatment and training within the confines of all the institutions were radically reformed. The first comprehensive revision of the Penitentiary Act since its enactment in 1883 was introduced under my administration. The intention of the government was to salvage as many offenders as possible. Rehabilitation, not punishment, was our aim. This could not always be achieved and the public had to be protected; but I might observe that every dollar saved in custodial cost was a double blessing to the paying citizen.

The Capital Murder Bill introduced in 1961 divided murder into two categories: capital and non-capital. Under this legislation the death penalty was attached only to murder of a planned, deliberate nature or to a homicide in the course of committing a crime. Under this legislation, only the person who committed the act resulting in death was to be subject to the death penalty. Life sentences became the penalty on conviction of a non-capital murder charge. My government considered that the killing of a police or penitentiary officer in the discharge of his duty was capital murder. Never once did I, as Prime Minister, allow the fact that capital punishment was personally repugnant to me deter me from making certain that the law was carried out. When a capital case came before Cabinet for review, as it must under the law, and where there was no recommendation of mercy from the jury, no extenuating circumstances, and no new evidence to cast doubt on the guilt of the convicted individual, the law took its course.

Further, the Royal Canadian Mounted Police Act and Regulations were completely revised in 1960. Thus, for the first time since 1894, the provisions governing the organization and discipline of the Royal Canadian Mounted

Police were modernized and streamlined. Several new concepts were incorporated: pensions as a matter of right; provision that disability as well as retirement pensions might be received where injury occurred while on duty; and allowance of a deferred annuity when a member retired before reaching pensionable length of service. We reduced the restriction on the right of a member to marry from five years to two years of service. Administrative procedures were improved. One hundred and twenty-one new detachment and headquarters buildings were completed between June 1957 and January 1962, and the total strength of the Force was increased. More important has been the repute of this great organization. The North West Mounted Police–Royal Canadian Mounted Police have created a great part of the Canadian legend, and have given to our history elements of myth and poetry. More than any other group or institution, the Force symbolizes Canada, whether at home or abroad. I was not prepared to see its brilliance tarnished by the anti-labour actions of the Smallwood government in Newfoundland.

In February 1959, Premier Smallwood pushed through his Liberal-dominated legislature a bill decertifying the International Woodworkers of America, whose members were on strike to back demands for a fifty-four-hour work-week at $1.22 per hour. Violence broke out. The RCMP, under a contract between the Newfoundland and the Canadian governments, served as Newfoundland's provincial police force (as in every province except Ontario and Quebec). Smallwood wanted to use the RCMP to break the International Woodworkers of America union.

In early March 1959, I received a request from the Newfoundland Premier that fifty additional RCMP constables be sent to that province. As I told the House on 16 March:

While this government has no intention of infringing on matters under provincial jurisdiction, I feel impelled to say that the premier of Newfoundland has greatly aggravated the present situation in that province by intervening in a labour dispute in a way which apparently goes beyond the usual role of government. The result, as might have been anticipated, has been a violent reaction on the part of the workers concerned. Under the circumstances we have concluded that it would be provocative and likely to cause further outbreaks of violence to authorize the sending of further members of the RCMP at this time.

We feel that the Royal Canadian Mounted Police has performed its duty with fairness and efficiency. The situation in Newfoundland will be kept constantly under review and if the Mounted Police, in the proper discharge of their duties, are subject to or encounter intimidation or threats by lawbreakers reconsideration will be given immediately to this decision.

The year was 1959. Unions had certain legal rights. The demands of the IWA had the backing of the provincially appointed conciliator in the dispute. We were being asked to provide RCMP reinforcements to recreate a strike-breaking scene from the 1930s. To have done this would have amounted to an intolerable social and political retrogression. I was aware that the Newfoundland economy was in a perilous state, and that if the loggers' strike resulted in the closing of the two pulp-and-paper mills, the result might be serious indeed. I also knew that Smallwood's was a spendthrift government and that his ill-considered economic policies had cost the Newfoundland people dearly. I was not prepared to sacrifice the national reputation of the RCMP to save either Mr. Smallwood or the reactionary corporations which owned the Newfoundland forest industry.

Unfortunately, this controversy was clouded by the decision of Commissioner L. H. Nicholson of the RCMP to resign over the issue. The Honourable Davie Fulton summed up his and the government's views in a letter to Commissioner Nicholson on 16 March:

The fundamental difference between us, as I view the matter, centres around your conclusion that there has been a breach of the clause quoted by you from the contract between Canada and Newfoundland.

The obligation imposed on Canada by that clause is to increase the number of members of the force in the province if, in my opinion as Attorney General of Canada, "having regard to other responsibilities and duties of the force", such increase is possible.

In reaching my conclusion on the question whether "having regard to other responsibilities and duties of the force", such increase were possible, I, of course, as you know, gave the most careful and anxious consideration to your views that additional members could and should be sent to Newfoundland without prejudice to other responsibilities and duties of the force. However, upon a consideration of all the factors, including especially the importance of preserving the character and capacity of the force to discharge its duty in connection with law enforcement in all of Canada, I came to the conclusion, after consulting my colleagues, that, as the situation existed at that time, it was not possible to send the additional men requested without prejudicing the other responsibilities and duties of the force.

This decision was my responsibility. I reached it only after the most careful consideration of your views and of all the other factors that, in my judgment, were relevant. I regret profoundly that you came to the conclusion that, by reason of that decision, you should resign.

Much as I regret your decision to tender your resignation, under these circumstances I have no alternative but to accept it and am prepared to make a submission to the Governor-in-Council accordingly.

I could only agree with I. Norman Smith, who wrote in

the *Ottawa Journal*:

It will be argued that Commissioner Nicholson's interpretation of this particular clause in this particular agreement was right, the Minister of Justice's interpretation wrong. The argument will be irrelevant. The interpretation of the Minister of Justice may be wrong, the interpretation of the Cabinet wrong, but wrong or right it was their sole responsibility to make it. Certainly if we come to the position where final interpretation of the meaning of agreements or treaties between the Government of Canada and other governments, plus what action should be taken on them, must be left to the heads of government administrative departments or branches or agencies, then our whole concept of government, of where government responsibility must rest, goes under.

Our mandate, above all else, was for the good government of the nation. I was interested in winning elections too, but I was determined to justify the faith of the people in my party and leadership. There was a price for political success that no Conservative could pay. Premier Smallwood might win provincial elections, as he did, campaigning against me. But this was at best clever politics. His record stands, and stands much to the detriment of his native province whose interests he was sworn to advance. Critics accused us of courting the support of organized labour during the Newfoundland loggers' strike. Had we been interested in this, we would have followed the advice of those who advocated that we disallow the provincial legislation that had resulted in the labour violence as contrary to the national interest. I considered it of questionable constitutionality, but as I have already pointed out in Chapter Three, I was wedded to the principle that it was the role of the courts to decide questions of constitutionality. The result was that Mr. Smallwood campaigned vigorously in the next Newfoundland election against John Diefenbaker (a contradiction that requires no further comment) and won; the federal Liberal Party thanked its lucky stars that they were not in government and could thus limit their role to irresponsibly fanning the fires of controversy. Ex-Commissioner L. H. Nicholson retired to a comfortable pension. My government was the political loser, but what was the alternative? Would Canada have been well served had every working man and woman come to regard the Royal Canadian Mounted Police as a strike-breaking force? "History," Lord Acton observed, "is a hanging judge." So be it.

Looking back over the record of the Conservative government in the years 1957 to 1962, there are so many policies that should be discussed. We took the necessary action to establish undisputed Canadian sovereignty over the Arctic Water and Islands right to the North Pole. We established a $5 million annual fund to promote physical fitness and amateur sport. We took the first important step to environmental control and clean water for Canada when we agreed to finance up to two-thirds of the cost of municipal sewage-treatment plants. I might add that these loans were repayable over a fifty-year period and that we added the incentive of agreeing to write off twenty-five per cent of the loan if it were spent on work put in place by 1 April 1963. I could go on and on. These, however, are matters that must await my next volume.

I have elsewhere indicated the concern of my colleagues and myself to preserve and strengthen our Canadian inheritance. "Canadianization" in the Liberal sense meant the political neutralization—perhaps better, "neutering"—of our history. In their view, there seemed to be no part of our past that may not be sacrificed for political gain; hence, they are the homogenizers of Canadian culture. A Conservative is one who conserves, and "Inheritance," to quote Edmund Burke, "furnishes a sure principle of conservation and a sure principle of transmission; without at all excluding a principle of improvement." He also observed: "The science of government being therefore so practical in itself, and intended for such practical purposes, a matter which requires experience, and even more experience than any person can gain in his whole life, however sagacious and observing he may be, it is with infinite caution that any man ought to venture upon pulling down an edifice, which has answered in any tolerable degree for ages the common purposes of society."

INDEX

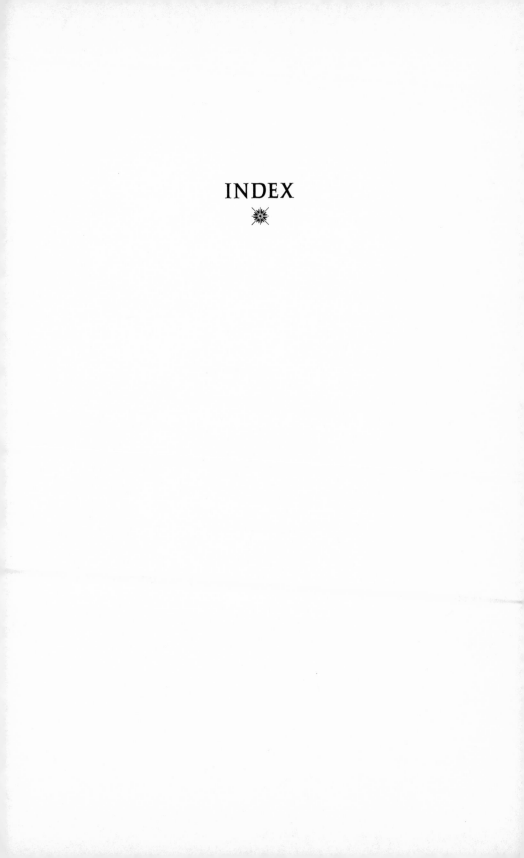

INDEX

✳

THE CANADIA[N]

An Act for the Recognition and Prote[ction...]
Statutes of Canada 1960, 8-9 Elizabe[th...]

THE Parliament of Canada, affirming that the Canadian Nation is founded upon principles that acknowledge the supremacy of God, the dignity and worth of the human person and the position of the family in a society of free men and free institutions;

Affirming also that men and institutions remain free only when freedom is founded upon respect for moral and spiritual values and the rule of law;

And being desirous of enshrining these principles and the human rights and fundamental freedoms derived from them, in a Bill of Rights which shall reflect the respect of Parliament for its constitutional authority and which shall ensure the protection of these rights and freedoms in Canada:

THEREFORE Her Majesty, by and with the advice and consent of the Senate and House of Commons of Canada, enacts as follows:

PART I
BILL OF RIGHTS

1. It is hereby recognized and declared that in Canada there have existed and shall continue to exist without discrimination by reason of race, national origin, colour, religion or sex, the following human rights and fundamental freedoms, namely,

a) the right of the individual to life, liberty, security of the person and enjoyment of property, and the

right not [...]
process o[...]
b) the right [...]
law and [...]
c) freedom [...]
d) freedom [...]
e) freedom [...]
f) freedom [...]

2. Every law [...]
declared by a [...]
shall operate [...]
be so construe[...]
infringe or to [...]
infringement [...]
ognized and d[...]
shall be constr[...]
a) authorize [...]
ment or e[...]
b) impose or [...]
unusual t[...]
c) deprive a p[...]
 (i) of the ri[...]
 for his a[...]
 (ii) of the ri[...]
 out dela[...]
 (iii) of the r[...]
 determi[...]
 and for [...]
d) authorize a [...]
authority [...]
denied cou[...]
other cor[...]

A MARI USQUE AD MARE

PARLIAMENT BUILDINGS · OTTAWA